SHIFTING HORIZONS

Lynn Beaton

Shifting Horizons

©Lynn Beaton

ISBN 0 9509967 3 4

Published by Canary Press
First edition October 1985

Typeset and printed in England by
Grassroots, London NW6.
01-328 0318

Set in 10/12 Plantin.
Cover design by Graphics International, London N1.
01-833 2988

Sole trade and mail order distribution by
Housmans Distribution, 5 Caledonian Road, London N1.
01-837 4473

CONTENTS

Lynn Beaton is an Australian who before travelling to England during the miners strike worked in a 'Working Womens Centre' attached to the ACTU, the Australian equivalent of the TUC. During four years work she researched and published bulletins on a variety of subjects related to women at work. In Australia she has written for Trade Union journals and papers. She also wrote and produced a manual for trade unionists to help them deal with cases of sexual harassment. Her history honours thesis was on women's employment in Australia during the Second World War and was published as a chapter in *Worth her Salt* (Hale & Iremonger. Sidney. 1980).

ACKNOWLEDGEMENTS

I want to thank the whole of Blidworth striking community for enabling me to stay with them and write the book. In particular I want to thank Pip Humber and Alan Radford for their support and friendship. I know there must have been times when they got sick to death of me forever spiriting their wives away to do yet another interview, and I know there were times when they felt some infringement of their personal lives to have intimate details relayed first to me and then to the world. But throughout they both went out of their way to make sure I felt at home and had everything I needed. I want to thank Karen, Laggy and in the last month Ricki Langford, David, Paul, and Mark Humber and Amanda and Michael Radford for making me feel so at home in their homes that I became 'one of the family' in both houses.

All three of us would like to thank also those strikers and their families and members of support groups who play a part in this book; Alison, Allan, Noreen Baker, Ann Bradley, Dennis Browne, Sylv Browne, Cambridge Support Group, Mick Carter, Chris, Claire, Clare, Terry Dunne, Fletch, Gay, Nicki Glegg, Margaret Groves, 'Yorkie' Groves, Annette Holroyd, Howard Hayman, Mal Howarth, Pauline Howarth, Louise, Sue Maddock, Maureen, Alison New, Maureen North, Gareth Pearce, Ann Petney, Ken and Sue Petney, Ralph, Tony Rose, Jim and Sarah Ryan, Betty Savage, Peter Savage, Doug Shaw, Simon, Lois Smith, Sue, Paul Thomson, Chris Tucker.

I also want to thank my own family for their incredible support and perseverance. In particular my daughters Lucy and Chloe whose understanding of the importance and demands of my work has amazed me. First of all they understood the necessity for me to be away from them for much longer than any of us wanted and secondly they have provided enormous support and help in the final compilation of all the material.

I want to thank the many people who gave me support and encouragement throughout the time it has taken to complete this manuscript. Many of the people who visited Blidworth as supporters of the Strike and many of my own friends in London and in Melbourne have provided me with all sorts of support, encouragement and inspiration which has enabled me to continue.

I want to thank Gerry Beaton, Mary Clarke, Loy McCarthy, Bernadette O'Connell, Betty Sturtivant, Martin Walker and Von Woodhead for help with the production of the manuscript itself.

Introduction

I went to Blidworth because of a chance meeting with some miners at Brighton during the week of the TUC Congress.

When I reached the Nottingham Bus Station I wasn't at all surprised that there was no-one to meet me despite having been assured less than twenty hours before that there would be. I had even said to the man on the phone, whose thick Nottinghamshire accent I had a lot of trouble understanding, that if no-one was there I would just catch a bus. I was convinced that the striking community of Blidworth would have much more on their plates than to come into Nottingham to meet someone who had described herself as an Australian journalist, coming to write some articles for Australian journals. In fact I was afraid that my presence would be a nuisance and I determined to make myself useful and not become an added burden.

But my estimation of my reception couldn't have been more wrong; as the bus pulled into Blidworth, I was shocked to realise that there were two women waiting there to meet me. Even more shocked to discover that these two women had been to Nottingham, but a communication error had sent them to the train station while I had arrived from London by coach. One of the things that amazed me most of all about Blidworth was the extent to which the striking community accepted me without question. I suppose that even if you think you are clear about the issues of something like the Miners' Strike, you are still to some extent influenced by the media presentation of things. One of the biggest surprises in going to Blidworth, was the extent to which everybody was real. Some of my first impressions of life in the Strike Centre were the interactions between the adults and kids. I arrived there at about two o'clock, at three, some of the younger kids came in from school. It was like being in any house when the kids get home from school, except this wasn't anybody's house, it was a Strike Centre and because there were so many families there, there was, of course, inter-action between all the kids and all the adults. I realised I was witnessing an experiment in communal living. But this experiment had not been born, like others I'd known out of a conscious effort to change lifestyle, but out of a necessity to survive unexpected attack from a Government determined to smash the mining communities.

Because over half the village were scabbing, the only refuge was in the Centre.

Late one night Pauline and I sat in her kitchen as she described some of the events of the last few months. The house was in that state of eerie quiet that comes late at night when everyone else has gone to bed and you talk softly to make sure you don't disturb them. The soft steady tones of Pauline's voice were in stark contrast to the content of her words. Her descriptions of police intimidation the likes of which no-one in Britain could quite believe were not new to me, I'd read accounts in the left-wing press and since I'd first arrived in Blidworth nearly two weeks before I'd heard the stories a number of times. What made this night so powerful was that in those two weeks Pauline and some of the other women in the village had become close friends. The stories were no longer something that had happened to someone somewhere, I had lost the ability to maintain a distance between me and the stories because the striking community of Blidworth had become a part of my life. Later, as I lay snug in Pauline's caravan I kept thinking that everybody should know what had happened here, in the way I now knew.

The next morning I asked Doreen and Pauline what they thought about me trying to write a book about it.

At first my suggestion was met with off-handed agreement, I knew the two women well enough to know that the off-handedness didn't come from disinterest but from the fact that I was proposing yet another venture which neither of them could have imagined possible before the strike had started. The strike at this time was six months old, and the whole six months had been a series of challenges, which the women had met, but each accomplishment was accompanied by a disbelief that such things could happen.

Having decided we would write the book, we then had to decide how we were going to do it. I was determined that as much as possible the story must be told in Pauline and Doreen's words so we started a series of long tape recorded interviews.

The interviews became a very special event in themselves, I think in a way we all enjoyed them, but they created moments of tension as well. We'd spend hours sitting in one of the houses or in the caravan with the tape recorder between us. At times it was hard to make the time available to do it but Doreen and Pauline's commitment to the project always made it possible.

I became part of the community and for six months, lived its ups and downs, its tensions and its energies.

In the normal course of living, we would often discuss things, and then, during an interview, I could bring it up. There was always a tension between interviewer and interviewee, but all of us somehow understood it as a part of the process and it never really got in our way. Doreen often expressed exasperation at my constant,

'How did you feel about that?'

'What were you doing just before that happened?'

'What did you think about such and such at the time?'

She would yell, 'How do you expect me to remember, it was four months ago.' But she would always remember, sometimes days later, she'd come and tell me some small detail that had slipped her mind during an interview, or answer a question I'd asked that she hadn't been able to answer at the time. Pauline's attitude to it was to laugh, she began to anticipate my questions.

'I know.' She'd say, 'you want to know how I felt'. But the whole book was really only possible because of the friendship which grew between us all. For six months, our lives were intertwined. We lived together through what is undoubtedly one of the most significant periods of all our lives. The resultant closeness is more than mere friendship, I feel now as if I have two new families.

Months after I had the interviews I was still unsure about the best way to present them in writing. I wanted a book that would be accessible to all but I also wanted to maintain as much of the personalities of the two women as possible. It is after all their story and as much as possible I wanted it told in their words. But spoken and written language are really quite different and so I was forced to edit, rearrange and sometimes completely re-word the taped conversations. In doing so it was always uppermost in my mind to try and represent as accurately as possible the style of speech and the language of Doreen and Pauline. Obviously I have been unsuccessful to some extent because my own language and style of speech are so different from theirs. I don't believe that it's possible to capture the charm of the Nottinghamshire accent on paper, but I have tried to maintain some of the flow and character and I hope that the reader will not find my efforts too clumsy.

As each chapter was written it was immediately shown to the two women, a discussion always followed and often changes were made. I became very excited by this way of working, it seems to me quite novel as a method, at the same time it seems no coincidence that a new method of approach should be born in the heart of the Miners' Strike which brought with it many social and cultural innovations.

I have presented the day to day lives of two women in the strike, in doing so I want to emphasize that Doreen and Pauline as two individuals involved in the strike have particular experiences and particular re-actions to them, and so we are not claiming that this story is necessarily representative of the story of all miners' wives during the strike. At the same time I want to say that I could have chosen any two miners' wives and found their stories just as exciting and inspiring. Doreen and Pauline are representative in so far that they show the incredible strength, determination and courage which was common to thousands of women during the dispute. They met challenges to their lives daily and in meeting them changed their entire world outlook, and in that they are also representative not only of thousands of miners' wives, but of thousands of miners as well.

I am also aware that this book has a weakness in that it doesn't attempt any analysis of the strike or even detail very many of the events which shaped the broader struggle. I would have like it to do this as well but I decided it was more important to have this printed and available for reading as quickly as possible. I'm sure in any case that much will be written about the strike, and perhaps my own contribution to that fund of knowledge will come later.

There was much in the lives of Doreen and Pauline during twelve months of the strike which has not been included, but I hope that the events which *have been* covered give an idea of the enormous range of experiences met by each woman. My main regret about these omissions is that I have done Doreen and Pauline a disservice because they actually coped with a lot more. The tensions of the strike made everyone's personal lives quite delicate and the demands of the strike often left no time for the resolution of problems which arose.

For some time we have been aware that women are capable of much more than they are often given credit for but all of the women in the strike were capable of much more than I had ever believed any individual could tolerate. I don't want to suggest that this was in any way magical or mystical. Their enormous capabilities came from their unswerving commitment to the fight they had taken on and their intuitive understanding of its importance as a watershed in British history. The situation demanded superwomen to deal with it and they rose to meet the demands put on them.

My final regret is that I couldn't have written a book about the whole of the Blidworth striking community. Every one of them made a deep and lasting impression on me and every one of them earned my undying respect and admiration, but more, every one of them will live with me as a dear friend for the rest of my life. To the women, men and kids of that community how can I every say thank-you for allowing me to share your lives and for giving me your friendship. I have to say that although my life has seen many rich moments there is not another six months that compare with the six I spent in Blidworth.

Lynn Beaton
1985

·1·
PAULINE
GETTING STARTED

My first memories are of Doe Lee in Derbyshire. We lived in a colliery house which my Mum and Dad moved to almost straight after I was born. They'd lived in a caravan until then, in the middle of a field which they shared with a horse. Our Carol, my older sister, was born in the caravan and I was conceived there, but I was born at my Grandma's house in 1959. The house at Doe Lee was very basic, the toilets were outside at the end of the yard. There was no hot running water and so my Mum used to put us in a boiler for a bath. Then we got one of those old tin baths and my Mum used to put that in front of the fire and bath us all in it together. There were four of us, by then I had another two sisters.

Everybody had a front room in those days, it was usually the best room in the house, but ours wasn't, ours was a junk room where we kept all the toys. There was an old gramophone and we used to play 'My Bonnie Lies Over the Ocean' and dress up in old hats, dresses and high-heeled shoes. We'd dance and sing to the music waiting for my Dad to come in from work. I used to wait by the window and when I saw him coming I'd run and open the door. As soon as he got in I'd tell him what I'd been doing and then ask him to tell me a story. He'd laugh and say, 'Wait on, let me have me dinner first.'

We used to love my Dad's stories. We'd all sit around, open mouthed and listening while he told them. He often recorded them on a tape recorder at night after we'd gone to bed and the next day my Mum, who must have had her hands full with four of us under six, would put the stories on when we were playing up. We'd all sit around quiet and listening. In the middle of the story he'd say,
'Are you enjoying the story, kids?'
And we'd all say,
'Yeah, Dad' as if he were really there. Then he'd say, 'Are you being good for your Mum?' And we'd all say,'Yeah,' and then he'd

go on with the story. When he'd come home from work he'd ask us if we enjoyed the story and we'd all talk about it to him and ask him questions about it. His homecoming was always something we looked forward to, that is if we'd been good. Sometimes he'd come home from work and we knew we'd been bad. We'd all disappear because we knew my Mum would tell him and we'd all get a good hiding.

I remember ever so clearly my Dad coming home one day with some keys for a new house, we were going to move. I never understood why but I think it was because Glapwell Pit, where he worked, was going to close down. We all went over to see the new house which was in Pleasley, just on the Nottinghamshire border. It seemed like a palace compared to the old one, it had an inside toilet, a bathroom and hot running water. But despite all these things, we were never really happy in that house.

At first I had the back bedroom and it had a latch on the door like a coalhouse door. I never liked the bedroom, the latch seemed to make it eerie and I used to have terrible nightmares. Little men with hatchets would come up the stairs, lift the latch and come into the room. They'd climb all over me and hit me with their little hatchets. The dreams were so awful that after a while I was too terrified to go to sleep so my mother moved me into another bedroom which I shared with Carol. We had two bunks and I had the top one, but I didn't stop having horrible dreams. This bedroom had a sliding door and one night I was lying in the top bunk and the door was half open. I heard my Dad, coming up the stairs but when I looked at the door, it wasn't my Dad it was a skeleton with a hatchet coming to hit me. I closed my eyes and when I opened them again, it was gone. I used to scare myself to death with my dreams and my imagination, I don't know why.

One day my parents went to Mansfield and left us out playing. I had a best friend I always used to play with, her name was Pauline too and somehow we felt it was very special that we both had the same name. This day we stood in the street looking up at my bedroom window. I said, 'Look, the curtains are moving.'
  'Oh yes, I wonder why?'

'Do you think there's somebody in there.'

'Could be, I think I can see something.'

We went on like that, just staring up at the bedroom window until we were convinced somebody or something evil was there and we were scared to death. We went into the house and stood at the bottom of the stairs, both petrified. Our Carol came in with a ping-pong bat and asked what was wrong. I said, 'Ooh Carol, there's somebody up there, in our room.' 'Yes, there is,' Pauline confirmed, 'I can see 'em.' Suddenly there was an almighty bang, it was Carol with the bloody ping-pong bat, but I screamed and ran out of the house and wouldn't go back in.

When my Mum and Dad came back they wanted to know what was wrong and I told them that I wouldn't go into the house 'cause there were ghosts in it. I got the biggest thrashing I'd ever had. Afterwards my father dragged me around the house, room by room, saying, 'Look, no ghosts.' Then he chucked me into my bedroom saying, 'I hope this'll teach you to be so stupid as to imagine bloody ghosts in the house.' I had to stay in my room for the rest of the night without any tea. I hated that bedroom and it was horrible being forced to stay in it. But I never pretended there were ghosts again.

It wasn't only me that didn't like that house, my Mum didn't either. I don't really know why, I know we had trouble with neighbours. One of them was an old miner who worked nights. During the day when we were playing outside he'd open his window and yell and scream at us and we'd have to go inside which must have been hard for my mother. While we lived in that house we used to go away a lot camping for holidays and at weekends. In the summer we'd go over the Moors and we all loved it. It was always so open and fresh and summer seemed so hot and so long. We'd walk along, picking bluebells, climbing over the big rocks and splashing through the streams and when it was time to eat we'd stop for a picnic beside a stream and go paddling. If the stream was a bit deep my Mum and Dad would come in the water with us. My Dad would tickle fish, you know, catch them in his bare hands and throw them out and then we'd poach them. We had a Bedford van and we loved piling in it to go off for a day's adventure or a camping holiday.

But when we weren't out things were getting on top of my Mum and really getting her down. She was very nasty tempered and was looking really old, older than she looks now. They decided to look around for another house. My Mum fell in love with a house in Ramonsthwaite, a part of Pleasley where all the houses seemed really big and posh. They were all semi-detached as well and so had lovely gardens and seemed so spacious compared to our little terraced pit house. My Mum wanted that house more than anything. She'd say, 'It's mine, I'll do anything to get that house.'

So we all tried very hard to save up for the deposit. For about six or eight weeks while we saved up we went without sweets or cakes and happily denied ourselves the bag of crisps we usually got whenever the baker came. We didn't buy anything at all, not even a pair of shoes. None of us complained, it was a sort of conspiracy we were all involved in, because we all understood how important it was to our mother.

When we moved into the house I was about seven. It seemed so big compared to our other one. It had bay windows, three large bedrooms and a bathroom upstairs, a garage that you could get into from the kitchen, three big lawns, a green house, a shed and a really big rose garden on the front. But to live there we had to make a lot of sacrifices. The Bedford van was sold and my Dad had to work seven days a week to keep up the repayments which meant an end to our trips out. My Mum was very happy though, she devoted herself to the house and worked really hard to make it just as she wanted.

One thing didn't change. My Dad kept telling us stories. As we were all getting older the stories would more often be about real life. These were even more exciting than the make-believe ones 'cause we felt somehow, listening to the stories that we were being allowed into a world which was usually for adults. We'd hear about my Dad's childhood and the early days of my Mum and Dad's courting and marriage and about things that happened at the pit. These latter were always gruesome, about people losing hands and legs and one bloke who got the cuff of his overalls caught in a machine and it just took him in and minced him to bits. He'd also tell us about the time that he went down the pit and they asked him if he'd clean out under the cage (the lift that goes down into the pit) because there was a lot of rubbish caught at the bottom of the shaft. While he was under the cage, cleaning all this rubbish out, the winder, who operates it, let it down. My Dad was pinned underneath the cage and there was just enough room for him because he'd already cleaned most of the rubbish away, otherwise he would have been squashed to oblivion. The cage was resting on his chest and he was screaming and praying that somebody would come and let him out. Lots of really gruesome horrible things happened and it painted a picture for me of a black dark dirty hole and lots of sweat and blood.

The worst experience he told us about was one day when he was with a group of men who were crawling on their bellies a few hundred yards to reach the face they were working on. As they crawled they could hear this rumbling above them, the roof was rumbling. He said it was very frightening, you could hear wood splitting and creaking as chocks were being crunched. They'd just got to keep going and hope it wouldn't cave in where they were, but then they heard this deafening noise. My Dad froze where he was but the others in front of him tried to scramble ahead and as they did all the roof came down and they all disappeared beneath it. My Dad could hear them shouting and screaming and started digging away at the fallen rubble with his bare hands. He called to some other men further down the tunnel for help and they started to come up but it took ages 'cause they had to inch along on their bellies. My Dad was trying to get through the rubble and was pulling lumps of muck and pieces of wood away. He pulled one big piece of muck away and it made a hole big enough to see through. When he looked in through the hole he could see one of his mates, knelt down with his hands together praying. He could hear him saying, 'Please help me God, I don't want to die now. Please let somebody dig me out. Please God, save me.'

It took them ages, but they did eventually get them all out and there were no serious injuries but a lot of broken bones and shattered nerves.

When I was about ten and we'd been in the new house for about three years, there was a threatened closure of Pleasley pit where my Dad worked. He was offered £100 transfer money to move to a place called Blidworth. None of us were very happy about it, we'd all got our friends in Pleasley and my Mum was very upset to be leaving the new house.

'I wouldn't mind if only I could take the house with me,' she said to my Dad.

'Well you can't do that duck,' he said. 'But I wish you could.'

They'd spent such a lot of time and money on making that house something beautiful, something that was a part of them. I felt sorry for my Mum because that house was something that she'd always dreamt about and worked so hard towards. Now she just had to up and leave it and go to a strange place with a strange sounding name.

We came over to see the house at Blidworth, it was nice enough but it was nothing like the one in Ramonsthwaite. It was smaller, we were back to small bedrooms again. The school was at the bottom of the garden and I didn't like the look of it, I especially didn't like it being so close, I thought, 'No more pretending I'm sick.'

To replace the Bedford van we'd bought a little three wheeler Bond and we moved in that. All of us piled in with loads of boxes and baggage. On the way we had to go up an enormous hill and none of us thought we'd make it. But we did. When we got there all the neighbours must have thought we were a terrible sight, all six of us climbing out of the little three wheeler, we must have looked like sardines.

My Dad decided that we should get to know our new village, so every Sunday we'd have to go on long walks all round the area. I thought it was a daft idea, I hated walking. We'd all get dressed up and off we'd go, we used to walk ten miles or so. I was a fat little girl and my legs used to rub together when we walked so far, and they used to get sore and bleed and I used to cry. But my Dad still made me go and used to shout at me if I moaned.

One morning, after we'd been in Blidworth about three years, there was a knock on the door just as I was getting out of bed to get ready to go to school. It was very unusual at that time of the morning so all of us kids crowded out onto the landing and peered down the stairs as my Mum opened the door. It was an ambulance man and my Mum started to cry and say, 'Oh no, no, bloody 'ell, what's 'e done.' We all came running down the stairs just as me Dad came walking up the path, his head was covered in bandages and another man was helping him to walk. He came in for a few minutes before they took him to the hospital, for stitches and x-rays. He'd refused to go straight to the hospital he'd insisted that they bring him home to see my mother first, so she'd know he was alright. We all started crying, there was blood seeping through the bandages and he looked awful. My Mum got dressed and went with them. We didn't go to school but sat around crying and talking to each other about what had happened and wondering whether he'd be alright or not. All the stories he'd told us about accidents at the pit made us frightened that something might happen to him and now it had, our imaginations ran away a bit, like kids do when they don't really understand what the situation is.

We talked about how upset my Mum was and that seemed to worry us as much as the sight of my Dad. We tried to comfort each other and made ourselves busy cleaning up the house so that when my Mum got back it was nice and tidy and she wouldn't have to do anything. She got back about dinner timeish and said that he was badly hurt, but that he'd be alright. He'd nearly scalped himself and had thirty stitches in his head. We thought he was going to die, scalping himself seemed so awful to us. You know what kids are like, bad things seem worse and good things seem better. Next day he came home and the stitches were right around his head like a horseshoe and his back was badly hurt. We asked him to tell us how it had happened. He was riding on the belt and it was his turn to jump off. But just where he jumped, the bulb in the light had gone and he wasn't able to see at all, so he tripped on something and banged his head on a steel bar. He ended up getting quite a lot of compensation for it but he was off work for a long time. After about three months he went back to work but only for a week, he was getting really bad headaches and had to come off work again for another week. Since then he's had lots of time off with headaches and a bad back.

It couldn't have been too long after my Dad went back to work that I heard my parents talking about stocking the pantry up in case there was a strike. By then I had moved up to Whittaker Comprehensive which was in the next village. I didn't like it all that much but all the kids from Blidworth went there together on the bus and we were like one big family. My Mum started going out and buying extra food each week which she'd put in the pantry and she used to buy extra sacks of potatoes and store them in the lobby. Then they were on strike. Instead of my Dad going to work he'd go out picketing and come home and tell us about it. They'd go off in buses to the power station where there was a big tent set up for bad weather. Next to that was a sort of shack they'd built with a stove in it, they threw potatoes on it and made soup. They used to do long shifts then of six or eight hours. There weren't so many police then as there are now, my Dad never talked about the police, I don't remember that they were a factor at all.

The strike was solid then. Everybody was out, not like now. The pit was closed, so they didn't need to picket there, that's why they could all go to the power stations. Lots of kids at school had Dads on strike and we used to talk about them going picketing. We had free meals at school and that was fun in a way. I never felt singled out or victimised because of it, I know there's supposed to be something shameful about having free school dinners but I didn't feel it at all. There was a big group of us, we were all friends 'cause your friends always lived in the village and all their Dads worked down the pit and were on strike. We'd queue up everyday for lunch and laugh and joke and actually we felt quite important, we knew our Dads were involved in something important.

After a couple of weeks all the food my Mum had stocked up was gone and there was nothing in the house. My Dad used to bring home a little bit of picketing money and we got social security benefits but it wasn't enough to live on. My Mum used to buy lots of potatoes and we'd have potato all sorts of ways. We started going up to the soup kitchen in the Youth Club with my Dad. I can remember it ever so well, it was very exciting, something completely new and different. There'd be men playing table tennis and darts and sitting around talking about things that sounded very important. We used to really enjoy going up, I can imagine the kids in this strike thinking it's great going up to the centre. I think that the kids must feel proud now to know that their Dads aren't scabs. I know one thing, our kids won't ever have to ask where we were in the '84/85 Strike, they'll know because they were there with us and they were part of the strike. Scabs' kids won't remember 'cause nothings different for them.

My Mum wouldn't go up, none of the women did, it was very different to our Strike Centre, I can't ever remember seeing a woman there. It was only men and kids. They didn't serve cooked meals like we do now, it was all snacks, chip butties, bacon cobs and soup. All the cooking and serving was done by men. The whole strike was like that really, it was just men's business and the men didn't involve the women at all. We used to go up with my Dad, or sometimes, if he was away picketing we'd go on our own. We used to nag my Mum to let us go and she'd give us a bit of money, 'cause you had to pay for the food. It wasn't very much, only 2d or 3d for a bacon cob. While we were there we used to watch everything that went on. Sacks and sacks of potatoes would be brought in through the big double doors and the men would sit there with their buckets of water and potato knives, peeling them and chipping them. That was a bit similar to the way they do it in our Centre. But a lot of the food then was donated from local shops. The butcher used to give them bones for soup and the green grocer sent round bits and bobs of vegetables. All the shops donated food because all the miners were on strike and we, after all, were their business. The men used to cope quite well with the cooking, but it was nothing like the standard of food we've got now, just snack meals. But it did help us get by.

One of the biggest hardships was lack of coal. At night we'd empty potato sacks and carrier bags and sneak out with my Dad to go over to the pit tip where we'd rake the slack coal with our hands to find little lumps. It was freezing and we'd come back absolutely filthy but we'd have a bag full of coal and it was such a luxury to come back and light a fire and stand around it getting warm. It was the only way to get coal then, because there was none being moved. Often people got caught pinching coal from the pit tips. One night when we went we saw these flashing lights coming our way. We all ran for our lives but we wouldn't leave our bag of coal, we were running with the bags trying to squeeze through the little gap in the fence and when we got home we told our Mum.

'We nearly got caught tonight.'

We were all flustered and excited and my Mum worried and said that we couldn't go any more, but of course we did.

Then, the strike was over. I don't remember really what it was about but I remember that it was a victory and everybody was celebrating. There was another Strike in '74, but it didn't last so long and I don't remember much about it. I knew that it brought the Heath Government down, I didn't really know what that meant, but I knew it was very important and that there was a lot of talk about it on the television. I also know that the men were really proud going back to work after that.

My life changed a lot between the two strikes which is maybe why I don't remember much about the '74 Strike.

My older sister, Carol, had started babysitting. The husband's brother took a fancy to her and they started courting. I was very intrigued and excited by that and used to want to talk to her about it and somehow share in it. But we were never very close really and she treated me even more than ever like a silly younger sister. Suddenly she seemed so grown up and I suppose that made me feel a little more grown-up as well, but most of all I was fascinated by what it was like for her. She started doing things with David instead of with the family and it made her seem a bit apart. One day, we all went out and our Carol didn't come. When we got home my Dad went into the toilet and came back into the kitchen quite angry.

He said to my Mum, 'Have you seen what's in't toilet?' My mother went into the toilet and came out looking shocked. I was completely bemused, I thought, 'Whatever can be in't toilet.'

Then my Dad said, 'That's what they're up to when we go out.'

I had no idea what he was talking about, I was ever so confused, I guessed it had something to do with our Carol and her boyfriend but I couldn't imagine what on earth they'd be getting up to in the toilet.

Me and my younger sisters were all sent to bed early, my Mum and Dad sat in the kitchen talking ever so seriously. I shared a room with Carol and the other two shared a room so when my Dad had gone back into the kitchen I crept out onto the landing so I could listen to what happened. I heard Carol come in.

My Dad says, 'Is that you Carol?'

'Yeah.'

'Come in here, we want you.'

I heard my Dad say, 'What have you and David been up to?'

And Carol says, 'What do you mean?'

'Well, you've been having sex haven't you.' And I thought, 'Ooh, that's what it were.' My Mum and Dad had always been very open with us about sex. When they were first courting my mother was looking after her whole family - her mother and father were both away, in prison. They'd had no money to buy Xmas presents for the children and my Grandad was a postman so he stole some postal orders and my Grandma signed them all. They'd both been sent down. My Dad started staying nights and my Mum got pregnant but she didn't know anything about sex and I don't think my father knew much more. Anyway she lost that baby, she lost it sitting on the toilet and my Dad was with her. It was a little boy. They didn't want us to get caught like that so they used to sit with us late into the night telling us about how sex was a lovely thing, a beautiful thing but that you must do it at the right time and only if you loved each other. My Dad told us that if we were getting serious with a boy we were to come and see my Mum and she'd make up an appointment to get us on the pill.

So when my Dad said they'd been having sex, I knew what he meant and I was quite titillated. They started having a row.

My Dad said, 'Well at least you're using something, but them things aren't safe you know. Me and ya Mum used them and they burst and they're no good. If you're gonna use something, use something proper. Anyway I don't like the idea of you having sex with him. You're too young.'

There was a pause and then he said, 'And he's too old.' There was seven years difference between them and my Dad was worried that David was taking advantage of Carol because she was so young, she was still at school and hadn't yet turned sixteen.

The door opened then and I scuttled back to bed. Carol came up and got in beside me and I said, 'What's the matter?'

'Nought, get to sleep.'

'Has me Dad been shouting ya?'

'Mind your own business and get to sleep else I'm telling me Dad on ya.'

So I tittered to myself and thought, 'I know what you've been up to.'

But I really wanted to ask her what it was like because I really wanted to know if it was as nice as my Mum and Dad said it was. But I daren't.

As it turned out Carol did get pregnant, she missed a month and my Mum seemed to know and asked her about it.

Carol said, 'Yeah, I think so.'

It was two weeks before her sixteenth birthday and so my Mum said she should wait till her birthday and then go to see the doctor. When the pregnancy was confirmed my Mum said, 'You don't have to get married just for the sake of the baby.'

But Carol said her and David had talked about it and wanted to get married anyway.

When the baby was born, because Carol was so young and hadn't had any life, she wanted to go straight out to work and she asked me if I'd look after the baby for her. I thought it was a great idea, so I just stopped going to school and used to go around to Carol's house every morning and look after the baby. They were magic times, I had this tiny little baby and it was just as if it was my own. I was only fifteen and it was a wonderful feeling to be responsible for it and to think that the baby depended on me and that what I did would reflect on that baby. I used to go around to Carol's house at half seven every morning and they'd go off to work. I'd get the baby up, feed her, change her, put her in the pram and take her for a walk to the shops where I'd buy the things that Carol wanted for dinner, she always left a shopping list. Then I'd come back and play with the baby for a bit, get her off to sleep, tidy around and get the dinner ready for Carol and David when they came back from work. I was like a mother to that baby. They used to come back about half past five, David would run me home and then at half seven I'd come back to babysit while they went out. I was living the life of a housewife and mother and taking on all the responsibility as well. I was really enjoying it, but after about a month my Mum and Dad started to worry about me. I was getting tired, I wasn't getting home until half eleven and then I'd be up at seven again in the morning. I never went out or mixed with young lasses of my own age.

'You ought to be out enjoying yu'sen,' my Mum started to say to me, 'Not tied down with a baby, ya just like a married woman, it's not your baby ya know, our Carol had the baby and she should be responsible for it.' 'I know, but I enjoy it and I said I'd do it, I can't very well just stop now and make her give up her job can I?'

My Mum arranged for them to bring the baby to our house instead of me going around there, so she could help me with it. She thought that would take a bit of the strain off me and that I might start to go out a little bit. But I wouldn't go out, I wouldn't let my Mum help me, I was so possessive with that baby, I insisted on doing everything for it myself. My life circulated around the baby. One night my Dad came in and I was fussing with her and he took one look at me and shouted,

'Get out of this bloody house, get out of here, now, before you go round the twist.'

I walked out, slammed the door behind me and walked to the park and sat on a bench and just cried. When it got dark I didn't know where to go, I felt sorry for myself, I didn't want to go home but I hadn't really got anywhere else to go. I knew that what my parents were saying was right, but at the same time I felt happy just being with the baby and scared about forcing myself to go out and make friends.

I'd had a couple of experiences with boys and both times, they'd tried to make me have sex with them. The first time it was with this fellow that I was really madly in love with, like you are when you're young. He seemed at the time everything a woman could dream of. I used to see him at a pub I used to go to with my Mum and Dad. For a couple of months, we just stared at each other all night. Then one night he went to the door and nodded to me to follow him. I got very excited, with butterflies in my stomach cause I'd never been out with a lad before. He started chatting me up in the passage and he asked me straight away how old I was. When I told him fifteen he seemed shocked and I thought that was going to be it. But he kept chatting. He said, 'I've had my eye on you for quite a while.' I didn't know what to say so I said, 'I've had mine on you.'

'Yeah, I know,' he said and he kissed me and it was lovely, it made me sort of melt. After that, every week he'd give me a nod and we'd stand in the passage snogging and fondling each other.

One week he asked me to go out with him. I was over the moon. He came to the house to pick me up and took me to the pictures and we sat in the back row, snogging. Afterwards, he asked me what time I had to be in. When I told him, no special time, he asked if I'd like to go for a drive around. I was very naive and thought that was literally what he meant, but of course soon we were parked in one of the country lanes. He pushed a button and my seat went back to the lying down position and then his seat went back as well. I was terrified, I really liked him a lot, but I was scared of what would happen and knew that this situation was all wrong. In the end I told him to stop. He was quite nice about it and asked if I wanted him to drive me home. I said, 'I think you'd better, yeah.' So he drove me home, the perfect gentleman, but I never saw him again.

Another time I was at a club with a friend who had got off with a Teddy-Boy. One of his friends asked me to dance and it was a smooch. He started kissing me and I hated it. He was ever so tall and lanky and he had a really big nose and mouth. His mouth was so big that when he kissed me it covered my nose as well as my mouth. He asked me to go outside with him for some air and I naively agreed. That just led to his hands being all over me and me struggling to get away, cause I didn't even like him.

So I was beginning to think that all men ever wanted was your body and I wasn't very keen on it. A few weeks after I'd sat and cried on the park bench, our Carol asked me to go to a party with her and her husband. 'No, I'm not gatecrashing no party.' 'Don't be silly, it'll do ya good to get out.' Carol insisted.

'Yeah,' my Mum said, 'Go on, take her out wi'ya and get her off wi' somebody.' Then she said to me, 'Come on, ya ought to go, you've got that new dress you've never worn, get yu'sen upstairs and put it on. 'That persuaded me. By that time I'd got a job working as a trainee machinist in a hosiery factory that made ladies nighties. This was just after Xmas and all over Xmas I'd hardly had any money 'cause almost as soon as I started working they put us on short time. Having a new dress was quite a treat and I did want to wear it.

When we got there our Carol started trying to set me up with the only available male that was there, but I just didn't fancy him. He didn't seem attractive to me at all so I spent hours trying to avoid talking to him with our Carol trying to push me at him. I hated it and wished I'd never come. A bit after midnight a group of men walked in, they were all old except for one who looked all right, although he was a bit spotty. I thought, 'He's probably married.' I don't really know why I thought that, maybe because he was wearing a suit, something about him definitely looked married. Carol and David introduced me to him, he was called Alan, Alan Radford. Carol said to him, 'Are you gonna dance with Pauline.?' I felt so stupid but we did dance and then he started chatting me up. He asked me where I worked and I asked him where he worked. He was an apprentice welder in a street furnishing factory. 'What's street furnishing?' I asked. 'Oh, you know all the things there are in streets, lamp-posts, litter bins, park benches, all that type of thing, we make it all at our factory.' I kept on thinking he was probably married, but I never asked him and he kept on dancing with me and everything seemed alright. Then a smooch came on and he went and sat down and wouldn't dance with me. I was just standing there feeling silly and awkward when this great big fat old bloke came up.

'I'll dance with ya duckie.' As he said it he put his arms round me and started mauling me, I felt quite sick.

Carol was standing next to me and she was saying, 'Don't dance wi' him, don't dance wi' him, get back wi' Alan, look he's sat there on his own, go and dance wi' him.'

She was talking so loud that the bloke I was dancing with must have been able to hear her and I was very embarrassed even though I didn't want to be dancing with him. I sort of whispered to Carol behind this bloke's back that Alan wouldn't dance with me.

'Well, go and sit next to him,' she said.

I did, I felt really stupid and pushy but I was also very keen to get away from this bloke mauling me. I sat on the floor next to Alan's chair and after that dance finished everybody went into the other room for supper. Alan didn't move and I didn't know what to do so I just stayed where I was. The next thing, Alan bent down and kissed me and I thought, 'Ooh, he's fast.'

We left the party after Carol and David had had some supper and they gave Alan a lift home. He sat in the back seat next to me and put his arm around me. He asked me to meet him the next day to go to his house for tea. When I got back to Carol's my other two sisters were there, they'd been baby-sitting. I climbed into bed next to them and they started asking me loads of questions about Alan and what had happened.

'Oh, he's alright,' was all I'd tell them, 'a bit spotty, but alright.'

Next day I set off to meet him as we'd planned in the market square in Mansfield. He was a bit late and I'd decided that he wasn't going to turn up. He lived in Sutton which is a village not far from Blidworth and we had to catch a bus to get there from Mansfield. When we got on the bus, Alan had no money so I had to pay our bus fares. Then when we got there I discovered that his parents didn't know that I was coming, but they made me very welcome and I thought they were very posh because we had our tea in cups and saucers. After tea Alan asked me if I'd like to go up to his room to listen to his records. When we got upstairs, there was nowhere to sit except on the bed, so I plonked myself down and he put a record on and then sat down beside me. Next thing, he was all over me, he pushed me down on the bed and his hands were everywhere. I got really cross then, it wasn't only Alan, it was the others as well and I'd had enough, so I hit him as hard as I could across the face and told him to stop it through clenched teeth.

His response surprised me, he was ever so sorry, he couldn't apologise enough and promised that he'd never do it again. I stayed for a while and we sat chatting and listening to his records. It was very comfortable and I started to feel quite relaxed. When I left he gave me a kiss and we arranged to meet the following week. After that I saw him once a week for about a fortnight, then twice a week and then almost every night and weekends. We just got on really well and being together was easy and seemed right somehow.We grew to love each other and at Easter got engaged. By then of course, Alan had broken the promise he'd made that first day in his bedroom, but it was different then, sex grew between us in a natural and really lovely way. One night we almost had intercourse but stopped ourselves because we had no contraception.

The next day I said to my Mum, 'I'm going to make an appointment with the doctor.'

'Why,' she said very surprised, 'aren't you well.'

'No, no, there's nothing wrong wi' me. Only, me and Alan's getting serious and I think it's time I went on the pill.'

'Ooh,' she sounded a bit shocked and a bit embarrassed but she said, 'Well, I'm glad you've decided to do that and not take the same road ya sister did.'

In March the following year we bought a house and we used to spend all our time doing it up. We stripped it from top to bottom and Alan's Dad, who's a painter and decorator, helped us with the decorating. We had quite a lot of arguments about it. I thought Alan's Dad interfered too much, at one stage he even tried to tell me where to put the bed. I was working at Sutton where the house was and so I used to stay overnight quite often on my own. Alan's parents would have thought it improper for him to stay there too. It was ever so scary, sleeping on a piece of foam in the empty house, but it seemed silly to go back to Blidworth because we wouldn't finish working on the house until eleven at night and I had to be back in Sutton for work at half seven the next morning.

In July we got married and moved into our house, we didn't have a honeymoon, but we both took two weeks off work and spent them in the house, making it just how we wanted and relishing living together in our own home. In October I stopped taking the pill and got caught the following month. It was a very easy pregnancy and a long but straightforward birth. That's when my role as housewife and mother really started. Before that I'd been working so I'd had my own independence, but I didn't mind losing it, I was perfectly happy to fill my new role. I absolutely idolised Amanda, she became everything. I really enjoyed just spending hours and hours playing with her and watching her growing up. I was blissfully happy, we had settled into a comfortable routine and everything seemed very secure.

But then, when Alan was nearing the end of his apprenticeship there were rumours that there would be redundancies where he worked and it seemed likely that he'd be put off when he got his papers. I told my parents about it and a few days later my Dad rang up to tell us that there was probably going to be a vacancy for a pit-top worker at Blidworth. 'It's not official yet,' he said. 'But I know that one of the welders is leaving. Get yu'sen over here t' see Manager on Saturday morning. 'When Alan got the job, I couldn't believe it. Most of the jobs on pit-top go to older or injured miners who can't get down the pit any more. So it's a very rare thing for someone to be employed for a pit-top job and I was very excited about it.

At first Alan used to ride over on his motorcycle but when the winter and the snow came he couldn't always get through so he put us down for a pit house in Blidworth. They showed us two houses before they offered us this one. They were both awful, I couldn't have lived in either, but as soon as I walked into this house I felt at home in it and I knew I could make it mine. I started travelling over on the bus with Amanda to clean it all up, it wasn't in very good condition. There was no sink in the kitchen which had a brick wall that wasn't even plastered, but they agreed to plaster it and put a second hand sink unit in. I cleaned the whole house through and it was ready to move in.

It was like coming home for me, I was very pleased to be coming back to Blidworth where I could be with my family again.

When we first moved in we kept ourselves to ourselves, I noticed that there seemed to be loads of kids living at the house next door, but I didn't really know anything else about them except that Pip, the husband, was an electrician at the pit. Occasionally in the summer when I was hanging clothes on the line, Doreen, would be hanging hers out too.

'Morning', I'd say.

'Hey up, think it'll dry 'em today.'

Bit by bit the conversations got longer and some days when it was very hot and we were both sitting out in the sun we'd chat a bit over the hedge. Then occasionally Doreen would come around for a cup of coffee but we never really talked personally, it was just neighbour chat, about the street and so on. We were both quite wary of each other.

At about this time I found I was pregnant again, we'd been trying for nine months so I was ever so pleased. When I was nineteen weeks I went to the doctor for my regular check-up and told him I wanted to have my baby delivered at home. I wanted to share the experience with Alan and Amanda, it seemed so artificial to get carted off to hospital to have a new baby when it was really a part of the family that was at home. That night Alan was working and my youngest sister came to stay the night to keep me company. We'd just got into bed and were starting to settle down for the night. I was feeling my tummy, feeling him moving inside. I do that a lot when I'm expecting. Without warning I felt a gush of water and knew at once that my waters had broken.

I called out to my sister.

'My waters have broken.' I jumped out of bed and grabbed for a bath towel. My sister got up and when she saw me standing there clasping a bath towel around myself she said:

'What on earth are ya doing?'

I just looked at her and repeated, 'My waters 'ave broke.'

'Ooh, those waters.' She said, her face showing sudden understanding before it broke into a wide grin. 'Oh, bloody 'ell, I thought you meant the water tank, I thought the house was flooding. What does it mean, what we going to do.'

'I don't know.' We were both very confused and went downstairs and made a cup of coffee and talked about what we ought to do. The water gushed again. I grabbed another bath towel and rang the doctor who came straight out and suggested I go straight into hospital. They kept me in overnight. They tested the water and said the tests were negative so it couldn't have been my waters breaking. 'You must just have wet yourself,' one of the nurses said to me. I felt really awful,

I was worried about the baby. You know when you've wet yourself, and when you've already had one baby you know what your waters breaking feels like, there were two bath towels at home both ringing wet. But how could I argue with their tests. It made me feel very frustrated.

The next morning I was on the ward walking around and I asked one of the nurses for a sanitary towel because I was still loosing water. She seemed quite cross with me.

'What do you want one of them for?'

'I'm still losing water.' She shrugged her shoulders in response and just walked off.

Soon after the doctor came and tested me again, this time the tests showed positively that the waters had broken. They sent me off to have a scan and then I saw Michael moving about on the screen. It was so fantastic to see his little body moving around inside me, I'd always loved feeling him move, but to actually see him was brilliant. Back up stairs I wanted to see a doctor to find out what it all meant, what was going to happen now that the waters had broken. Alan was with me, they drew curtains around the bed.

'I'm sorry Mrs. Radford, but we think you're going to loose your baby.'

I just went to pieces, I can't tell anybody how I felt, I'd just seen him moving around and alive inside of me. I couldn't believe I was going to lose him, the thought of it just broke me in two.

Within a few days I was home, but my waters broke again. They brought my bed downstairs and my Mum and sisters came around during the day to look after me. I was confined to bed and that went on for four weeks. It was a hard four weeks, the central heating was installed and some new windows were put in the house I'd got Amanda to look after and Alan had to go to work, he took some time off but couldn't take the whole four weeks off. It was during this time that I realised what a good friend Doreen was. She used to come around and see if I was alright. Whenever there was nobody with me she'd make sure that the phone was at the bottom of my bed and tell me to ring her if ever I needed anything. That was especially comforting at nights when Alan was at work. People tend to shy away from you when you need help or when you're in trouble, but Doreen didn't. We hardly knew each other yet she was a great support to me.

As far as the baby was concerned things were getting worse. I started loosing blood, the doctor decided it was safer to leave me where I was, they thought I was going to have a miscarriage. One night I lost such a lot of blood I had to phone the doctor again and he sent the Flying Squad out. They came into the house and took over, they put a drip in my arm, took blood samples in case I needed a transfusion and then raced me off to hospital in the ambulance. For fifteen days I was kept in the hospital, not allowed out of bed at all, I had to have bedpans and bedbaths. I was very weak, very worried and very tense. It was the first time I'd been away from Amanda, Alan used to bring her into the hospital but it broke my heart. I used to say to Alan 'I'm missing Amanda growing up.'

She'd been my life, every little thing she did was a great joy to me and suddenly I'd been taken away from her. When she came into the hospital she'd do things she'd never done before and it broke me up to think that I was not going through all her new developments with her.

I went into labour three or four times and each time they managed to stop it but one evening after tea I started contracting and although they pumped me full of pethodine the labour continued. They took me down to the delivery room and sent Alan home saying, 'The baby won't be born yet, Mr. Radford, your wife's just constipated.'

But at three that morning I knew the baby was coming. I could feel within me that powerful urge to bear down. The birth itself was reasonably straightforward and quick.

At first I kept saying to them, 'What is it? A little girl, or a little boy.'

They'd only say, 'It's very small Mrs. Rradford, it's very small.'

When Alan arrived a little later the baby was on a resuscitation table and there were no signs of life coming from him. Alan came and sat down beside me and we held hands and prayed and prayed and prayed. It was the first time we'd ever prayed together, it was the first time we'd let each other knew that we believed in God. It took twenty-five minutes before he cried, and then they rushed him straight away and I was taken back to the ward.

The next day they put me into a wheelchair and took me down to see him. I was very weak, I was losing lots and lots of rubbish, the afterbirth was absolutely deteriorated and smelly, one of the nurses said to me:

'However he's lived in that, I don't know.'

When I saw him I couldn't believe that anything so small could survive. Although he was there and I knew he was mine I was frightened of getting attached to him. Earlier before his birth I was lying in bed at sleep time and I could hear a woman screaming and crying. Although no-one told me I knew her baby had died and the pain in her screams really terrified me so I held back my feelings. Her baby was called Michael and somehow I wanted to make up to her for her pain, so I called mine Michael too and prayed that he wouldn't go, that I wouldn't lose him.

I stayed in hospital for another ten days and he was growing stronger each day. I used to go down to the nursery and put my hands into the incubator and stroke his little face. When I left they gave me photos to take home with me. Of course, Michael had to stay in the hospital. We used to go in every day to see him. I learned how to tube feed him and when he was a month and a half they let me hold him. It was fantastic, looking down at him in my arms and knowing that he was mine and that one day we'd take him home with us. But he had a set-back, he got a heart murmur and so they had to keep him in hospital until he was two and half months and five pounds.

It was wonderful when he came home, but that was short-lived too, after twelve days the heart murmur returned and he had to go back into hospital. That was another very traumatic time, we thought we might lose him again, but he was only in for a couple of days and then he came home with the all clear.

Life started to return to normal. Doreen and I had cups of coffee together more frequently and a closeness began to develop. I told Doreen all about Michael's birth and my trauma through that. Doreen was having a very hard time, her husband had been off work, ill, for nine months, they had a lot of financial worries and five children to feed. Neither of us felt we could go out to work because we both had very small children but we talked about needing more money and the possibilities of taking work in at home.

One day Doreen came around with a newspaper advertisement for machinists to work at home. We both decided to give it a go. It was slave labour, we used to work from eight in the morning till ten at night for about forty quid a week. But we were both making a bit of money and of course we got to know each other much better too, we found out that we could work together. We were brought even closer because my experience with Michael's birth had led me and Alan to start going to Church and Doreen started to come with us. Life developed a pattern which included a lot of toing and froing between the two houses and a deep and trusting friendship between Doreen and me. A small gap in the hedge between our two back yards widened with the number of trips we made in and out of each other's back doors.

Not long after Michael turned two his eyes started puffing up and his tummy started swelling. I took him to a doctor but he dismissed the symptoms as being those of a cold. When I got home I was still worried, you know your own children and I felt in myself that it wasn't a cold. I was frighted in case it was the heart murmur again so I rung my own G.P. and he admitted him straight into hospital. Within half an hour the hospital had diagnosed that Michael had a chronic kidney disease which they called Nephrotic Syndrome.

·2·
DOREEN
CHASING DREAMS

When Pauline and Alan first moved in next door I wasn't the tiniest bit interested in neighbouring. Their house had been empty since we moved into ours and so it seemed like a loss of our privacy to suddenly have someone else living there. The two houses are a semi-detached pair so when Pauline's house was empty we felt free to make as much noise as we wanted and the kids used to flow over into the yard as if it were part of their own. Not surprisingly we felt a bit put out when suddenly we had to contain ourselves to our own side. I was keeping myself to myself in any case, I'd only moved to Blidworth a couple of years before when I had come to live with Pip from my own brand new detached bungalow in Kirkby. It was strange for me to be living in a pit house in a pit village where almost all the men worked together at the pit.

But living with and among miners was not a new experience. Both my Grandads were miners, in fact my very first memories are of my Mum's brothers coming home to my Grandma's house, black with coaldust from working at the pit. That was in Kirkby, I'd lived there all my life until I came to live in Blidworth.

When I was first born we lived with my mother's parents, my Grandad had moved to Kirkby in Nottinghamshire from Cambridge 'cause at that time there were lots of jobs in Notts. pits. My only memory of him was a very frail old man who was very tall and very very thin. My Grandma said that he used to be a big strapping man but I only remember him sitting on the front doorstep and you could see his bones and his ribs sticking out, he was dying of cancer. My Grandma had a great big copper and when my Mum's brothers were due home I'd help her fill it with water and we'd put a tin bath in front of it for them to wash themselves in, there were no showers at the pit then, like there are now, so they'd have to come home to wash the coal dust off themselves.

My Mum had seven brothers and they were all miners like their

Dad, they all used to sit around and talk about life down the pits. I used to listen, fascinated, but my Mum told me that she'd seen too much of what goes on at the pits and she vowed when she was very young that she wouldn't marry a miner.

We moved into our own house, the house my Mum still lives in, just after the first of my brothers was born, I must have been two years old. I continued to visit my Grandparents a lot and I always got on especially well with my Grandmas. I remember my Dad's father very well, he didn't die till I was eleven and I used to visit their house often from when I was about three. They used to live in a row of pit houses in Kirkby and when it was time for my Grandad to be coming home from work, my Grandma would take me to the front door and we'd watch for him to come walking up the street. When he got near enough my Grandma would let me run down the street to meet him.

He was a very grumpy man, he had my Grandma really under the table, she was really terrified of him. Whenever he came in, he expected his dinner to be ready and on the table and if it wasn't he'd scream at her. Every Saturday my Grandma and I used to go shopping. My Dad used to drop me off at my Grandma's at nine in the morning and I'd spend all day there. I'd walk around the shops and help my Grandma carry the shopping. We always used to call on the way back for fish for Saturday dinner, but it had to be ready, with the table set and everything by three o' clock when my Grandad came home from the Club otherwise he'd have a fit. Whenever you were there you had to sit and not murmur while he was watching television, he was that blooming grumpy.

My Grandma had to do everything for him and if it wasn't just how he liked it, he would yell and scream at her. The way he treated her used to upset me. If she poured him a cup of tea and put in his sugar but didn't stir it enough, he'd create and chuck the cup to the other side of the table. If ever she went out for any length of time, he wouldn't make himself a cup of tea or anything, he'd just sit in his chair, sulking, because she'd gone out.

When I was still very young he had an accident at the pit and had to have both his feet removed. When he got over the accident he still had to go back to work on pit tops because they didn't get thousands of pounds in compensation like they do now and so they had no money at all and he had to keep working. I remember him hobbling off to work on his sticks everyday and coming home exhausted just from the effort of having to walk.

I was sure that my Grandad didn't like me because he was always yelling at me.

I used to say to my Grandma, 'I know he don't love me 'cause he's always shouting at me.'

'Don't love you', she'd say. 'How can you say that, you know very well how upset he got when you had your accident.' Then she'd tell me about the time I'd fallen off the slide when I was about seven and been rushed to hospital unconscious. While I was waiting for an ambulance to come my Grandad had walked up to our house on his sticks to see how I was. At the time my Grandma was visiting her sister in Derbyshire and she loved to tell me that when she got home she found my Grandad sitting, crying, in his chair.

She said to him. 'Whatever's the matter Frank, what ever's up wi'ya.'

'It's our lass,' he said, 'You'd better get off up there, ambulance is come, they've raced her to hospital, you'd better get off quick, she's going to die, I know she's going to die.'

A few years ago I went to a spiritualist, I don't really believe in them, I went for a bit of a lark, but I was missing my Grandma who'd died only a couple of years before and I sort of hoped I might be able to talk to her. The spiritualist said to me. 'There's a man who's had an accident at pit.' Then her voice became irritable and cross and she said, 'Don't you drink that cream soda. You can have the pop but don't touch that cream soda.'

I knew it was my Grandad, every weekend my Grandma used to buy twelve little bottles of pop, six of them were always cream soda for my Grandad and the other six were for her. But my Grandma never got hers, she always gave them to me but my Grandad would never let me have his cream soda. He was like a baby, they had two drawers in the kitchen, one was my Grandma's and the other was Grandad's. I loved going to my Grandma's drawer, she had a little black cat and I used to love to take it out and turn it in my hands three times because she said that would bring me luck. I wasn't allowed in my Grandad's drawer, of course, but every so often when he wasn't looking I used to sneak a look in it. He kept some cough toffees in there and sometimes I'd pinch one, but he always found out, he was such a cantankerous old bugger that he used to count them.

In the end you had to feel sorry for him because he was so pathetic, he wanted everything his own way. When I was about eleven and he was about seventy-six he took very badly. One day he was lying in his bed in the front room, the doctor was there and I went in to see him.

He said, 'Hey up lass, you'll not be seeing me much longer, I'll not be on this earth long now.'

The doctor, who was a friend of the family, said, 'Don't be so bloody stupid, you'll be here a long while if you stop feeling so sorry for yourself.'

But he kept getting worse, my Mum and Dad used to come up a lot and my Grandma was sitting up at nights with him. He started having horrible fits and shouting and yelling out and talking nonsense. The last time I saw him he really terrified me, I was standing at the bottom of his bed and he was shouting and going at it and my Grandma said,

'Come on out, he's too far gone to know you now.'

I came out and cried and cried because my Grandad hadn't known who I was. A couple of days later we were all sitting around in the living room and Auntie Phyllis, Grandad's sister, was in the room with him.

She came out and said, 'He's gone.'

My Dad sat down on the floor with his legs outstretched and said, 'Poor old Frank.'

I said 'Has Grandad died?'

'Yes.' My Grandma said, 'He's gone to Jesus.'

The night after the funeral I asked my Grandma if I could stay with her and I ended up staying with her for about four months. We used to sit and talk and talk, she talked a lot about the old days, about her life and about my Grandad. After four months, my Mum made me go back home, I would have been happy to stay with my Grandma, I used to get spoilt there. I had three brothers at home and I don't think my Mum liked to see me getting spoilt and not them. Still I continued to go often to visit my Grandma, I was as close to her as I was to my Mum.

I think my Mum was quite hard on me because I was the only girl and she expected a lot from me. Sometimes I know that she felt sorry for something she'd made me do and she'd try to make up for it. I remember one time very clearly, my Mum was expecting my youngest brother, Stephen. She was very pregnant and as well as that she was looking after her own mother who was living with us but was very very sick. My Mum was very nasty tempered at that time. One night she wanted a loaf of bread from the shop which was just up the next street and she wanted me to fetch it for her. It was dark and there'd been a lot of talk about a rapist in the area. I said I daren't go, I was too frightened but my Mum really lost her temper and made me go.

I ran all the way, the street was deserted and I was petrified. I got the loaf and as I turned out of the shop to head home I looked up and at the bottom of the street ahead of me was this scary looking shape. I thought it was the rapist with a blanket over him and I thought he was coming to get me. Then I realised that it was my Mum standing there looking enormous in the dark because she was so pregnant. She'd come out to watch down the street to make sure that I was all right because she felt really upset and hurt that she'd made me go knowing I was so frightened.

Every year, ever since I can remember, we used to go on the train to Skegness and stay in a caravan for a week. They were really old fashioned caravans on legs, and they were all lined up in a field. My Mum used to save her Family Allowance every year and that used to pay for our holiday, without it we could never have afforded a holiday at all. In 1953 when I was about eight there had been terrible floods which had caused a lot of damage. Right next to the beach there were bungalows and the floods had ruined them. When we first arrived that year, we went down to the beach to have a look at the damage and it was eerie. The families in the bungalows had just left everything and fled and the beach was scattered with belongings, I especially remember seeing dolls and dolls' prams, ruined and stranded on the sand. One day we were on the beach packing things up to go back to the caravan. I said I'd run back to the caravan by myself, but everything had changed so much that I got lost. I was walking round and round a caravan site and there was nobody about because everyone had gone inside out of the rain. It seemed like hours and hours and I started to cry because I couldn't see anything that looked familiar. In the end a woman came out of one of the vans and walked around with me till we found my Mum who'd come looking for me. I'd ended up right on the other side of the site to where our caravan was because everything had changed so much because of the floods.

I was a very busy little kid, I went to Brownies, the Girl Guides, Life Brigade and I was very involved in the church, there weren't enough nights in the week for all the things I wanted to be involved in. I went to Sunday School from the time I was three and always loved it. As I got older I started going to more and more activities organised by the church. One of these was a Gazette Class, we were given papers to take around to peoples' houses to sell. They organised a day-trip to York one November. I was really looking forward to it, but when the time came it snowed and I had no boots, the only shoes I had were a pair of sandals and so it looked as if I wouldn't be able to go. I felt very sorry for myself, it seemed as if I did everything else with the church and that when it was time to have an outing I couldn't go. When my Mum saw how upset I was she borrowed the money to get me a pair of boots so I could go.

We never had much money, my Mum only ever had one dress to go out in and I can remember she used to have to wash it, iron it and put it straight on if she was going out.Every year, the two Sundays leading up to Whit Monday were Sunday School Anniversaries. They were brilliant, the church was always full, morning, afternoon and night and the Sunday School kids always helped with running the Services. Then, on Whit Monday there was always a big rally and march around Kirkby and all the churches would take part in it. It was a really big event, there were banners and streamers and everybody got dressed up in their best. Every year my Mum saved her Co-op dividends to buy us all a new outfit for the Anniversaries. The lads always got a new suit and I always had two new dresses.

During the Anniversary Services I always read a poem. One year, when I was about twelve, they asked me if I'd read the Twenty-third Psalm and if I'd take elocution lessons to help me to speak out clearly. I was very flattered and pleased, it was a great honour. A week or so later the Superintendent came to our house to see my Mum and Dad to ask if I could read the sermon from the pulpit on the second Anniversary Sunday. Each year they chose two of the teenagers to read the sermon each Sunday. My Mum and Dad called me into the room and asked me if I'd like to do it. This was the greatest honour of all and I was only twelve and had been asked to do it, I was over the moon. I was to recite the Twenty-third Psalm and read the sermon, I felt as if all the hard work I'd put into the church was being recognised.

When we went to buy our new clothes that year I saw a red nylon dress with white flowers on it, it was so pretty, I could just imagine myself standing up in the pulpit with it on. It was very expensive, I think it was three pound ten, and I could have had three or four dresses for that, but my Mum was so proud of me that she let me have it.

The Anniversary Celebrations that year were really fantastic for me, I'll always remember them. I stood up in the pulpit on the second Sunday and proudly read the sermon. It was just after tape recorders first came out and they recorded it, which made it seem very impor-tant. I felt wonderful, as I was reading I looked down at my Dad and the look of pride on his face as he looked up at me made me feel really excited. The next day at the Whit Sunday Parade they asked me to carry our church banner because I'd read the sermon and so I marched all around the main street of Kirkby in front of everybody else carrying our church banner.

After that I started going to scripture classes twice a week where I had to take examinations. If you did this for so many years, and got high enough marks in the exams, then you automatically went on to become a Sunday School teacher. I did it every year and always got prizes and highly recommended but when I was about fifteen they closed our Sunday School down because they couldn't afford to keep it. I went to Wesleyan Methodist Sunday School a couple of times, but I didn't like it, after that I sort of drifted away from the church and only ever went to christenings, weddings and funerals. Whenever I went into a church I always enjoyed it but I never committed myself again until I turned back to the church a couple of years ago.

I used to enjoy school a lot, especially primary school. I can remember my first day. My mother took me up and left me there crying. I had to find my own way home for lunch and then go back again on my own. That was it, she never took me up again. But I settled in pretty quickly, I was a reasonably bright kid and got reasonably good reports. When I went up from infants to juniors I was in the A stream. The only thing I remember hating was the milk we had to drink, it made me sick. I failed the eleven plus, so I went to a Secondary Modern and I was in the A stream there as well. I loved reading, writing, spelling, composition and history, but I didn't like maths and physical education, I was never a very energetic kid. I used to worry about maths, I can remember sitting up at nights, trying to learn my tables and I was pathetic at it, it just wouldn't come. I used to read lots and lots, I think I must have read every book written for kids over and over again.

When I went into third year, the class had to elect a Prefect and a Vice-prefect. Somebody nominated me and I was elected Vice-Prefect. I couldn't believe it, I had no idea I was liked enough to get that position. Later, when my daughter Karen came home from school one day really surprised that she'd been voted class prefect, I understood exactly how she felt because the same thing had happened to me and I could talk to her about it knowing exactly how she felt.

When I was fifteen I left school and got a job machining in a factory. I didn't particularly want to, but my Mum said she needed the money. For the first three months I was training, I learnt to operate all the machines in the place. Then I started on as a fully trained machinist. I earned three pounds ten and used to give my Mum three pounds. As I got better at it I earned more and did lots of overtime as well, so I had quite a lot of money for myself. There was a union there and when they asked me to join, I didn't know what to do, so I went home and asked my Dad.

'You join it,' he said. 'You've got to join your union.' So I joined, but it was a small private firm and if you ever had any problems you could always thrash them out with the boss. So we never went to the union at all the whole time I was there.

At one stage something really got at me and I bottled it up and bottled it up and then finally applied for another job and got it. The next morning I put my notice in and the boss called me into his office.

'What's this?' he said, waving my notice at me.

'It's me notice.'

'Have you been and got another job?'

'Yeah.'

He asked me where, and when I told him he picked up the phone and dialled a number.

'I understand you've got Doreen coming to work for you.'

He waited a while and then said, 'Well, she's changed her mind, she won't be coming after all.' And he hung up the phone.

'What have you done that for, because I am going.'

'No you're not, you're going to sit down here and we're going to thrash out whatever's the matter with you and we'll sort it out.'

That's how he was, very fair with everybody, it was a good firm to work for. They used to take us all on holidays, we went to Belgium, Holland and France. He paid for everything and gave us some spending money as well. You could take a friend too, of course they'd have to pay something towards it, but it was great. I know people used to say that they'd get the money back on tax, but still not all firms gave you a free holiday.

One weekend we went to Blackpool and saw Cliff Richard for the first time. The trip was going to be to Bournemouth, but we all wanted to see Cliff Richard. He was at the top of the Hit Parade at that time and was doing some concerts in Blackpool. He'd always been my idol and to see him was fantastic, he was even better than I'd expected. I'd never seen anything like it, everybody was nearly hysterical with excitement and we were all there along with the rest, screaming and yelling and going at it. I really enjoyed working at that firm, when the Manager left, everybody put in to buy him a clock. There were about three hundred workers at the factory altogether and I thought it was a great honour that they asked me to present the clock to him.

When I was fifteen, just as I started work, I also started courting. We got married when I was nineteen. During that time we hardly ever went out anywhere, we spent most of our time at my house or his, mostly his. We saved and saved and talked about getting married and having our own house.

It was all that seemed important, the one thing we shared was wanting our own modern bungalow. We had a great big white wedding and I suppose at the time I couldn't see past that. It seemed to me that all I'd ever wanted was to be a bride, have a big wedding and my own house. It felt as if my dream was coming true.

For the first year of our marriage we lived at my mother's house and it wasn't a very happy year. Karen was born while we were there and then, when she was three months old we moved into our first house. By the time I was twenty-one, Paul had been born and so I had two children and my own house. My dream had come true but I was far from happy. I was really very bored, we never went out, the house was new and so the housework didn't take long. I didn't feel as if my life had any meaning, it consisted of cleaning the house, knitting and watching television.

We had moved out of Kirkby and so we decided to move back into the village and have a brand new bungalow built to our own specifications. When we moved into it, Karen had just started school. But moving into the new house didn't change anything much at all. I was still very bored with my life as a wife and mother. When my husband came in from work, he would just lie down on the settee and go to sleep. If I ever asked him to take me out he made me feel like some kind of freak that wasn't worth bothering about. Whenever I tried to express to him how I felt being stuck in the house all the time, he'd say, 'I must be crazy, being stuck with you.' After a while I started to get an inferiority complex. I started to believe that there must be something wrong with me and that I really wasn't worth bothering about. It got so bad that I wouldn't go out of the house because I thought people would laugh at me and were talking about me. I started taking nerve tablets and at one stage went to see a psychiatrist about it, but nothing seemed to help.

Then someone offered me a job in an outside catering firm. I started going out and working at nights while my husband stayed in with the kids. It was during the time of the mini-skirt and I used to wear a black mini-skirt and white apron. I was the youngest woman working there and I started to notice that I was meeting people and talking to them and I was really getting quite a lot of attention, particularly from men. I had been feeling so bad about myself that all the attention went to my head and I started to have an affair. It got quite serious and I left my husband and took the kids to live with this bloke. But that didn't work out either and after two years I moved into my mother's house again with the kids.

Being back at my mother's was not easy either, I suppose I'd had my own house for quite a while and I was used to doing things my own way. My mother was very opposed to me leaving my husband in the first place and so was my Grandma. I'd continued to be really really close to her through all these years. By this time she was living with my mother and it broke my heart that she'd turned against me. She was always the only person I could really talk to and now I felt unable to talk to her because she was so upset about what I'd done. I felt completely alone in the world.

Once I moved into my mother's, my husband started saying that he wanted me to go back with him. One Sunday he came down to pick up the kids for the day and left a note saying that he wanted to see me. Later that day, when I went up to get the kids we had a long talk, he said he really wanted to give it a second try.

I said, 'Well, if I do, would you agree to me being able to work as soon as Paul's settled into school. I don't want just to be a wife and mother, just being there at your beck and call like I was before. I'd want to go to work so I could have my own independence.'

He said he'd do anything, if I went back to him, so we decided to go out together that night for a drink.

I asked my Dad if he'd look after the kids for me and he was over the moon. I think it had been as hard for them to have me and the kids there as it was for me. Their kids had all grown up and they were used to just being on their own, so suddenly having two little kids in the house again was quite a shock.

That night my husband and I seemed to get on really well. Things seemed very different from how I'd remembered them, we talked and talked and I really enjoyed myself. The next day while he was at work I went up and let myself into the bungalow. As soon as I walked in I felt more at home than I had for two years. It seemed that this was where I belonged so I decided to move back in.

We both tried very hard to make it work. Once the kids were both at school I got a job and for a while I started to enjoy my life again. But there was one thing missing, although I tried and tried I couldn't get any intimacy back into the marriage. That was my fault, I just couldn't feel that way about him any more. Although he was trying ever so hard and I wanted it to work very much, that side of things just wasn't right. Even when we were courting I found that side of things difficult. He was the first man I'd been with and he wanted sex all the time, whereas I needed lots of loving and he couldn't somehow see the difference. I knew even then that something was wrong but I was so tied up with all the plans we'd made and my own dreams that I'd allowed myself to get carried along by events and ignored the warnings that were deep inside me.

For about two years the reconciliation was quite good but then things started to drift back into what they had been before. But this time, I had a bit of independence, I had a wage and I had a car. The kids were growing up, I started to get sick of not going out at night. I was quite happy with my job, and with coming home and looking after my kids and cleaning up my house, but then I wanted to go out a bit. I wanted to feel as if I was living a little bit.

I used to say to him, 'you're only on this earth once, you've got to live.'

We started falling out over it, we started falling out over all sorts of things and then we started to go out separately. I used to go out on Thursday nights on my own and he used to go out on Friday nights. In the end we were living separate lives. He used to go out and not come back for a few days, I knew he was with other women but I didn't think I could do anything about it.

I thought it was my fault. After all if I could give him what a wife should, he wouldn't need to go with other women, but at the same time I didn't much care. I was determined not to leave him again, I couldn't bear the thought of putting the kids through all the upset the first separation had caused. But I used to go out too and I always enjoyed myself when I did. There were outings from work I used to go on and I used to go drinking every Friday night. After a while I started having affairs too and we started falling out about it, but we never admitted to each other that we were having affairs.

This went on for years and years, I wasn't really happy, deep down I felt very guilty about what I was doing. I sometimes wondered what God must think of me, but at the same time I'd feel very bitter towards God for giving me so much suffering. Whenever I felt myself getting serious about anybody, I'd break it off, the last thing I wanted to do was to move with the kids again.

One night I went to the Miners' Welfare at Rainworth. A group of us were standing around talking. Someone introduced me to this bloke who I could feel had been looking at me for some time. When the music started for the last dance I said to him:
  'Well, are you going to ask me for last waltz or not?'
  'I can't dance,' he said, but somebody whisked his pint off him and we had the last waltz. As it ended he asked if he could see me to the car.

We sat in the car and he started all over me.
  'Look,' I said, 'I want to get one thing straight. I might be here at Rainworth Welfare on my own and I might have a stormy marriage, but that doesn't mean I'm going to have sex with anyone unless I really know them.'

We made arrangements to meet again then started seeing each other quite regularly. He was a miner called Pip and I could feel myself getting quite involved emotionally and I decided to call it all off. I didn't trust relationships, the two I'd had had both in their different ways been disasters and I wasn't prepared to put the kids through a lot of trauma again.

When we next met I said, 'I've got sommat to tell you.'

'What.'

'Well, I want you to understand......'

But he wouldn't let me finish, he said,

'If you're going to say what I think you're going to say don't say if before you listen, 'cause I've got something to say 'n all.'

'What's that.'

'Oh, it don't matter, it's your decision, you're going to tell me you want to break if off, aren't ya?'

'Yes, why, what do you want to say?'

'Nothing, it don't matter, if that's your decision.'

'So you're quite happy with that decision then, are you?' He said, 'No, I'm not happy with that decision'. He hesitated, he isn't a man to throw words around and I already knew him well enough to know that he found emotional things hard to talk about, but he managed to say,

'No, I'm not happy with that because I love you.' I could feel myself suddenly filled with fear, I said,

'Well, that's really put the kybosh on it then hasn't it?'

'Why?'

'I didn't want you to say that.'

'Well,' he said, 'It's true and I want you to go home and think about it. I won't ring you or anything, I just want you to think about it.'

So I drove him home and as he got out of the car he said: 'Remember what I've said, 'cause I mean it.' That night I couldn't sleep, I tossed and turned and didn't know what to do with myself. The next morning after my husband had gone to work at seven o' clock I sat with a cup of coffee and tried to make some sense of my feelings and my situation. It was a very difficult situation. I was living with a man from whom I'd become estranged and who'd never really made me happy. Now another man was offering me happiness, he had his own house, his wife had left him some time before and he had told me that he loved me and I knew I loved him. But I still wasn't sure if I trusted that enough to risk the security that I had with my husband

and could give my kids. As I was sitting there trying to work it all out, the phone rang. It was Pip.

I said, 'I thought you weren't ringing me any more.'

'I can't help it, have you thought about what I said last night.'

'Of course I have, I can't think of anything else can I, you've put me in a funny position.'

'Well I don't want us to pack it up.'

I told him that I would have to think about things some more and ring him back.

At this time a friend and I were making children's clothes and selling them at the market. We also used to do parties in people's houses to sell them. I went to the market and rang Pip up and we had a talk on the phone and I arranged to meet him in a few days after one of the parties. All the time I felt it was wrong, I thought I should leave it alone, but I couldn't.

I was very tense over the next few days, and when I finally got over to Pip's house he was very miserable. He told me that he'd been listening to a record and that he was going to buy it for me. Just then it was played on the radio. It was Andrew Gold, 'Never Let Her Slip Away'. As I listened to the words I started to feel differently about everything, the confusion lifted and I knew what I had to do.

To protect myself I decided not to move in with Pip straight away, but to get a council house and live there on my own with the kids for a while to see how things worked out. I knew that lots of new council houses were being built in Kirkby at that time and so I put myself onto the waiting list for one. I was told to expect about a three months wait. I told my husband what I had done and that I was going to leave him as soon as I could get a house. Things between us then started to deteriorate even more, they got very bad.

Pip and I introduced our kids to each other. Karen was twelve and Paul was nine. Pip had two boys David, who was eleven and another Paul who was also nine. We decided to take them all out for a picnic. When I picked them up in the car, Pip sat in the front with me and all the kids piled into the back. None of the kids said a word. Pip and I were as nervous as anything and I could feel Pip looking at me and whittling because they weren't getting on. When we got to the picnic spot, I took a football out of the car and the three boys quickly joined in playing football, and were soon the best of mates. But Karen was very reserved and didn't want anything to do with it. Pip was worrying about her and asked her if she'd like us all to go back to his place for some tea.

'What is there?' she said, very off-handed.'

Well I've got a piece of steak in the fridge, if you'd like that.' Karen's face lit up, she adores steak, Pip had won her heart, after that the atmosphere relaxed, it had been a big test but it had worked out well.

After that I used to take the kids to Pip's and often we'd all stay the night. The kids were really at home there. In fact, they were happier there than they were at home because things between me and their father had got so bad. One day after an especially nasty fight between me and my husband I decided that I couldn't live with him any more. I asked the kids if they wanted to move into Pip's house and they were dead keen. So I rang him up at work that morning. 'Hello, Pip, we're coming.' That was all I said, I didn't know what to say.

'What, for your tea' he said.

'No, I'm coming and I'm bringing the kids.'

He said, 'What, for good?'

'Yeah.'

'Oh, I better ring me Dad and tell him I can't come down and help him with his car then hadn't I. What time will you be here?'

Pip wasn't all that surprised, although I'd never said that I'd consider moving in with him before a council house became available. He knew that the situation at home was getting worse and worse.

That was in June. Once I'd moved in with Pip and it was working quite well, I knew I'd never move into a council house on my own, so I took our name off the waiting list. But the first few months were by no means all plain sailing, we did have our problems. It took some adjusting for us all to live together, it was quite different from just visits, but we were happy despite the difficulties. At Christmas I said to Pip, 'How about you and I have a baby of our own?'

'Don't you think we've got enough mouths to feed,' he said, not very keen on the idea.

'Yes I do, but we've two of your and two of mine, if we had one of our own, it would really bring us all together, we'd all really be related and I think it would help the tensions between the kids.' Eventually he agreed and within three months I was pregnant.

We'd always said that we weren't going to get married. I was getting bigger and bigger with Mark and one evening as we were laying on the settee together, which we always did in the evening, I said, 'Shall we get married?'
'What for?'
'Shall we?'
'Well, it's only a piece of paper.'
'Yes I know, but shall we?'
'Do you really want to?'
'Well, I don't know, because if we get married we don't want to lose what we've got now. That's the only thing, sometimes when people get married they take each other for granted. I want you to know, that if we get married and we lose this, I shan't stay with you. So don't feel that by getting married you can take me for granted and feel that you can treat me any way you like, 'cause you can't.'
'Well, are we getting married then?'
'Do you think they'd mind me coming to the registry office as big as this, seven months pregnant?'
'I don't know, I suppose not.'
'All right, I think we might as well do it then.'

At that time we were living in Pip's house, the same one he'd lived in with his ex-wife. Even though we'd redecorated it and I'd bought all my own furniture and stuff over, I never really felt comfortable there, I always felt as if it was someone else's house. Because it was a rented pit house, it was a bit of a problem, because the pit wouldn't find us another. I decided to put a notice up in the Post Office to see if anybody wanted to do a swap. That's what happened, we got married in July and moved a couple of weeks later.

Mark was the most spoilt child you've even seen, all of us doted on him. He was the link between us all, all the kids felt that link. Mark was everybody's brother. He never whimpered without one of us would be there picking him up and making sure his every need was met. Pip absolutely adored him and became very involved looking after him. Our naps on the couch now included Mark and often Pip would lie for hours on the sofa half dozing with Mark half dozing beside him. It was wonderful for me to really share a baby with it's father the way Pip and I shared Mark. My first husband had never had anything much to do with the kids when they were babies and so I enjoyed just watching Pip and Mark together.

The house next door was empty but then Pauline and Alan moved in and at first we all kept ourselves to ourselves. After a bit Pauline and I would occasionally chat with each other.

I was very busy with four teenage kids and a baby so I didn't have much time anyway. I knew that Pauline was having a lot of trouble with her second pregnancy so I used to go around and help her. After that we were a little closer, but still not much.

Then Pip got ill, he had hurt his knee at work and had to have his cartilage removed. He had to wait ages and ages for the operation and then when he finally had it done, he came out of hospital on a Friday only to be rushed to Mansfield General Hospital on Monday in terrible pain and having trouble breathing. It turned out that he had a blood clot on his lung and he nearly died, it was really a terrible time. I was worried sick about Pip, rushing into the hospital whenever I could to be with him. Having to keep things going at home and looking after the kids was taking it's toll on me.

One night, the hospital rang and said I'd better get straight in, he was in a very critical condition. Later I came back home, he seemed to be all right but was still in a very dangerous condition. When I got home I sat in front of the television blankly staring at the screen wondering what I would do if Pip died. Suddenly my old teenage hero, Cliff Richard came on the screen. I can remember him saying, 'Jesus Christ is knocking on the door of your heart, he only wants to be let in.' That night I went to bed and prayed for the first time for years and years. I prayed for Pip to be alive, I said, 'What will I do with five kids and Pip dead?' The next day Pip was much better.

A couple of weeks later I went around to have a cup of coffee with Pauline and I told her about Pip's illness and how worried I'd been about him. She started to tell me about Michael's birth and about how her and Alan had turned to God when he was born and she thought that his birth was a miracle, because he had actually died and when her and Alan had started to pray he had started to breath.

She said to me, 'You might think I'm being stupid, but I'm not, that's just how it was for me.'

Pauline and Alan had started going to church, we talked for a long time about religion, but I didn't do anything about it. Pip was getting better and I was busy keeping things at home going.

Pip went back to work eventually, altogether he'd been off for nine months and during that time he'd paid no maintenance. He was supposed to pay his ex-wife fifteen pounds a week maintenance because when she had left she had taken their two youngest children with her. We weren't very happy about the maintenance anyway. Pip's ex-wife had remarried a miner who was probably making as much money as Pip was, so the situation didn't seem very fair.

When Pip went back to work they wanted to put him on light work for a while but he wanted to get back to his own job. The first week he almost lived at the pit, he worked so much overtime that at the end of the week he'd made £290 before tax. But all he brought home was £20. They deducted the rest for the maintenance payments that were owing. For three months Pip brought home twenty quid a week. It was impossible to make it spin out, to feed seven of us. The result was that Pip was very nasty tempered because he felt that he wasn't able to bring home enough money to feed us. I was nasty tempered because I was trying to make twenty quid a week feed a family of seven.

It was one of the most difficult times of my life. I was very bitter that we were struggling so hard just to make payments to another woman who I didn't think needed or deserved them. I didn't believe that the courts could be so callous to our needs and leave us to try and survive on such a pittance. The kids seemed to pick up the atmosphere. Teenage kids are always difficult and I was increasingly finding that having a mixed family could be very trying. With both Pip and I being very tense things in the house were very difficult.

The kids were trying to establish themselves as grown up, and that was complicated for everybody by the fact that Pip and I were each step-parents to two of them. Bringing your own teenage kids up is difficult but trying to bring someone else's up is very hard, because you've got to be so careful. It fell mostly on me I think, being the woman. It was harder for me with Pip's kids than it was for him with mine. Things got so bad that Pip and I were going to split up, not because there was anything wrong between us, but because things with the kids were so bad. I really felt that I couldn't cope, I felt at the end of my wits. I was on nerve tablets and I just didn't know where to turn.

I went around to visit Pauline and the Pastor from the Church she went to was there. He knew straight away who I was. He said to Pauline as I walked in.

'Is this your neighbour from that side.'

Then he looked at me and said, 'How are you, alright?' I was so low, I couldn't even casually say yes when someone asked how I was, so I said 'No, I'm not.'

'Why don't you come to church' he said.

'I can't come to church, I haven't got the time, I've got five kids to look after.' I said, but after he'd left I said to Pauline.

'I think I might come to church with you on Sunday.'

'Are ya?'

'Well what have I got to lose, things can't get any worse, it's either that or the nuthouse. There's only that left and if it helped you, it might help me.'

The following Sunday I went, and I sat there right through the service and got nothing at all from it, not a thing. Through that week things got worse and worse, I had an enormous row with David, Pip's eldest son and he moved out to his Grandparents' house. Pip wanted him to come back, he wanted to come back, but somehow I just felt too depressed about everything to make a decision or to imagine anything but more rows. I was beside myself feeling that I just wasn't coping with the situation.

The next Sunday I decided to go back to church with Pauline

and Alan. I don't know why I went, it was a Pentecostal Church, people were throwing their arms up in the air shouting, 'Praise the Lord' and 'Allelujah'

I thought, 'Oh, these people are mad, whatever am I doing here, I must be crazy.'

All the way through the service I kept wishing it would end, thinking, 'There's no way I'm coming here again, I think I'm crackers, but these are worse.'

When the Pastor gave his sermon, I listened and a lot of what he said seemed to reach out to me, and have meaning for me. As I listened I thought, 'Well alright, but I feel so stupid sitting here, there's no way I'll come back unless I have proof that Jesus Christ exists.'

The service ended and Alan went off to take his Grandma back to Sutton. Pauline and I were talking to people and this man who I knew vaguely because he worked at the pit with Pip said,

'What's made you come to church, Doreen?'

'Problems.'

'I'm glad to see you here.'

'Well, there's no way I'm coming again unless I find that there's some truth in what you all keep saying.'

'What do you want out of life? Do you want to find peace and contentment?'

'Yeah, that's what I come hoping to find.'

'Do you believe?'

'I've always believed, or rather, I've never not believed, although I think that God's given me a raw deal. I've always believed that he's there and can see everything I'm doing.'

'Well, what do you want then?'

'I want help from him, and I want proof that he's there.'

The Pastor came over then and asked me to go and talk to him in his back room. He asked me what was the matter and I told him.

He said, 'Well, what way do you want to go, do you want to find out if God's really there and if he can really help you?'

'Yeah, I do.'

He started to say a prayer, at first I felt really stupid, I thought, 'Ooh, people will think I'm crackers, I hope nobody hears about this', but as he went on and as I started to say the prayer with him, I felt something happening to me. It started in my toes, then went right up my body and right off the top of my head. All the depression had gone. I came out of there and I was singing and I was laughing, Pauline and I walked up the street dancing. I felt as I had never felt before. As we were singing and dancing up the street I didn't care if people saw us and I didn't care what they thought, all of that self consciousness had gone too.

I started to go to church regularly and got very involved in it. Things keep happening that gave me more faith, it seemed that everything I asked for I got. It wasn't so much that anything changed, we still had very bad money problems. There were still fights with the kids and between the kids, but I felt that I could cope with it all. I'd been taking nerve tablets for years and over the last few months a lot of them. I just stopped taking them, without even thinking about it I just stopped. Whenever things got really bad there seemed some way out, I no longer felt trapped in an endless tunnel.

Pauline went away for a week to a Christian Camp, and one day while she was away, I was sitting, machining and singing some of the choruses we sang at church. Suddenly I started thinking about a Sunday School. It was like a sudden thought or a voice or something. It was as if it was saying to me that I'd got to do something about a Sunday School. It confused me quite a lot because I thought there was already a Sunday School at the church and yet I was having this very powerful feeling about it. It kept playing on my mind and started to drive me crackers.

When Pauline came back, I said to her, 'I've got a problem.'

'What's that?'

'Well, while you were away I got this thought into my head that I had to something about a Sunday School, but there's already a Sunday School at the church in't there?' She started to laugh.

'What's funny?'

'Well, its really strange, 'cause when I was at Hollybush I had a message, somebody said that I had to do something about helping with a Sunday School.'

We invited the Pastor up to the house and said we wanted to get a Sunday School together.

'That's great,' he said. 'It's a wonderful idea, but you know you're new members to the church and it might upset people if I just let you come into church and set up a Sunday School. Besides, there aren't any kids. Perhaps you should bring Amanda and Mark down to the Sunday School that is there and see what you think about it.' The next week I took Amanda and Mark but I didn't like the way the Sunday School was run. Mark hated it, he didn't want to go any more.

A couple of weeks later that Sunday School just closed down, the two kids stopped going. We asked the Pastor again and he said, 'If you can get thirty-five kids together, you can have a Sunday School.'

So we started, all of a sudden kids who we'd never seen in the village before came knocking on our doors asking to play with our kids. They came five and six at a time, all in about three days. These kids used to come and play and me and Pauline would be sitting out on the garden, or the kids would come into the house for something and we'd talk to them. We asked them if they'd like to come to a Sunday School in Pauline's house. The first Sunday we had thirteen kids, the second week we had eighteen, then twenty and it grew and grew.

Eventually the Pastor agreed to give us the key to the church so we could bring the children in for Sunday School. The Sunday School thrived, but there were a lot of people in that church who weren't very pleased about what we were doing.

Just before Christmas we suggested that we bring the Sunday School kids into the church to do a Carol Service, singing the Carols that we'd taught them. We thought it would be a good way to bring people to the church who'd never been before and we knew that was one of the main concerns of the Pastor and the other church members. On the appointed day the church was full, they were fetching seats out of another room. There were people standing at the back and more people sitting in the aisle on the floor. People who'd never been in that church came to see those kids. There'd never been more than twenty people in that Church before and for the first time it was full to the brim. There were parents, aunties, uncles, grandmas and grand-dads, it was one of the biggest things that had happened in this village for years. The Pentecostal Church was full because of this fantastic Sunday School that had opened up. The kids all stood at the front with Pauline and me and sang beautifully, everybody was thrilled.

Things continued on for a while and we decided to have an open service, on a Sunday afternoon to let people know what the kids were doing at Sunday School.

This Sunday afternoon we had exactly the same response as we'd had to the Carol Service, the church was packed out again. But this time there was no-one there to preach. There was just me and Pauline and forty kids and all their families.

We didn't preach at all. I started the service by welcoming everybody into the place, then I thanked God for bringing the kids into our Sunday School and said a little bit about how we'd got the Sunday School together. Then Pauline talked a bit about the things that we did at the Sunday School and then we let the kids take over. The bigger kids gave lessons from the bible and they sang songs and we got one of the women to read a story. It was really fantastic, it'd never happened before.

Despite the enormous success of our two major events we met continuing opposition to everything we suggested. We wanted to take the kids on a Sunday School outing, but the Pastor said that he didn't have any money to put towards the bus. As we worked on the idea, people started coming to our doors asking if their kids could come on the outing and offering to pay towards the cost of the bus. We raised enough money and we took the kids and some of their parents and everybody had a great time.

As Harvest time approached we wanted to bring the kids into the church to the Harvest Festival and have them bring fruit and vegetables up to the front and sing Harvest songs, but we were told that would be too much trouble. Then we wanted to have a bonfire, but they said that would be too much trouble and cost too much money. So we got fed up with asking. We started talking about leaving the church but it was a big decision to make and we were very worried about it. But we felt we had no choice really and decided to leave. To our amazement most of the kids wanted to come with us, so we continued with the Sunday School in our own home as it had been in the beginning.

Soon after that I saw vacancies for machinists advertised in the local paper and rang up about them. Pauline decided she wanted to try to get one too. With the two men working shift work we were fairly sure we could work out child-care arrangements between us all. The money was much better than working at home and money was very short. The men were working with an overtime ban, miners depend on their overtime for a decent standard of living. Without it Pip, who is a qualified electrician and therefore one of the better paid workers at the pit, was only bringing home between eighty and ninety quid a week. On top of the difficulties that had arisen when he was off work we could barely manage on the money and so I was quite keen to go out and make some more. I wasn't all that happy with the Miners' Union, I felt that they hadn't helped Pip when we were in such trouble and I wasn't at all impressed by Arthur Scargill, I thought he was just out for a strike. He'd called two ballots and lost them both, then they put the overtime ban on and it seemed to go on and on.

Pip didn't ever tell me much about what went on at union meetings, he thought I wasn't bothered. He'd just tell me if something happened that was to affect us. When the overtime ban came on I remember he came home and just said, 'There's going to be an overtime ban and it'll go on for a long time.' One day a few months after Pauline and I had started going out to work Pip came back from a union meeting.

'Arthur Scargill's coming to Blidworth, to our next meeting.' he said.

After the meeting attended by Scargill, Pip came home and said, 'He's right you know.'

'He isn't right at all and I don't want to listen. If he's turned you his road I don't want to listen.'

'But you don't even know what I'm going to say.'

'I don't care, I don't want to hear.' To tell the truth I was terrified he would tell me that there was going to be a strike. My mind was so poisoned against Arthur Scargill by the media and I was so terrified of a strike and what it would do to our already disastrous finances that I just wouldn't listen. But Pip kept on and on, in the end he made me listen.

At the meeting someone has asked Scargill what he was going to do about the overtime ban. People were becoming impatient with it and some of them thought we should go for a strike instead and settle the issue more quickly. Scargill had said that it was not time to strike now, that with summer approaching we should wait and consider a strike in November. Pip said,

'I agree with that. I think he's right. And I think if we don't get any result from the overtime ban by the beginning of winter we should think about a strike then.'

I said, 'Oh well, if that's what you think, you do what you think right. You know more about it than I do.' But I added,

'How are we going to manage, all I've had to do since I met you is struggle and now we'll have to struggle again by the sounds of it.'

But on the other hand I'd been watching the television and I'd seen different places closing down. There was a great outcry when it was announced that there were a million on the dole but still I kept seeing that they were closing down this and closing down that and making cuts to the other. I wondered where it was all going to end and I also wondered when it would be our turn. Somehow we all knew that sooner or later the Government would turn on the Miners and then what would happen because everybody so far was calling on the Miners for support.

Little did I know that it would only be another six weeks before I would begin to find out the answers to these questions and to learn what these things would mean for me and my life.

·3·
PAULINE
BREAKING THROUGH

Doreen and I were standing in the backyard to chat and enjoy the sunshine. Mark and Michael were playing with some trucks nearby. I looked over at their happy little faces and suddenly felt a surge of joy at the sight of Michael looking so fit and healthy and playing just like any other child. 'Look at him, Doreen,' I said. 'Isn't he lovely now, he's really looking like himself.' There'd been so much illness in Michael's life and all the anxiety I'd felt about him was washed away for that moment.

Since they'd diagnosed Nephrotic Syndrome he'd been a very sick little boy. The first attack had kept him in hospital for two weeks, and the two years since then he'd had about six relapses. It had been a very hard time for all of us, just when we were confident that he would be fit and healthy we were suddenly confronted by the fact that he had a very serious disease which could only be held in check by giving him regular doses of steroids. The steroids themselves had all sorts of side effects including a tendency to obesity and hyper-action, so the hospital was reducing the dosage to try and find the best balance.

We had to test his urine every day to measure the amount of protein in it. Too much protein was a danger sign, it meant that his kidneys were not retaining it as they should and therefore he was likely to have a relapse. We also had to take him to the hospital every week for tests. Those hospital visits had become more and more tedious over the last year, we always had to wait hours and hours. I never felt at ease in the hospital, there were always so many people bustling about and I felt as if they didn't really have time for us. Somehow you almost felt guilty just being there, but we had no choice, Michael's illness was very serious. It was awful, just waiting and waiting with a lively little boy getting cantankerous because he was so bored. We used to get quite annoyed about it. One day, one of the doctors was walking about obviously half asleep, Alan asked him what was wrong. He told us he'd been on call for the last forty-eight hours and that all the staff were really run down because there'd been so many cut-backs in the hospital budget. We were quite shocked, we'd heard about Government cuts to the Health Service but it hadn't really hit home before that it was affecting us. Alan said, 'How can the Government and Health Authorities expect you to give a full hundred per cent to these children in your care; sometimes it could be a matter of life or death.' The doctor agreed, he said, 'You're right, but what can we do.'

As the steroid doses got lower, Michael began to return to his proper weight and as I stood with Doreen watching him and Mark playing I was overcome by how beautiful his wiry little body really was. The next day when I tested his urine it was showing too much protein. I wasn't really worried it was only 2+, when it gets up to three or four it becomes really dangerous. But the next day it was right up to four. It was a Friday, we rang the hospital and they said they'd ring back. But they never did.

We rang again on the Saturday morning, but there were no Consultants there over the weekend and they told us to leave it till Monday. By Sunday night he was screaming with pain. We wrapped him up in a sleeping bag and rushed him into hospital. When they examined him, they said they couldn't feel anything in his tummy but they'd keep him in because of his high protein count. They said they'd call the Consultant and they settled him down for the night and then sent us home. After that he started swelling again and he just swelled and swelled. They increased the doses of Steroids, but things seemed to stay the same for about a week. There were no signs at all that he was getting better.

Everybody was worried about him, some evenings we'd call in to see my parents on our way home from the hospital to let them know how he was. They kept asking if we were sure that he was getting proper treatment, they wanted us to get a second opinion. Alan's parents were saying the same sort of thing so we decided that we should have a word with the Consultant when we saw her the following Tuesday if nothing had changed.

That week the Government announced that Cortonwood Colliery in Yorkshire was to be closed on Monday, 12th March. The Cortonwood miners walked out on strike on Friday, 9th March to prevent the closure from taking place. The rest of the Yorkshire pits followed suit.

There'd been discussion for some time about a strike, no-one was very happy with the situation, but the NUM executive had lost two ballots. When we first heard the news about Cortonwood, we were very surprised and confused, but worry about Michael overshadowed it. By the weekend we were fairly sure there would be a strike. Alan and I discussed it.

I asked him, 'If there's a ballot, how will you vote?'

'I'll vote for a strike, I'm against pit closures, I'll vote for a strike.'

'Well, you do what you think best,' I said. I had confidence in Alan's judgement, I knew that if he was in favour of a strike it must be necessary, he wasn't a militant and he knew that we really couldn't afford a strike. So for him to vote in favour of one the situation must be very serious. But I was worried. I didn't think Arthur Scargill was the right man to lead the union. He'd had so much bad publicity, I'd listened to the reports and read the papers and as far as I was concerned he was a bad man – just out for a strike. I was also worried about Michael being in hospital and how a strike could affect him.

The next Tuesday we saw the Consultant and Michael was transferred to Nottingham City Hospital. I rode in the ambulance with Michael, and Alan drove the car. It was awful in the ambulance, I was so worried about Michael. His little body was so swollen and distorted he didn't look like himself. It was monstrous to see him, he was like a pregnant three year old. He had stretch marks on his tummy and his privates were so big that the skin was transparent and you could see right through it. This was the worst he'd ever been and my anxiety was all the more intense because I had so recently begun to feel that he was beginning to return to normal.

I decided to stay at the hospital. There were units for mothers to stay in and I wanted to be near Michael all the time. Somehow the bigger Nottingham hospital seemed so strange I didn't want to leave him there on his own. It was also further from home and it would have taken us longer to get there if we were called. Alan was working nights so he went off to work. The first day Alan came in at about lunch time after he'd had a sleep and we just sat about all afternoon wishing there was something we could do. We'd never seen Michael like this before, he wasn't only swollen but he was very poorly as well. Other times he'd at least been up and playing with other children, but this time he just wanted to lie down, he was very miserable with himself and it was heart-breaking to see him and feel unable to help him.

Alan mentioned that everybody at work had been talking about a strike and it seemed definite that it would come.

I said, 'I hope it don't happen yet, if we can just hang out till Michael's better, then I don't care.'

I expected Alan back at the hospital the next day at lunchtime again so I was very surprised to see him walk in quite early in the morning.

'Hey up, you're early, what's the matter.'

'The Yorkshire lads came down last night and I didn't cross their picket line.'

My stomach sank, I knew all at once that I was terrified of this strike coming before Michael was better. If Alan went on strike we wouldn't be able to afford to visit Michael, we had to find petrol money to drive to Nottingham, money to buy food while we were at the hospital and money for bits and bobs for Michael. We had no money at all put away because the overtime ban hadn't left us any spare. Almost against my own better judgement I said,

'You're gonna have to go Alan, even if you just make a few shifts to get us through this patch.'

I knew the importance of the principle of not crossing a picket line. I'd always learnt from my Dad that holding these principles was just part of being a miner. I also sensed that the issue of pit closures was not something we could let go by. But my anxiety about Michael's welfare, my need to make sure that he had everything he needed to get better and that we must do everything we could to make him better, overpowered everything else.

Later that afternoon Doreen and Pip came into the hospital. I took Doreen down to show her the mother's unit where I was staying. As we walked along the miles of corridors to get there, we talked a bit about the strike. Doreen told me about the Yorkshire lads forming a picket line in Blidworth saying that it was against union rules to cross it. We had a bit of a heart to heart about it. We agreed that we would stand by our men if they had to strike, but we were both very worried. Me, because of Michael and Doreen because she was scared of another struggle over Pip's maintenance like they'd had after his illness. When we got to the unit, I showed Doreen the little cooker that was there for cooking toast and bits and bobs. She said, 'Do you want me to get some things and send them in to you, it'd be cheaper wouldn't it, if you could cook your own meals?

So I made out a list of things that I could use and she said she'd get them for me. That's what Doreen's like, she's very supportive and practical. She's been a brick all the way through. All along with my pregnancy with Michael and then with him being in hospital, she'd ask if there was any washing and she'd have Amanda at night for me. She was a brick, I wouldn't have got through without her. She was the one person that stood by me and gave me support when my own family didn't. And it was the sort of support that I needed. It was firm support because that's what Doreen's like, she's a firm person. She used to say, 'Come on, keep your chin up, you're gonna be all right.' It wasn't the sort of sympathy that can make you feel worse when people say, 'I don't know how I'd manage if it were me.' You don't need that, you need someone to stay strong and say, 'Look, it'll be all right, Michael will be all right you'll see.'

It was good of Doreen to come and visit Michael. And I know that it's been hard for her. I know the first time she saw him with his little body so swollen, she choked up at the sight that met her eyes, she didn't know what to say. It's good to have friends like that, you need friends like that.

The next few days sort of went by uneventfully really, my overwhelming concern was with Michael. I might have heard more about the strike but in the hospital with everything being so upsetting all you think about is where you are and what you're doing and the child that's in front of you. I couldn't really think about the strike, if people talked about it, it didn't really sink in.

That Friday, March 16th, the Notts. area of the National Union of Mineworkers held a ballot of its members to determine whether it would support the strike. At Blidworth the ballot was held, to the surprise of many of the men, at the pit itself. The National Coal Board had made a room available.

After the ballot Alan came into the hospital and told me that he'd voted for a strike, then later, Pip and Doreen came in. Doreen and I went to have a cup of coffee and again we talked about the strike. Doreen told me that Pip had taken a bag of potatoes up to the Yorkshire lads on the picket line the night before. She said, 'At first I said to him, what about us, we need those spuds, but then he told me that they were starving and cold and all huddled around a fire and so he'd put some spuds onto their fire for them.'

Doreen continued, 'I felt awful then, I asked him if they needed ought else, bread and butter or ought. But he said that Yorkie and his Missus were there and she'd gone to fetch some.'

'Who's Yorkie? I don't know him.'

'You must have seen him, he's a tall lad, and he's from Yorkshire but he lives in village and works at pit. I don't know him, but I've seen him about.'

'I don't think I have.'

'He's on the union committee, I've heard Pip talk about him before. Anyway, they were on the picket line with all the Yorkshire pickets. I couldn't sleep then, last night, whittling about those lads up there. I asked Pip if they needed somewhere to sleep, but he said they'd be having shift changes and going home.'

We talked some more about our worries if there was a strike. We knew it would be a long one and we tried to look at it as best we could. Doreen seemed resolved that it would happen.

She said, 'I've heard that your mortgage gets frozen and your H.P. Thing is, if they don't go on strike, they'll as likely not to have a job soon enough, it's important now.'

She could tell that I was still worried about it and said, 'We'll manage, we're both working and that'll help. Because we can go to

Tesco's and get what we need to eat and everything else will just have to go.'

'Yes Doreen, but while Michael is in hospital if we don't get any money, Alan won't be able to afford petrol to get in to him.'

'Well, he oughtn't to cross a picket line. Look, if worst comes to worst he'll have to come and stay in here with you. We'll look after Amanda. We'll just have to sort it out between us like that.'

But underneath I was still worried and I knew that Doreen was too. We were both very torn, neither of us wanted a strike and somehow hoped that there'd be some way out of it.

When we got back to the ward, we all watched the television news and they said that Notts. had voted and it was expected that seventy-five per cent had voted against joining the strike. It threw us all into more confusion.

'What do we do now?' Alan asked, as if talking for all of us.

'Well,' said Pip. 'What I want to know is, how come they know the result. We don't even know us'ens yet. I think we should wait till Monday and see what's going off.'

Although we were all confused we were clearly angry with the result of the ballot and talked about Notts. being scabland in 1926. It was very strange, none of us wanted a strike, yet we all had a sense that it was necessary and that we didn't want Notts. to let the rest of the NUM down. We discussed it for quite a long time and both Alan and Pip were disgusted with the Notts. Executive for not making a clear call to strike in the very beginning.

'At least then we'd know where we were.' Alan said, 'This way we don't know what we're supposed to be doing.'

Over the weekend Michael seemed to get worse and I got more and more worried about him. I forgot all about the strike again but I did say to Alan that he should try to make at least a couple of shifts the next week, just to tide us over.

On Sunday night I was exhausted, I wanted to get home and do some washing but most of all I was worried about Amanda. She was pining, she'd hardly seen me and I thought I should spend a bit of time with her. Michael seemed used to the routine at the hospital and so I decided to go home for the next few nights. On Monday night, Alan went up to the pit to see what was going off and he went in to work. No-one seemed to know what was happening or what we were supposed to do–most of the men who had been on strike the week before were going back in. The ballot results were not official, but it seemed that Notts. would not go out. Going to work must have been difficult for Alan because the next night as I was getting his snap ready he started talking about whether he should be going in or not.

I said, 'Well you ought to, because we can't afford for you not to and it's not fair on Michael being in hospital.'

He started shouting, 'You don't have to cross them lines, you don't have to go by them men. They're my mates. I don't like to go through.'

Then we started arguing and it got around to family. My Mum hadn't been in to see Michael, she'd just sent him a card and said that because it looked like they were going to be on strike they couldn't afford the petrol money to go into Nottingham to see him. Alan knew that had hurt me, so he threw it at me.

'Your parents are not bothered to go and see Michael are they? Your fuckin' family don't care a toss about you and you're too bloody blind to see it.'

That made me really mad so I said, 'You pissin' bastard. You can piss off back to your mother's,' and I lashed out with my fists and started hitting him on the back. He picked up his snap bag and just walked out and slammed the door. After he'd gone I wondered whether he'd rather cross the picket line or come back and have the argument with me. I waited up for a while and he never came back so it was apparent that he had crossed the picket line. But I sat there crying and feeling awful that I'd made him go to work against what he felt.

The next morning I got up when I heard Amanda wake, Alan had slept on the sofa but he came into the kitchen when he heard Amanda and I having breakfast. We all got ready to take Amanda to school and then go straight to the hospital. It was very tense between us, we only spoke when absolutely necessary.

At the hospital I looked straight away at Michael's chart, I always did that because we'd had a lot of trouble with him taking medicines. The chart showed that he'd taken them with force. Then a nurse came up and said that they wanted to put him on a drip and that a doctor would be along soon to talk to us. The doctor said that his condition was not improving and so they wanted to put him on albumin which would make him direece. We knew that direecing would bring him relief so we agreed that he should have it. Apparently, it's a very expensive drug which they had to send off for so they couldn't give it to him until later that afternoon.

Of course in the face of Michael's predicament the tension between Alan and I just vanished. I gave him a kiss and said I was sorry and he said he was sorry and then he went off to have a sleep before he picked up Amanda. At about half past two, they came with a drip. Michael hated needles and as soon as they came near him he knew what they were going to do and he started crying.

'No Mummy, no Mummy, don't let them hurt me.'

I sat holding him down and stroking his head and they had hold of his arms. They tried three times to get the vein, each time piercing his skin but then having to try again. Then, when they thought they had it and set the drip up they discovered it wasn't in properly and so they had to start all over again. Michael screamed and screamed.

'Mummy, don't let them do it again, Mummy please stop them.'

I was crying and Michael was crying and I was holding his little hand and they were taking the drip out of one arm and trying to put it into the other. It took another three or four attempts to find the vein again and each time they'd try I'd think, 'Oh come on, please let them get it this time.'

My overwhelming instinct was to tell them to 'go away and leave him alone,' but I knew that what they were doing was necessary and so I just had to try and help them and comfort Michael all at once. I had to leave as soon as they'd finished because I was so distraught. I went into the television room. There was another woman there who gave me a cigarette and I sobbed and sobbed and told her what had gone off and she just sat with me for a few minutes. I've never experienced a child going through pain like that, and there's just nothing you can do about it. You can't take that pain off them. As much as you want to, you just can't take the pain off them. I think it's one of the worst situations to be in, to see someone, that you feel responsible for and that you love so much, suffering like that and not be able to stop it.

Half an hour later I went up to see him and he was sitting up in bed singing Sunday School Choruses. That just did it, that was marvelous. I went and sat with him and sang the choruses with him and thanked God that he was on the mend. That was the turning point. Later when Alan came in after picking up Amanda from school I hugged him and cried and cried. I said, 'You should have been here, he's gone through hell.' And I explained what had happened. As I did I kept crying and I can remember saying that he had already made two shifts that week and that he didn't need to go to work tonight. We could manage on two shifts and I needed Alan with me at the hospital. So for the rest of that week Alan would come in and stay with us all day until he had to go and pick up Amanda and then to save petrol they'd both stay at home at nights.

Over the next few days we had a few setbacks and a few more traumas with Michael, but by the weekend he was well enough to take home. It was such a relief to all be together again. Amanda, Michael, Alan and me.

Once we were home life started to resume its normal pattern. Doreen and I decided to hold Sunday School the next morning. She came around early so we'd have time to catch up on each other's news before the kids came. But as soon she started talking I realised that life wasn't going to return to normal at all. All Doreen could talk about was the strike. She and Pip had been rowing about it. She was terrified that they would have to go through the nightmare of the maintenance back-payments again. The Notts. officials had announced the result of the ballot, seventy-two per cent had voted against a strike and it seemed that we weren't involved. But still we all felt that it was wrong to cross a picket line. Pip was quite ill with worry, crossing the picket line made him badly but facing the financial worries which Doreen was presenting him with was just as bad.

Doreen also told me about the police arriving in the village. Alan had mentioned that they'd been up on the picket line, but he'd not said a lot. Doreen had been driving back from work when she noticed eight police vans on the road, four in front of her and four behind. When she got into the village she was shocked to see the car park of the Forest Folk pub full of police vans.

'Pauline, there must have been at least twenty of them,' she said. 'They were all full of coppers. Ooh it were 'orrible. I was fair frightened. I couldn't believe it were Blid'th I thought it must of been Poland. I couldn't believe it were England. I've never seen police like that before, ever.'

'What were they all doing here?'

'They're still here, they've come up because of pickets, aren't they. All the pickets from Derbyshire and Yorkshire, they reckon they shouldn't be here, they can't do that can they?'

That week both Pip and Alan went into work, I started back at work again too and it was really awful. Doreen and I were sickened by the attitude of the other women there, most of them were married to miners who were working and didn't support the strike at all. They kept slagging the Yorkshire pickets and saying that they should go back to Yorkshire where they belonged. And they were calling Arthur Scargill everything under the sun. Although our husbands were sometimes going in to work Doreen and I argued with them about it because we just didn't agree with the sort of things they were saying. In some ways listening to them made us realise what side we were really on and it made us ashamed that we weren't really living by what we believed in.

Pip and Doreen rowed all the next weekend. Doreen was worried about Pip.

She said, 'Crossing picket lines makes him as low as a snake's belly.'

She'd given him an ultimatum, she'd said to him, 'If you want to go on strike, you've got to ring a solicitor and get your maintenance taken care of. If you don't do that, you don't go on strike.'

Doreen had found out that the reason Pip had to pay so much maintenance was because he was still being classified as a single man and that he needed to have his new situation presented to the Court.

Once that had been done they would never have to pay back so much at once again.

When we got home from work on Monday, Pip said to Doreen, 'I've phoned the solicitor, I've got an appointment tomorrow morning. Alan's gonna drive me.' She said, 'Is that it then?'

'Yes, that's it, me snap tin's in that cupboard there and it's not coming out until we've won.'

When Doreen told me this a couple of hours later she was glad that he'd made his mind up.

'I knew as soon as he'd phoned the solicitor. You know Pip, he's not the sort to come up to me and say,"look, there's no way I can cross them picket lines" but as soon as he said he'd phoned the solicitor then I knew that was it.'

Pip had been through a very hard time. On the Friday before, he'd not been in to work but spent the morning talking to some of the union officials from our pit, he'd decided then not to go in any more. But on the Monday morning after rowing all weekend with Doreen he'd gone off to work. When he came off his shift they'd put a special picket line on for him and his mate, Howard. After talking to them for a while Pip had kicked his snap-box across the field in front of the pit and said, 'That's it.'

Doreen was fully prepared to support him.

She said to me, 'He's gonna need my support now in't he?'

I agreed.

She said, 'What's Alan gonna do now?'

'I don't know I suppose he'll come out.'

'Well, she said. He oughtn't to be crossing picket lines.'

'But he's not at the moment 'cause he's working those odd shifts and there's no pickets there when he goes in.'

'Well, maybe they oughta put a special picket line for him like they did for Pip and Howard.'

The next night they did put a special picket line on for Alan and he refused to cross it. That was it then, we had all put our everything in with the strike and we felt good about it because we knew where we stood. Now we were standing up for our principles and that made us feel proud. That week so much seemed to happen, our lives really began to change. The first obvious change was at work.

Doreen asked the Manageress if we could work our own hours to get as much overtime as possible because our husbands were on strike. She agreed that as long as we did the five hours we'd signed the contract for, we could work what we wanted. We had a supervisor called Pat who was very unpopular with everybody. She was always picking on the young lasses and she was very two-faced. If you did something wrong, instead of bringing it back to you to fix it up she'd take it straight to the Manager so you'd get into trouble. If she didn't like you she'd bring someone else's repairs and say they were yours, so you'd waste time cause you didn't get paid for doing your own repairs. She particularly hated Doreen and me because we just came along to earn money and we sat next to each other and we'd always be having a laugh and a joke. We did our work easily and hardly made a mistake and that really used to annoy her.

The other thing that annoyed her was that if we wanted anything we'd go over her head and straight to the management. When Doreen asked for overtime, she made a whole lot of snide remarks to us at first. But when she found out why we wanted it her attitude changed. We were very surprised when she came up to us, sat in front of our machines and asked how Michael was. She stayed and talked about Michael's illness for a long time and then she said to Doreen:
'Why didn't you come to me about extra hours?'
Doreen said, 'I didn't think it mattered, I thought Marie was the one to ask.'
Then she asked why we wanted extra hours and when Doreen told her she said, 'Well, I'm really proud to know you.'
Then she told us that she came from Yorkshire and was fully behind the strike.

After that we all became good friends and Pat used to make sure that we got all the best jobs, and the ones that you could make most money on. Sometimes she'd bring us some repairs of someone else's and if they took a quarter of an hour, she'd mark it down as half an hour. The scabs' wives got really mad about that and used to make snide comments all the time.

'Oh look at the favourites.'

'You can tell who's in this week.'

I started to bring a radio in to work with me so we could listen to the news about the strike. Every hour me and Doreen would stop our machines and Pat would come up and listen with us. At first all the others thought we were really funny for listening to all the news broadcasts but then they got quite nasty and stopped talking to us, or else they'd sneer and make snide remarks.

'Arthur Scargill wants shooting.'

'He's tried before to get the men to strike, those with any sense won't strike now either.'

'All them lazy idle strikers should get back to work and keep their families.'

If they weren't making comments like that they'd talk in loud voices about all the things they were buying with their husbands' wages. It got so they never spoke to us unless it was uncivil. But the three of us used to have a laugh and a joke about it all the time and we knew that we had the bond of the strike and that was more important than all their pettiness. Later when we got more involved and started taking a lot of time off we used to come and say to Pat, 'We weren't well yesterday, but really we were at that rally in Barnsley,' or 'We went to a meeting to raise money,' or 'We had to stay in t'village 'cause our centre opened today.'

Pat used to say, 'Good lasses.' She was pleased that we were telling her the truth and also that we were out working hard to support the strike.

One day at work this joke came up and we all laughed about it for ages. There was this scab's wife who used to sit behind us and she was always telling jokes in a really loud voice. Often they were about the strike and strikers but sometimes they were just jokes. This day I heard her say, 'What's the most useless thing in the world?'

I turned to Doreen and said, 'A Nottinghamshire miner.' We thought it was so funny we creased ourselves laughing. The real answer was a prick, because it's got no arms, no legs and a hole in the head. When we got home that night I went next door and told Pip the joke. He laughed and then I told him the real answer and I was just finishing saying 'and a hole in the head' and Alan walked in.

Pip said, 'Tell Alan that one.'

Well Alan thought we were talking about him and when I said 'What's the most useless thing in the world, Alan?' he said, 'There's nought wrong wi' me.'

Well, we just fell about in hysterics, we laughed and laughed. It became a sort of standard joke then and all any of us had to do was mention it and we all burst out laughing.

Alan was getting up and going picketing every morning at about four o'clock and I always used to lie there and listen to the men shouting on the picket line. It was quite frightening and I used to worry about it. There was also something exciting about it and I used to wonder exactly what went on up there. On Wednesday Alan came back from the picket line and said to me, 'I seen ya Dad go in this morning.'

'Ah well, he's got his principles,' I said, 'if he wants to do that, let it be on his conscience not ours.'

But I couldn't understand his attitude at all. This strike was over things that I knew he'd always believed in. All my life my father had been a strong unionist and it was because of what he'd taught me that I knew it was wrong for Alan to be crossing a picket line. I can remember him in the 1970's strikes when he was solid and behind them and used to talk about what a terrible thing strike-breaking was. I couldn't understand how his attitude had changed so much. I hadn't seen my parents in the last ten days since Michael had come out of hospital. Alan had told me that while I was in hospital my Dad had called him a scab because he'd gone in for a couple of shifts. My Dad had been out for the first full week but had apparently gone back after that and not missed a shift since. I could only think it must have been over money. They'd bought a holiday bungalow and a new car. I suppose he felt that he'd worked hard all his life for what they'd got and he didn't want to risk losing it. But it hurt me and I was bitter about it. I thought, after all, we've only got one house to lose. I knew then that it would be a long strike. I thought maybe about six or eight weeks.

The next morning I was woken up by a commotion outside our house. I could hear people laughing and joking and I got out of bed and looked through the curtains. I saw a couple of vans and loads of blokes standing around them. Somehow I could tell they were pickets. It was only about quarter past three but I woke Alan and said,

'Hey, pickets are here.' I was really excited that they'd come to our house.

Alan hardly woke up and just grunted.

I said, 'They're out there in the cold.'

'Argh.'

'Didn't we ought to get up and make a cup of tea?'

'No, not at this time of the morning, get back into bed.'

'But it's cold out there.'

'Oh shurrup and get back into bed.'

So I lay in bed listening, but I couldn't stay there and when I looked again I saw a police van go by and all the pickets dived back into their vans. Then I saw a neighbour looking through his curtains and I thought, that ratty old bloke he's called the police, so I said.

'Alan, George's sent for t' coppers. We ought to let 'em in 'ouse. It's freezing and now there are coppers going by.'

Alan said, 'Well, go on then.'

And so I got up, put my clothes on and went out and asked them if they wanted a cup of tea. That was the first step to me getting involved really. It turned out that they came from Derbyshire and that was quite nice because my uncles were on strike in Derbyshire and I thought any of these could be my uncles.

I've got a great big teapot that Alan's Mum had given me for Sunday School and a whole lot of plastic cups. I filled the enormous teapot with tea which took two electric kettles and then put milk into it and took it out to the men. Alan got up then and some of them came in the house and we all chatted about the strike. It was very exciting, I nipped in next door. Doreen was just getting up and I told her all about it. She'd heard the noise as well, but was too sleepy to get up. Doreen likes her bed more than me in the mornings.

All the men went up to picket. I told them to come back for another cup of tea after picketing and by the time they did it was nice and sunny and so they all sat around the back yard on the patio steps. Doreen and I had to leave for work, but we really wanted to stay and talk to the pickets and listen to their stories about the strike.

All the way to work and all through the morning we kept talking about it.

'Fancy them coming to our house.'

'I wonder if they'll still be there when we get back.' It was lovely to feel involved and it made us feel important that they'd come to our houses.

After that they used to come every morning and either I'd make them a cup of tea or Pip would. When they came back from picketing they'd always talk about what happened and be really excited if they'd turned someone back. We all thought then, that if we could just get all the Notts. Miners out we'd win the strike. Doreen used to get up to go to work and the house would be full of pickets spread all over the floor and up the stairs. And they'd be all over our house too. By this time the police were aware that the pickets were coming in and they started following them all around the village. Doreen would open their double gates so the pickets could drive in and then the police couldn't touch them.

More and more I was wishing I could go picketing, but I just didn't think it was the sort of thing that women did. I suppose I remembered the '72 and '74 strikes and knew women weren't involved so I assumed this would be the same. But I also knew that I'd found those strikes exciting as a child and that stimulated my interest and my wanting to get involved now that I was a woman.

On Sunday night, Alan and I were just getting ready to go to bed when he heard loads of shouting next door. Doreen and Pip were really going at it screaming and shouting.

I said to Alan, 'Ooh listen, to 'em next door, they're really having a barney, all hell's let loose. I wonder what's gone off.'

Alan said, 'Oh, probably they've had a drink or two.' 'Bloomin' 'eck, she sounds like she's gonna kill 'im.'

The next morning Pip came around and said that Doreen wasn't feeling well and wouldn't be going to work. I knew damn well they'd had a fight the night before but I didn't let on and Alan drove me into work. When I got back I was dying to hear what had gone off so I was eager to listen to Doreen when she came around a bit later for a coffee.

'What did they say at work about me not coming in, did you tell 'em I weren't very well?' She asked.

'No, I told 'em you had a barney last night with Pip,' I joked and we both laughed.

'Oh that bloody Pip' she said as soon as we'd finished laughing.

'He's a right bloody article he is. You know what he did last night. He begged me to go out wi' him, I weren't really bothered, but he begged me to go to Friar for a drink wi' him and then when we got there he buggers off and talks to a bleedin' scab all night.'

'Did he?'

'Yeah, but you know how obsessed I am about him sitting wi' me when we go out 'cause with all the kids we never get time together on our own at home, so I think that when we go out we should sit together. Well we'd only been there about a quarter of an hour when Pip goes up to the bar and starts talking to this scab. He were stood there for thirty-five minutes and I were getting madder and madder and in the end I got up and walked home. I walked right past him and he were so engrossed in his conversation that he didn't even see me walk by. And it took him twenty minutes to notice that I'd left cause he drove home and didn't get here until a bit after me. Anyway he says, 'What's up wi' you' and I said, 'Nothing' and he says,' 'Come on. So I told him. I were so mad wi' him, well, you heard us, so you know. He said that you gotta talk to scabs to let 'em know what it's all about and I says, 'rubbish, you stand on the picket line to talk to scabs, you shouldn't be talking to them when you take me out for a drink.' I said to him, 'I'm finished, if you're on strike, that's it. I'm backing you all the way and if you want to treat me like this, when you take me out, well then, I'm not going to work no more. If you want to stand around talking to scabs then I'll do your job and stand on the picket line.' He got really mad then, he said, 'I weren't just talking to scabs I was merely trying to convince them that they should be on strike and what's more if I catch you near the picket line I'll get you by the hair and sling you into the nearest police van.'

'Did he?'

'Yeah, he did. And I've a good mind just to go up there tonight, just to show him.'

'I'll come with you, I'd love to go up to the picket line.'

'Right, that's it then, let's go up tonight.'

I didn't really expect her to go but just after Alan had left for picketing Doreen came in with her coat on and said, 'Shall we go then?'

'I can't really, I've got the kids. I'd thought about it and it didn't really seem possible to pay a babysitter while I went picketing.'

But Doreen said, 'Well, Karen's looking after Mark, I'm sure she won't mind listening out for your two as well.'

When we first got there we were quite timid and stood on the corner a bit away from the main body of the picket. Gradually we edged closer and closer. As we got near to the back line we saw that there were some other women there as well. We didn't know them then, but it was Pauline Howarth, Sylv Browne, Betty Savage and Ann Bradley. Betty Savage said, 'Oh it's lovely to see some more women up here.'

'We'd have been up before if we'd known that there were women here, we thought it were just for men.'

'Oh no, duck,' Betty said, 'I've stood here every day since day one. We can do our bit too can't we? I think it's important that we do. It's our fight too in't it duck. I'm ever so glad to have other women join us.'

While we were there I listened to the conversations around me and I really began to understand the issues in a different way from before. The older women told me that their husbands were union officials. They said that Arthur Scargill hadn't wanted a strike now but that the Coal Board had forced the Yorkshire men into it by threatening to close Cortonwood Colliery. I'd never really understood that properly before. So for me, going up to the picket line really changed the way I saw things. I liked being there as well, I liked feeling that I was involved in it and was doing something.

When the picket finished a lot of the men came over to welcome us. I noticed Pip standing a little apart and looking quite sheepish when he heard Dennis Browne, who had become the picket manager saying to us, 'It's nice to see women up here. We're pleased to see you.'

I was pleased the men had made us welcome, it made me feel accepted, because of Pip's attitude I wasn't sure if we would be welcome and I was really glad that we were. I knew that the picket line was a place I belonged and I was relieved to know that others felt that way too. As we started to leave someone asked if we were coming back the next day. We explained that we had to work but said that we'd be up again the next night.

Betty said, 'Oh good, I'll bring you a pair of frilly knickers. Some nights I come up with seven pairs in my pockets.'

I looked at her, I didn't know what she meant. 'We wave them at the scabs and ask them if they want them – they're not really men are they?'

·4·
PAULINE
GETTING PLACES

Once the ice was broken we started picketing every night. Our lives became very busy. We'd be up every morning at 3.30 to make tea for the Derbyshire pickets. Occasionally we'd go up to the morning picket with them but mostly we'd stay at home getting ready for work. When the Derbyshire lads came back from the picket we'd make another cup of tea, chat to them about what had gone off that morning and then leave for work at about half seven.

We were getting lots of overtime at work so we used to stay until tea-time, then come home, have tea, bed the kids down and then go up to the picket line. Betty brought loads of pairs of frilly knickers and all the women would wave them at the scabs and shout.

'Come and get these, you might as well wear them, they're more suitable for you.'

We used to think that would make the scabs feel ashamed that they were less than men for crossing the picket line, we never realised then that we were putting ourselves down by doing it. I suppose we should have known something was wrong because the police used to laugh. When I think about those early pickets a lot of the things people shouted were to do with women and it makes me feel a bit ashamed now but at the time it never occurred to us we were doing ourselves an injustice. The men used to shout:

'Who's knocking off your missus while you scab?' Everybody would laugh. But we also shouted lots of other things that weren't sexist. In a way one of the exciting things about it was trying to think up new things to shout. One of the favourites was,

'Where's ya backbone, left it at home then?'

'Come over here where the backbone is.'

'You might find a spare one at the cemetery if you look hard enough.'

'Traitors, scabs.'

'You're lower than lino, you are.'

'Lower than snake's shit.'

One night a man crossed the picket line who used to go to church with me and Doreen.

Doreen yelled out to him, 'Judas. You're selling your soul for thirty pieces of silver.'

He turned around and looked at us, and Doreen said, 'Yes, its Pauline and Doreen here, we can see what you're doing.'

We used to talk to each other a lot on the picket line, we were all starting to get to know each other and there was an excitement in that. The strike was in its fifth week so in normal terms it was already quite a long strike. The hardship was really starting to tell and we women started to talk about the need to organize some way of feeding everybody. We decided to have a meeting of the women who'd been coming up to the picket line.

The meeting was arranged for Sunday morning at Pauline Howarth's house. Mal, Pauline's husband, had been the Union Branch Secretary before the strike and we all sort of looked up to Pauline as knowing more about things than we did. I can remember getting up that Sunday. It seemed so exciting. The idea of holding a meeting to really get things organized and the responsibility of being involved in that was thrilling. I'd never been involved in anything like it before. It seemed the sort of thing that other people did, people who were somehow different from me, people who had a lot of education. I'm not sure what it was I thought they had but it had never seemed to me that I was that sort of person, or even that anyone I knew was that sort of person. I felt awakened. It was as if I'd woken up in the morning and it had rained and everything seemed fresh and new. Knowing that we were going to set up a committee seemed a definite thing and I liked the idea that I was going to be part of the fight, that it was my fight as well as Alan's and that I was going to be a part of that. In some ways I suppose I must have sensed that things in my life were going to change, I felt the same as I did just before I started my first job. Knowing that I was taking something on that was an important thing, a responsible thing and something completely different in my life.

Through picketing together a group of about six of us had formed a sort of nucleus. Doreen and my neighbour from the other side, Annette, Betty, who brought the frilly knickers up to the picket line and Pauline Howarth, Sylv Browne and Margaret Groves whose husbands were all Union Officials and we thought that made them quite important compared to us.

At the meeting we talked about how we could arrange some food distribution. We had a bit of an argument about whether to give out food parcels or whether to set up a soup kitchen. We'd talked to some of the pickets from Yorkshire and the ones from Derbyshire and they were already getting organized distributing food parcels. I thought that if we could we should set up a soup kitchen. I could remember the kitchen in '72 and how much I'd enjoyed going there.

It also seemed to me to be more economical to serve hot meals than to distribute food in parcels. You can make things go a lot further if you cook it up in bulk than if you have to divide it all up into so many parcels. More of us seemed to favour a soup kitchen and we knew that in '72 they'd run it at the Youth Club. It seemed the perfect place, it is situated well back off the road, has excellent cooking facilities and is normally only used at nights. At that stage we had no money, nor really any idea how we could get any. At first we talked about writing to companies like Tesco and the Co-op to see if we could make some sort of credit arrangement with them, then charge a small amount for the food to cover our costs as we went along. People remembered the food that had been donated by local shop-keepers in '72 and since we all got on well with them we thought they'd probably do the same again.

We left the meeting feeling very positive about everything and as we walked home we chatted excitedly about the organization and our part in it. We were all very enthusiastic and determined. In that one week we had learnt so much about the situation and our will to fight and win had become very strong, we almost felt as if we could do anything.

The next few days Doreen and I worked very long hours, when we'd get up to the picket line each night the other women were always full of news about what had happened each day. Annette and Pauline Howarth had approached the Chairman of the Youth Club

Committee. He told them that they would probably have trouble getting the Youth Club because the Committee was half NUM and half NCB. He advised that the NCB half would probably raise objections.

A schoolteacher from Nottingham, Paul Thompson had been up to the picket line and talked to Annette and Betty about raising funds. He'd suggested writing a leaflet for distribution in Nottingham to launch an appeal. He'd also talked about the need for organizing a proper committee with a Secretary, Treasurer and Chairperson.

Betty had talked to one of the young miners who'd heard we were looking for premises to set up a soup kitchen and offered his house. He'd bought it just before the strike had started and now he couldn't afford to move in, so he was happy for us to use it. Annette and Betty went down to the house to see if it would be alright. There was nothing there but they cleaned it up and everybody pitched in with camping stoves and a camp table and we all brought plates and cutlery from home.

Once the house was set up some of the women used to go down and open it up in time to give the visiting pickets a cup of tea and slice of toast before the morning picket and afterwards serve breakfast, which was usually beans on toast.

Doreen and I started to get despondent about going to work, we seemed to be missing out on everything that the others were doing and we used to talk all day to each other and wonder what was going off back in Blidworth. Sometimes they'd serve stew or soup that someone had made at home. I remember going there one day after work and spreading butter on the bread for the kids' teas. The very first effort at actually cooking a meal for everyone was in that house. We didn't have much food and I remember they made a stew. It had baked beans and rice pudding in it. I couldn't believe that anybody would put rice pudding in a stew, but people ate it up and in a way it was a very significant thing and quite an achievement to actually attempt to cook a meal for everyone. But right from the start it was clear that the house wasn't big enough and the facilities weren't adequate so we kept on with the idea of getting the Youth Club.

Bits and pieces of food and money started coming in, people around the place were learning of our plight and sending help. The first shipment of food I remember arriving was very soon after we started using the house. A van pulled up outside the front door and everybody started unloading things. There was a box of bread, about twelve loaves, cans of beans and soups and peas, loads of dried milk and tea-bags. All kinds of things and a few little luxuries as well, some beer and a few tins of ham. We thought it was great. I remember kneeling on the concrete floor and sorting all the cans out. It was the beginning of our understanding about what support we'd got outside.

It was then that we started to get impatient about being able to use the Youth Club. We'd got food, we'd got donations, we'd got support from outside and we wanted somewhere bigger to serve the food up. We'd become so aware of the need to feed the men and children that we couldn't believe that anyone would try to stop us. At one stage we discussed using the three houses in Thorny Abbey Road, ours, Doreen's and Annette's because they were all next to each other. At the time I was quite in favour of it. I enjoyed having the Derbyshire pickets in the mornings and I thought it would be nice to extend that experience throughout the day.We decided that we should have a meeting with the union men to discuss various problems. We hadn't really talked to them officially about what we were doing, we thought it would be a good idea to discuss everything and get their ideas on it. Doreen rang around and everybody came here.

There were fourteen of us, Dennis Browne, the picket manager and his wife Sylv, Yorkie and Margaret Groves, Annette and John from next door, Betty and Peter Savage, Mal and Pauline Howarth, Doreen and Pip and me and Alan. We talked about raising funds and about whether we would go ahead and try for the Youth Club or not. Everyone was in favour of doing that. We all believed that we had a right to use it and that no-one had a right to stop us. It was decided that Annette and Pauline Howarth would continue to try to get permission. It was suggested that they go to Berry Hill, the Notts Area Union Office, and find out exactly what the situation was.

The men were all very enthusiastic about what we were doing.

We talked about holding a demonstration the following night and distributing the leaflets that Annette was working on with Paul Thompson. The leaflet was to let all the strikers in the village know about the house and food, but it was also a call for unity. Annette had rung the radio stations and the newspapers and they'd told her that they'd come out to cover it. Yorkie said he'd get us the big union banner. So we were going to march through the streets and demonstrate outside the meeting. Pip was against the idea. He said, 'You'll look daft, there'll only be half a dozen of you, there's not enough time to organize it.'

Doreen, Pip, Alan and I decided to go to Skegness for Easter, we'd done it the year before and had a great time. Doreen and I had brought home a good wage packet and Pip and Alan had got some holiday pay from the pit. We were fairly sure we wouldn't get another holiday that year so we thought we might as well take the kids away and all have a bloody good time while we could. We broke up on Thursday at dinner time and went out drinking with Pat from work and another couple of women. The husband of one had been made redundant and another used to talk to Doreen all the time about her problems. On the way home we were moaning about having to pack up to get away, but when we got there the men had done most of it. We were very surprised and very pleased. It was the first sign that while they were home and we were out at work they were really taking some responsibility for things.

The National Committee of the NUM had met that day and Pip's lad, Paul, had been up to Sheffield to the meeting with Pip's mate Howard. When we got back they came in just after us and were really full of it.

'Watch it on telly, Arthur Scargill's declared the strike official. All of Notts. will have to come out now.'

'Are you sure?'

'Well, they've got to, don't they, if strike's official?'

'Well that'll be it then, once all of Notts. scabby bastards come out, we'll win, it's only Notts. holding us back now.'

'I think it'll take a while, the NCB won't back down straight away. Depends on what coal stocks they've got I suppose,' Howard said.

Howard always seemed more politically aware than the rest of us and we always listened to him. We were all quite excited because we assumed that this would mean that all of Blidworth would come out again like they'd done at the beginning and the village would be united again.

That night we all togged up and met to march up to the union meeting. Pip had been right, there were exactly six of us, we hadn't got the banner and none of the press turned up. But we did have the leaflets so we went up to the Welfare, where the meeting was being held and gave them out as the men went in. Then we had a drink and walked up to the picket line buying chips on the way and eating them as we walked up.

Most of the men went into the pit through the main door which was next to the canteen. Only six pickets, known as the official pickets, were allowed to stand by the door. There were a couple of other entrances and there were usually two pickets on either one of them as well. Across the road from the main entrance there was a small green and the rest of us had to stand over there while picketing. There were usually seventy or eighty pickets altogether and about the same number of police in front of the pit, although they always had at least double their number in reinforcements around the back of the pit. The police spread themselves around the entrances and the rest formed a shoulder to shoulder cordon around the pickets standing by the green. The police used to march out like soldiers to take their positions up once a picket started.

When we arrived at the pit after eating our chips, we were the only ones there because the men were all still at their meeting.

We stood where the official pickets normally stood. None of us had ever stood there before, the men were quite protective of the position and competitive among each other to see who would stand there.

The police said, 'Oh, women's night is it, giving the men a break eh?'

'Yeah,' we said as sharply as we could. Whenever the police tried to make conversation with us we'd answer sharply and with as few words as possible, because we resented them being there.

It wasn't long before the men started to come back from their meeting and we left the official picket post and moved across to the other side of the road. The police were very heavy handed that night, in fact they were quite nasty. They wouldn't let the men go into the pit canteen to buy smokes or go to the toilet like they'd been doing. They were pushing us and bossing us about more harshly than normal. We were all quite surprised, up until now they'd always been quite polite.

Luis Smith, one of the young lads was walking across the road, coming back from the union meeting. He was standing in the road looking to see if all six official pickets' positions were taken. A copper made a grab for him, saying, 'You've had it, you can't go over there.' Luis moved his arm to try and get the policeman off him and about four or five more police jumped in and pulled him down. We all surged forward, shouting, 'Leave him alone, leave him alone.'

Everybody's emotions flared. One of our men had been attacked for nothing and we were all furious and indignant. The surge forward was very strong, everybody pushing and trying to see. As the front row of pickets were forced onto the cordon of police, scuffles broke out, I noticed a few police helmets flying about but I don't think any of us really knew what to do.

I was terrified at the same time as being angry, I was shaking in my boots and my heart was banging. I was clinging onto Alan, I was terrified they were going to get him, I kept saying to him.
'Don't go too far forward.'
Looking over the heads in front of me I could just make out that they were dragging Luis off. Suddenly, almost as quickly as it had started it was over. We discovered that they'd taken some more but nobody seemed to know how many. I couldn't understand why they'd acted that way, they're supposed to be the upholders of the peace and there wasn't any peace being broken, just a young lad crossing the road. We weren't breaking any laws, we've got every right to cross a road.

I started realizing that things weren't as I'd always believed them to be, the coppers, it seemed, could just take any of us if they wanted to, they didn't have to have a reason, they could always make one.

They could make a perfectly peaceful picket into a violent one. There had never been any violence on our picket line before and if the police hadn't been there, there wouldn't have been any trouble that night either. Later, when I saw the media showing violence on picket lines and blaming pickets for it, I knew they were lying, because I'd seen what had happened that night. And that made me rethink the truth of all that the media said.

Eventually the picket broke up and everybody started dispersing. There were women working in the pit canteen and a few of us decided that as women we should go in and talk to them about the strike and ask them to join it. We thought that since the men stood every day trying to bring the rest of the men out, we should go into the canteen to bring the women out. We came across Annette who was looking for her husband John. She was worried he had been arrested. We dismissed that as a possibility and persuaded her to come into the canteen with us.

As we walked past a group of cops on our way to the door of the canteen, Annette asked one of them, 'Has my husband been arrested?'

'No, me dear. What does he look like? Is 'e short and dark with a moustache?'

'Yeah, that's 'im.'

'No, we 'aven't lifted anyone that looks like that.'

We all ignored that, there was a lot going on, the men were telling us not to go into the canteen, not to cause any trouble.

'Come on, you'll get arrested.'

'Leave it for now, come on home.'

But we ignored them too. Then the police tried to stop us getting into the canteen. 'You can't go in there.'

'We're only going to talk to the canteen women.' We pushed straight past them.

When we were actually going into the canteen I was very frightened, my stomach was like a knot, I thought, anything might happen, but I just didn't care. We were fed up and angry and were prepared to take risks we wouldn't have taken before for what we believed in.

When we first got into the canteen there was only one young woman there and we started to talk to her and tell her about the strike, and why she shouldn't be crossing the picket line to come into work. We talked about what we were fighting for, that it was our community that would go if this pit was closed and that it was everyone's fight. Then another woman, an old battleaxe came out from the back yelling and swearing at us.

'Fuck off, you've got no business being in here. You lot ought to tell your bloody idle husbands to get back to work instead of coming in here causing trouble.'

We started arguing with her, calling her stupid and all sorts of things because this fight was as much hers as it was the men's. We said, 'You'll have no job if they close this pit.' About then the union officials, Dennis, Mal and Yorkie came into the canteen to try and fetch us out. We paid them no attention but kept on with our arguing. When the men saw what we were doing, they shrugged their shoulders and said, 'Oh, leave them to it.'

When they walked out it made us feel really good that they could see we were responsible and determined, it made us feel accepted by them and it was an acknowledgement that we could fight too for what we all believed in. Our pride in ourselves deepened when we walked out a little later with the young woman who had agreed to support the strike.

All the way home Annette was worrying about John. She kept saying, 'I'm sure he's been arrested.'

I said, 'Oh don't be so silly, I bet he's at home now with his feet stuck up, watching telly and you're wasting your time whittling about 'im.'

'That cop knew what he looked like, didn't you hear him?'

'Come on Annette, don't be so dramatic, what do you think they'd want to arrest John for?'

Anyway, we all went back to Annette's with her and John wasn't there. We rang Dennis Browne, the picket manager. He didn't know anything but suggested Annette ring Mansfield Police Station.

To my absolute amazement, when she got through to Mansfield they said they had him. He'd been charged with assaulting a Police Officer.

'John! Assaulting a Police Officer, never!'

'That's what they said.'

I could only laugh, somehow the idea of John assaulting a copper seemed so out of character that it became comical. Both Doreen and I were splitting our sides saying, 'Oh no, we were saying he'd be home with his feet up, and all the time he really had been arrested.' It still didn't ring true, but we were just beginning to get a taste of what the police were like and we had no idea that this was just the beginning.

They kept John in overnight and Annette kept ringing up to see if he was alright. The next day we were going away, so we started to pack up the cars and hook the caravan up. I was just sitting down to have a cup of tea and I looked up and saw my Mum walk by the window. She was coming to our house. I was quite pleased because I hadn't seen her since Michael had come home from hospital, but also a little apprehensive because I knew that my father was working. I felt a sudden leap of joy thinking that she must be visiting to tell me that he'd decided to join the strike, but as soon as she banged on the back door I felt it turn into disappointment.

'Come on in.'

She walked in and said, 'Hope you're bloody satisfied.'

'What are you talking about?'

We had a big row about my dad working and Alan striking. She told me that I shouldn't be going to work to keep Alan. In the end she walked out slamming the door behind her.

Doreen came in just after she'd left, my mother had been shouting that loud that she'd heard all the commotion. I told her what had gone off, then we walked up to the dinner picket with the kids while Alan hooked the caravan up to the car. He was going to meet us up at the picket line and we were going to leave from there.

It was a beautiful red hot day. We sat up on the picket in the sunshine. John arrived back from Mansfield, they'd charged him and we were shocked all over again. They had taken four lads the night before and charged them all, one of them went back to work a few weeks later and his charges were dropped immediately.

We asked John what had happened and how he'd been arrested. He said that he'd seen all the coppers on top of Luis and had gone to help him. They'd nabbed him before he got anywhere near Luis and chucked him straight into the van. He had a black eye with a cut over it and he told us that he'd been given some fist by the police. That worried me a lot. I'd seen films on telly where the police beat people up in the cells, but I'd never believed it. I'd always thought that they must have been causing trouble and that the police were just restraining them, but when I saw John's eye, I was quite upset. The more I was finding out about the police the less I was liking it.

After the picket we left straight away for Skeggy. We asked Annette if she'd keep an eye on our houses for us, we were worried in case someone put our windows through. We had a lovely few days. It was very relaxing and we did it all without spending that much money. But we couldn't leave the strike behind. We took a portable telly with us so we could watch the news every day. We saw Henry Richardson, the Notts. Area Secretary come on and say that the strike was official and that Notts. miners shouldn't cross picket lines. We were overjoyed. But our hopes were short lived. The television immediately showed interviews with Notts. miners who said that they were still going to keep working, they wanted a national ballot and until one was held they'd continue to work.

We came back from Skeggy on Tuesday night. On Wednesday when we came back from work and Doreen was in the middle of unpacking everything, Annette went down to her house in a flap because she was supposed to be going into Nottingham with Betty Savage to raise support and Betty couldn't go at the last minute. Annette wanted to know if Doreen would go with her. Since they'd first met the Nottingham school teacher, Paul Thompson on the picket line, he'd been back several times and was proving to be a great help. He was a member of the Labour Party and seemed to know how to go about organizing things. He had a lot of contacts in Nottingham and he'd arranged for Annette and Betty to go and see several people that day.

He was coming out to Blidworth to pick them up. Paul had also had a second leaflet printed that we'd worked on. The second one was to call on people for support. It was quite small, on buff coloured paper with red writing on it. It looked very professional. At the top in big letters it said, 'Support Us in Our Struggle to Save

Our Mining Communities from Destruction.' Then in smaller print it continued saying that the wives and children were suffering to save jobs from being lost, that our struggle was important to the nation. We called for urgent help and asked for food, money, clothing and advice on welfare rights. At the bottom it said, 'If the miners are beaten, so are we all.' Then it was signed by five of us as miners' wives and gave Annette and Betty's phone numbers.

When Doreen and Annette went into Nottingham with Paul they took the leaflets and distributed them everywhere they went. At first they went into a health food shop because Paul wanted to buy some sprouts. He introduced Doreen and Annette and said they were miners' wives. The people in the shop were very sympathetic and offered to give them some potatoes and food. Then Paul drove them around Nottingham introducing them to a whole load of people he thought might be sympathetic and helpful. They went to Radio Trent to see if they would put an interview on the air. Radio Trent said that the Miners' Strike was too political for them but contacted Radio Nottingham who agreed to do an interview the next day. An appointment was made for the next afternoon, the interview was to be pre-recorded and put on air first thing the following morning. That night Paul had arranged for the two women to speak at the Nottingham Trades Council meeting. Annette was going to talk, but when the Chairperson asked who was going to speak for the Miners' Wives, Annette said, 'Doreen.'
So Doreen made her first speech.

The next day she was very chuffed with herself. She told me all about it on our way to work the next day. 'Oh Pauline, you'd 'ave been proud of me. Annette were supposed to be doing it, but when the Chairwoman, this woman called Noreen Baker, she's fantastic, she gave us fifty quid of her own money, she asked if one us could tell the meeting what we were doing and Annette just said, 'Yes, Doreen will.'
'I didn't know what I were doing. I didn't have any warning at all. I just stood up and said we were collecting for striking miners' children and that we'd been on strike all this time and we were dead hungry and wanted all the support we could get. I said we had a Cen-

tre set up and that we needed money and food. You should have seen the support they gave us. They want to set up a collection centre in Nottingham for things, and altogether we brought back seventy-eight quid. You know when I was speaking I was ever so nervous, but after I finished it felt quite good, in fact it felt exhilarating. I was fair pleased with myself.'

When we got home from work that day we discovered that Annette couldn't go into Radio Nottingham for the interview because she had to go to Berry Hill with Pauline Howarth to sort out about the Youth Club. Doreen asked me if I'd go with her, so I agreed. As we drove into Nottingham I was absolutely terrified. I just couldn't imagine myself talking on the radio, I was sure that I'd just seize up and have nothing to say. Doreen was nervous too but more confident than me because she'd spoken at the meeting the night before. She said, 'It'll be all right, once you start talking it all just comes out. We have got a lot to say, haven't we?' When we arrived, the people at the station were very nice to us, they showed us into the little studio and started setting up the microphones and getting us to test our voice on them. The interviewer told us not to worry, that the interview was on tape and so if we made a mess of anything it could be changed later. Then he started asking questions.

'Is there anything really essential that you're having to go without?'

Doreen told him that we were working, but that many miners' wives in Nottinghamshire weren't able to work because they had young children and that they were going without all the essentials, there was nothing coming in and so we were trying to set up a Centre to provide all the help we could. Then he asked what sort of services we were providing from the Centre.

Doreen said, 'We're giving all the children hot meals and clothes and shoes that people have donated will be shared around.'

Suddenly I found myself talking, I said, 'There's going to be games organized for the children and all sorts of amenities like that.'

As the interview continued we got more confident and I found it easier to talk. The interviewer asked how much hardship there was and we both told him different stories that we'd heard about people in very serious plights. I talked about one man who'd rung a few days before, he was in quite a state because his wife had a heart complaint and it cost four pound every time he had to have a prescription made up. He didn't know where to turn and was thinking that his only alternative was to go back to work.

'That's the sort of people we want to help ' I said. 'Those that are desperate.'

The interviewer kept asking why the strike was so strong in Blidworth as if it shouldn't be and then he said,

'Obviously this long strike is causing a good deal of hardship, but shouldn't the miners' have foreseen it when they went into it?'

Doreen said, 'Well, nobody likes a strike, let's face it, nobody wants to be on the dole either. What choice do we have, we either fight and try to keep our men in work for the next ten years or we give up, that's our choice.'

The interviewer said, 'Seeing this dispute from the point of view of the miners' wives with families and homes to run are you hoping the whole thing will be settled very quickly?'

'Definitely hoping.' Doreen said, 'I mean, we don't want to see people on the poverty line do we? We want to be able to go out to work, to work and have what we're used to, we want a good wage, a good living so we can bring our children up properly.'

I added, 'And jobs for your children at the end of it as well. I mean we don't want to bring our children up to a life on the dole. We want some future for them.' Doreen talked a bit about her teenage lads all facing unemployment, then the interviewer cut her off. We got the feeling that he really only wanted to know about the hardship, he didn't want to hear about the importance of what we were fighting for.

That night when we got up to the picket line we told everyone about the interview, it was to be put on air at seven the next morning. Annette and Pauline had been to Berry Hill, they'd been told that it was the local union representatives who were against us using the Youth Club. They'd also said that as far as they were concerned we had every right to use it. Annette and Pauline had come back and tried to see the Chairman of the Committee to tell him that Berry Hill were in favour of us using the Youth Club. At first he tried to avoid them, pretending he wasn't home, but eventually they did get to see him and they had quite an argument with him. In the end he promised that the Committee would meet the following Monday night to discuss it and make a definite decision.

Next morning I got up and taped the radio interview. As I listened to it I was quite upset at the end. The interviewer said,

'We checked Doreen Humber's claim that 95% of men are out at Blidworth Pit. The NCB have a different story, they are claiming that more than three quarters of the men are working.'

It just went to show how ridiculous the Coal Board figures were, Doreen's 95% might have been a little hopeful, but it was certainly much closer to the truth than the Coal Board's figures. I felt cheated by the interviewer, he'd been so nice while we were there, but he'd checked those figures after we left and while we were there he didn't even challenge them. Still it seemed amazing listening to myself and Doreen on the radio. So much was happening to us so quickly, we were going from one new experience to another. In a way we couldn't really believe it all but there was no time to stop and think. Things kept cropping up and had to be dealt with there and then and each thing taught us something new. And each new piece of knowledge made us stronger in our resolve to keep fighting.

Doreen came in just after the interview. As soon as it had finished she'd had a phone call from a very posh sounding woman who said,

'Do you seriously believe that we are going to support the Miners' Strike? You must be out of your head.'

Doreen told her to get stuffed. But that was the first phone call of many, and it was the only nasty one, all of the others offered support. Support had started to come in from the leaflets. They had been distributed all over Nottingham and Paul had put one in a local newspaper. Letters and cheques started arriving in the mail and packages of food arrived more frequently. Altogether quite a lot was coming in, we still thought it was just our fight, we didn't realize how much other trade unionists in the country could see that it affected them too.

We were to have a meeting the next Sunday morning with Paul Thompson to set up an acting committee. It was to be at Annette's. We asked some other women to come who hadn't really been involved before but who were striking miners' wives and had said that they wanted to help. When Paul arrived at the meeting he had brought three other people with him. One of them knew a great deal about welfare rights, which was very helpful. Paul and the others introduced themselves at the beginning of the meeting telling us why they had come.

I remember Paul said, 'I'm very involved in the Labour Party and I recently went to a meeting where I became aware of the need to raise support outside the mining communities to get enough food and money to keep the strike going. I've come here to help in that because although I'm not a miner, I'm a school teacher, I'm a member of the National Union of Teachers and I understand that if the NUM is defeated in this struggle then I am defeated as well. In that sense there is no difference between me and you, we are exactly the same. Therefore your fight is my fight. You shouldn't regard me as putting myself out for you, I am merely acting in my own interests by coming here because I know that the mining union is the strongest union in the world and the oldest union and if they're defeated then we're all defeated and that creates the conditions for fascism and there is no way I want to live in a fascist country.'

It started to make sense then, why everybody was so supportive, I started to realise it was everyone's fight, and that made me feel very responsible. I was becoming aware of how much responsibility we had to make sure that we won this fight.

Paul said that he had prepared an agenda. Most of us didn't know what that was, so he explained that it was a list of things that we needed to discuss. He taught us to go through the Chair every time we wanted to speak, we had to put our hand up. I thought that was very funny, I felt like I was back at school again. But it was very exciting too. Then Paul said that we needed to elect an acting committee, that we all needed to have different jobs so everything could run efficiently. He said we also needed to keep an account of all the money and food we received so people could see where it was all going. He explained that that was the job of the Treasurer and that we needed a Secretary to send out letters to people and Chairperson to chair the meetings and be a spokesperson for the group. It was decided for the time being that Doreen would be the Chairperson and Annette would be the Treasurer and Secretary. We didn't seem to need a separate Secretary, we couldn't imagine that we had that many letters to write.

Tony Rose talked a lot about welfare rights and what we were entitled to from Social Security. He suggested that someone in the village should get to know all the details so she could help everybody. He suggested putting out a leaflet to let people know what their rights were. Margaret said that she was interested in that and so it was decided that she should find out all about it and work with Tony to get a leaflet out.

We also discussed the Youth Club premises again. By then we were quite angry with the Committee in Blidworth and all felt that they had no right to stop us from using it. Pauline and Annette reported that they'd been told at Berry Hill that it was the Blidworth Committee's responsibility to let us have the premises and that the Chairman of the Committee had agreed to call a special meeting the following night to discuss whether they were going to let us have it or not.

After some discussion we decided that if the meeting that night didn't amount to anything we'd occupy the Youth Club after the young ones had finished that night. We felt that we'd been given the run around about it. The Chairman of the Committee had continually put obstacles in our way, he was a miner and a Labour County Councillor and we couldn't understand why he was being so unco-operative. We were convinced that our need was perfectly reasonable and just and any opposition to our request seemed unbelievable and made us very angry. We decided to keep our plan to ourselves and didn't even tell our husbands. We had taken on the responsibility to find somewhere to feed the men and children, we felt that this was our fight and we would do it our way and on our own.

The Committee meeting was planned for seven-thirty that night. We all met at Doreen's, dressed up in layers of warm clothes in case we had to go ahead with our sit-in. Our plan if the meeting wasn't successful was to sneak into the ladies toilets until the Youth Club had finished, and then when they'd all gone home, to come out and stay there overnight and serve breakfast there the next morning. One of the strikers who was on the Committee agreed to let us know at Doreen's straight away what the meeting decided.

We hadn't been at Doreen's very long when our messenger arrived.

He said, 'They've called the meeting off again.'

'Why?' we all asked, not altogether surprised but very annoyed, this seemed like the last straw, they were still refusing to discuss it.

'When Les Jones arrived at the Welfare for the meeting, he saw two of the lads there having a drink. He said they had come to put pressure on the meeting. He said they were a picket line and that he wasn't going to be pressured into making a decision so he cancelled the meeting.'

It was just another feeble excuse. The men we found out later were simply having a drink at the Welfare waiting to hear the outcome of the meeting. It was outrageous, the Welfare was theirs, they could drink there anytime they liked, it was just another obstacle but we were ready to take it further and our resolve hardened.

We were all prepared and we set off. We marched up the street, about eight of us. Margaret had made some banners for the occasion and she raced back to her house to get them. The rest of us strode along the street, walking at a fast and determined pace. Underneath we were all quite nervous but none of us had any second thoughts, our nervousness became a sort of excited energy which fuelled our determination.

We walked down Thorny Abbey Road, down into the valley which is the centre of the village and then began to walk up again to the Youth Club which is on the other side of the valley. As we approached the Youth Club we saw one of the working miners, rushing towards the door.

'Quick, he's gonna lock the doors,' someone yelled and we all started to run as fast as we could. Annette got there first. She said, 'We want to talk to you about setting the support group up.'

He grabbed hold of her and dragged her inside the double doors and started hitting her on the back of the neck. She was struggling and fighting back. Doreen got there next and she was shouting, 'Leave her alone, you bastard.'

He seemed to be getting angrier and angrier and really started laying into Annette. I didn't know what to do, we were all so shocked that he'd done such a thing, I don't really think any of us believed it was happening. I rushed into the Ladies like we'd planned and locked myself in one of the toilets. A few minutes later I heard voices in the washroom I recognised as the rest of the women and so I stuck my head out to check. Everyone else was there. Annette was very shaken, she had a nasty cut on her neck where he'd pulled on a chain she'd been wearing and she had a black eye.

In the meantime the woman that runs the Youth Club came to the door of the Ladies and screamed and swore at us, 'What the fuckin' hell do you think you're doing, coming in here when the Youth Club's on, disturbing the youth. These kids don't want to see this going on.'

'Look, all we wanted to do was to come in and stay in the toilets till the Youth Club had finished. That working miner caused all the trouble, there was no need for him to lay into Annette and give her some fist like he did.'

She kept arguing with us and abusing us and then the men came bursting in. We were very surprised to see them, we didn't even know that they knew we were there. Apparently as the man was laying into Annette a couple of the kids that were at Youth Club had rushed over to tell the men drinking at the Welfare what was going off. Word got around like wildfire and men were appearing from all over the place.

When the men arrived the man who had attacked Annette tried to scuttle out of the way. We moved out into the main room where the kids were all playing table tennis and things and just as we did the police arrived. They told us that we'd got to get out or they'd arrest us. We all expected to be arrested and were quite prepared to be, we believed so strongly that we had a right to be there. We told the police.

'Well, you'll have to arrest us then, because we're not moving.'

Everybody told them about Annette and they interviewed her and interviewed some of the men and we edged our way into the television room and locked ourselves in there. By this time about fifty lads and men had come to support us. A copper came to the door of the television room and said he wanted to talk to someone about what we were doing. Doreen went out to see him.

'Look,' she said, 'all we're trying to do is to get a place together for a soup kitchen. This place belongs to us, we pay for the running of it and we're taking it over.'

To our surprise, he said, 'All right, if you promise me there'll be no trouble we'll let you alone.' The kids from the Youth Club started to leave, they'd never seen so much excitement, first the women barging in, then the men and then the police. The police were hanging around taking statements. Annette said she was going to press charges. The man responsible had slipped in his rush to get out of the way of the men and hit his head on the table.

We sent the men off to fetch sleeping bags and things for the night. Someone went out to get fish 'n chips for us all. The police were letting people out but then not letting them back in and so we were letting them in through the window. There were sleeping bags and food and flasks of tea and coffee and all sorts coming in through the windows and men climbing in and out. A lot of the men decided that they'd stay the night as well in case any more trouble broke out. Alan had arrived with some of the other men and I asked him to go home and get some sleeping bags. When he came back he wanted me to go home and stay with the kids.

He said, 'Look, this isn't a place for you, I think you should be going home, I'll stop and do the lie-in.'

I was quite indignant, I said, 'No Alan, this is our job, we're fighting for the Youth Club, we've come this far, you're not gonna kick me out now, I'm stopping. You go home with the kids.'

He could see that I was very determined so he left. I was frightened but I was very determined that we were going to get this place. We'd got to get it, there wasn't any choice, we couldn't do the meals at the house. These silly people weren't going to stop us from getting some decent facilities to serve food.

The women claimed the television room, we locked the door so none of the men could get in, watched telly for a bit and then all tried to settle down for the night. We made beds out of the tables and the chairs, I was laid on a coffee table and it was so uncomfortable that I got onto the floor. But the floor was made of stone and it was so cold that I couldn't get to sleep.

Somebody peeked out to see what the men were doing, there was no sign of them in the big room so we went into the kitchen and there were the men with the cooker on and the oven door open for warmth. They were quite snug so we went in and joined them. Everybody was still excited and we talked and joked all night, nobody got much sleep. By four o'clock the next morning we were up and cooking breakfast. Someone went up to the house in Grange Road to get some of the food and we had beans on toast and hot-dog sausages for breakfast.

The early morning activities were full of bustling energy. People started arriving, mostly people who hadn't stayed in overnight but wanted to make sure we were all right. We all passed the time cooking, eating and chatting endlessly about what we could do with the premises now that we had won them. We all felt quite confident that we had won. At about eight o'clock, someone came over from the Welfare to say that the Committee had met and wanted to talk to us about their decision. Doreen made it clear that she didn't want to talk to them alone, she wanted someone else with her, so she and Annette left us to talk to the Youth Club Committee.

·5·
DOREEN HOTTING UP

As we walked across to the Welfare to meet the Committee, Annette and I felt victorious but also very tired. We'd had our lie-in, they'd called an emergency meeting and now we expected to reap the rewards. When we got there we discovered that we were to have a meeting with Les Jones and the woman who runs the Youth Club, not the whole Committee. The two of them were sitting in one of the committee rooms and we were shown in. As we walked in Les Jones smiled and tried to be friendly, but we were not feeling friendly, we were only interested in the decision that had been reached by the meeting.

'What have you decided?' I said.

Les looked a little uncomfortable and said, 'We've decided to let you have the Youth Club to feed women and children.' 'What?' I said, 'just women and children. What about the men?'

'No, no men. Only the women and children.'

'You stink Les and so does this whole situation, you're supposed to be a Labour County Councillor and look what you're doing, people in the Labour Party all over the place are helping us and you're putting obstacles in our way.'

He said, 'Just tell me what you're going to do.'

'I can't, I'm going back over there to tell them what you've said, then I'll let you know what we're going to do.'

He started to look panicky, 'Oh no, don't do that, you know what'll happen don't ya.'

I said, 'Yeah.' I knew what he was getting at, but as far as I was concerned if the men were being singled out and denied food they must be part of the decision as to whether we accepted these terms.

Les's voice had become quite shaky, he said, 'They'll smash it up.'

'More than likely,' I said as we walked out the door.

When we got back to the Youth Club we reported on our meeting. Everybody was very resentful especially the women, but the men insisted that if we had somewhere to feed the women and kids we should accept that, for the present anyway. But as soon as that decision was made, we received a message from the Manager of the pit. We were to go and see one of the Personnel Officers to discuss using the Village Hall as a Centre. Annette and Pauline Howarth went straight up and came back half an hour later with the keys. We were able to use the Village Hall every day till five at night and on Wednesday and Thursday afternoons we had to make room for the Old-age Pensioners who used it regularly on those afternoons.

The Village Hall was not as well suited to our needs as the Youth Club, but it was more than adequate. It had an ample kitchen, joined to a large hall by a serving hatch. There was a small supper room at the back of the main hall with another connecting hatch and there was a large pantry. It was called the Glasshouse because the upper half of nearly all the outside walls was glass. That was a mixed blessing. It meant that the hall was light and airy, that any sunshine warmed the inside and it meant that we could see out at all times so we always knew who was coming and going. But it also meant that people outside could see in. Being so close to the pit meant that the scabs had to walk past it to get to work. It overlooked the pit itself, which was a constant reminder that the friction of the dispute was never far away. The power supply and heating were all connected up to the mains at the pit, and the hall was cleaned each night by the pit cleaners. It served our purposes very well. It lacked entertainment facilities which the Youth Club offered and we thought would be a good idea to help encourage everyone to be involved. While we'd been making breakfast at the Youth Club that morning we'd discussed what we wanted for our Centre. We had talked about wanting a Community Centre that served three hot meals a day, where we could all meet to discuss and plan events. We knew we wanted a Strike Centre not just a soup kitchen.

Now we had our own Strike Centre we were elated, although we never understood the irony of being offered an NCB property while the Youth Club, which we felt belonged to us, had been denied us.

Some of us had to attend a fund raising meeting in Nottingham that night. We were very tired and so decided to go home and sleep. Some of the other women who hadn't been at the Youth Club the night before immediately started to move all our things up to the Centre.

As I walked through the gates of our front yard, desperate for sleep, I noticed the New Testament I'd given my next door neighbour, who was working, as a present, lying on the grass. I picked it up. It had slanderous things written all over it. I didn't actually read them. I recognised them vaguely but felt too disgusted to bother. Apparently Pip did read it and he told me that it accused me of being the devil.

At last I lay down in my own comfortable bed to sleep, but next door started up a terrible racket, banging and knocking. I was sure they were doing it on purpose, but my mind was too busy to dwell on it. I was thinking about the events of the night before. I was amazed at what we had done, and that we had done it on our own without calling on the men to help us. In the end they had come of course, but it was us, the women, who had organized it and carried it off. There was a great feeling of strength and pride in that. The first time I had felt that sense of pride was when we'd gone into the canteen to bring the women working there out. That night, when the men came in to get us, and ended up just leaving us to it, it was like a confirmation that they realised that we were just as strong, deter-mined and able as them. It was confirmation to ourselves as well. None of us had ever done anything like this before and yet, we hadn't hesitated, there had been no second thoughts, we knew what we wanted and went to get it.

Paul Thompson had arranged a meeting that night at Snenton Labour Party at which I was going to speak. My confidence in public speaking had received quite a boost the Friday before. Paul had told us there was a public meeting being held in Nottingham about the Miners' Strike. He suggested that we should go to it. Quite a few of us went, men as well as women. When we walked in Noreen Baker who'd chaired the Trades Council meeting I'd spoken at was sitting up on the platform and she called out to me.

'Doreen,' she said when I got to the platform, 'would you like to sit up here and speak?'

'Oh, I don't know.'

'You've done it before and I think it would be good if you spoke. You could talk about the same things you talked about at the Trades Council. There's supposed to be a woman coming from Yorkshire but she's not here yet so we need a woman and even if she does come I think it would be good to hear what you've got to say.'

Pip had come to the meeting too, I'm sure he'd only come because he thought I wasn't going to speak, he was very nervous about my speaking and when he found out that I was going to speak he was frightened to death. He trembled at the knees.

Mick Carter, from Cortonwood was the first speaker. He talked about the beginning of the strike in Cortonwood, the policies of the Government to attack not just the coalmining industry but the NUM as well because it was the strongest union in the country.

'This Government,' he said, 'is determined to break the back of the Union Movement. It will try to do it by smashing the NUM, but it'll have a fight on its hands, the miners are not prepared to stand by and watch their industry, their union and their communities disappear without a fight, we are determined to fight to the end, and the end will be victory.'

Then it was my turn. Paul had been quite critical of my previous speeches. I always sort of stare into space, thinking about what I'm going to say next. Paul used to say, 'Doreen, you don't stare at the back of the room, you look at the people you're talking to.' So as I stood up I was determined to look into the audience and as I did I caught Pip's eyes. He looked petrified, his face was pale and his lips were sort of tight like they get when he's nervous. I started off by thanking the people there for letting me speak and then I said, 'We're a group of Miners' Wives that are starting up a Strike Centre. We've been on the picket lines and we've got a kitchen together to feed the kids. What we've seen has really made us determined to stand with our men in this fight all the way '

Then I talked about what we'd done and how we were starting to organise. I looked at Pip again, he wasn't under his chair yet so I continued.

'We've never been politically minded people but we have seen over the last few years the unemployment rising, when there was two million unemployed there was a big outcry and now there's three million, and if we don't fight for what we believe in, fight for our jobs and communities the unemployment number is going to double and treble because there aren't enough pits for us to go to and it's obvious that a lot of us are going to finish up on the dole. It isn't just Cortonwood and it isn't just Yorkshire, it's everywhere.

'Our pit at Blidworth was threatened with closure last July and it was only the union that saved it. The Coal Board said it was uneconomical, that it was losing twenty pound on every ton of coal produced and you know why? Because they opened two new faces and they spent a lot of money on new machinery.

'It took fourteen months to open one of those faces and that was the biggest joke in Nottinghamshire, that it took fourteen months to open a new face. The reason it took so long was because the Manager insisted that the men work the way he told them. A lot of them complained and said that it was a very long way to go about it. They all knew that if they had been able to open that face the way they usually opened new faces it would only have taken three or four months, but management insisted on the new method. So for fourteen months a lot of men were working without producing and that should have only been three or four months. Of course a lot of money was lost, and then on top of that the money for the new machinery had to be taken off the price of the coal that was produced.

'The union argued that once the two new faces were open and working the pit wouldn't be uneconomical and they got the Coal Board to agree to give them six months to get those new faces working, and then the pit would be holding its head above water. But they had everything against them. First the overtime ban and then the strike. We've heard now that it is still on a list of three Nottinghamshire pits which are marked for closure. The other thing about Blidworth pit is that it produces the best quality coal in Notts., you can't sell other coal without mixing it with Blidworth coal and there's at least another fifty years good quality coal there. Yet the Coal Board want to close it down. That's an example of their judgement on what is an uneconomical pit. And so that's what we're fighting against.'

I stopped for a moment and looked around the room, everybody seemed to be listening and really wanted to hear more so I started to talk about the police.

'Before this strike, we were just a small village with one village policeman. He never bothered us and we never bothered him, he just did his few hours surgery every day. Then suddenly we wake up one morning and the whole village is crawling with coppers. We can't go about our normal business anymore without being hassled by police. One of our women, Margaret, who is sitting just there, was stopped four times in an hour the other morning. She was just going about her own business and walking in the streets of her own village, doing such dangerous things as buying milk for her kids' breakfasts. Coppers kept stopping her and asking her where she was going and what she was doing and telling her that she couldn't go anywhere near the pit. That happens to us all the time. We walk along the street and suddenly we're being followed by a pair of Maggie's blue bobbies. The other morning my husband was going up to the early morning picket, it was still dark and he walked the quickest way up there which is through the allotments, two coppers jumped out from behind a tree at him and asked him if he was going to work. We don't feel at home in our own village any more, we feel like criminals but we've done nothing.

'On the picket lines men are arrested for nothing at all, if the police feel in a nasty mood, they just arrest someone. We don't know what's hit us, but we do know that we've got to keep fighting. It's in everybody's interest that we back Cortonwood and back Yorkshire and work as the National Union of Mineworkers and not be scabby as Notts. is known for being. If we go down, everybody goes down. We've seen her attack industry after industry, she brought McGregor in to butcher the steel works and now she's trying to get him to butcher the miners, if we go down, who will she attack next. So it's very important that we keep on fighting until we've won and that everybody in this country helps us to do that.'

I sat down, everybody clapped and a few stood up. I got very embarrassed, I still do when people clap after I've spoken, I don't know where to put my face. There was a miner from Ollerton sitting next to me who was going to speak as well and he said to me, 'That were great lass. But I thought you were going to lose your rings.'

All the time I'd been speaking my hands were behind my back and I was fiddling with my rings. The funny thing about that was that he had never spoken before and he was as nervous as I was. When he stood up to speak he took his watch off and put it on the table, then he picked it up and put it back on his wrist, then back onto the table and so on all the way through his speech. So when he sat down I told him about it and it's been a standing joke between the two of us ever since, that I fiddled with my rings and then he fiddled with his watch, because we were both so nervous speaking at those early meetings.

When we got home after that meeting we all went to Pauline's for a cup of coffee. Yorkie had been at the meeting and he said to me, 'The way you talk Doreen, you sound like a socialist.'

That really frightened me because I knew that socialists were like communists and I thought communists were something bad. You always heard people say, 'He's a bloody communist ' as if it was a bad thing, and then there was Russia and police states and all those things that somehow frightened me and were against what I thought I believed in.

I said, 'Is a socialist like a communist, 'cause I'm not a communist. Anyway what do you mean, I thought it was horrible to be a communist.'

Howard was there as well, he and his wife Marilyn were very close friends of ours and Howard and Pip and me used to talk a lot about religion and politics, because we were all believers.

Howard said, 'If Jesus Christ came back on this earth today, he'd be a communist because he believed in equality and that's what communism's all about.'

That made a lot of sense to me and from then on I started going into the whole question and every chance I'd get I'd talk to the men that were political about it. I knew some of the men were Communists and I began to realise that I nearly always agreed with them and respected the way they were organizing the strike. I started asking questions about what different things meant and about things that had happened in the past.

Somehow all the things that I'd seen before but tried to ignore fitted in and everything began to make sense. I'd seen unemployment rising and I knew that sooner or later it was going to affect everyone.

I can remember when they had one of the ballots to strike a year before and I'd been against it because we couldn't afford to strike, but at the same time I can remember watching television and thinking, 'That bitch, she's out to get us all in the same boat.' So in a way, I was thinking politically, and suddenly all of those things fitted into place with what was happening to us and I started to talk about them. At first I didn't think I was talking politics, I was just concerned for our own welfare but I started to realise that everything the Government did was against us.

I used to think that anybody that was political and made political speeches must have read a lot and must know a lot, then I started to realise that I knew a lot too. It's just that it all suddenly seemed to make sense and I realised that things I'd been hearing for ages and trying to ignore were still there in my memory and now they all fitted together and made some sense. It was like a lot of scrambled bits of information suddenly became sorted out and when that happened I started to realise that I was a political person. I remembered watching the Brixton riots on television. At the time I believed what the television said, that the police had to stop these race riots. Then when I saw what the police did to us on the picket line, and when I could see what the Government was doing to us I started to wonder what they'd done to those black people to make them riot like that. I was beginning to have some confidence in my knowledge, not just about the strike but about other things as well. We'd discussed the best ways of raising support with Paul and he'd suggested that each Notts. pit should twin with a community in Nottinghamshire and get support from that community. I don't know where he got the idea from, I don't think anybody else was doing it then, but it sounded like a good idea. So we were going to ask the Snenton Labour Party if they'd twin with us. Pauline, Annette, Margaret and Pauline Howarth all came to the meeting too and after I'd finished my speech Margaret suggested that we sit around in the circle so that everyone could have a discussion. Paul had forms that he'd had printed for people to fill in if they wanted to pledge a levy, so he handed them out and the meeting discussed how they could raise food and money for us. They agreed with our idea of twinning and agreed that their branch of the Labour Party would twin with us. There was a man there from another branch and we asked him if they would twin with

Rainworth, our neighbouring village. Our idea was that there were enough communities in Notts to support all the pits in the county. The support we'd got had been overwhelming and so we thought there would be enough. But as it turned out there wasn't that much support in Notts, but twinning did work out nationally.

The next day Pauline and I stayed home from work again. There was so much to do. Everything from the house in Grange Road had been moved up to the Centre. All the food that had been donated and that we'd collected was sorted out and put away in the pantry. We all took knives, forks, spoons, plates, cups and cooking equipment up from our houses to make sure we had enough. I stayed at home in the morning to phone big stores to see if they'd give us a discount on food. I didn't have much joy but the Co-op head office said we could have something like a 5% discount. Then I got in the car and went to see a milkman whose wife I knew and asked if he'd deliver to the Centre every day. I went up to the Village Hall. It was the first time I went to the Centre. As soon as I walked in I sensed the excitement.

People everywhere were shouting to each other and bustling about busily getting things organized. The Centre was from the outset, just as we had imagined it, not only a place where we could provide food but a place we could all be a part of, a place which belonged to everybody which would help to unite us and help us to get to know each other. It was like our big communal home and we became like a big communal family.

Some women from Rainworth had come up to see us and to see if we could help them to get set up. I told them about the twinning we'd arranged for them and gave them half of the money that we had and some bread, potatoes, eggs and milk to help them get started. Just then the phone rang and someone asked to speak to me. It was Central Television and they wanted to come out and film the Centre. I told them that I'd have to check with everybody else and when I asked around nobody objected so I told them they could come up the next day.

Over the next two days, Pauline and I had to work very hard

to make up all the time we'd missed, so we missed out on a lot of the activity at the Village Hall. Central Television came and made a feature about the Centre, they showed the women cooking and serving and everybody eating the first hot meal we served there. Annette and Betty Savage were interviewed and excited kids ran all over the place in the background. Our Centre was the first opened in Nottinghamshire and one of the first in the country, so it was quite a big deal and lots of people were really interested in it.

Pauline and I felt left out of it during the day while we were at work and work started to become a real drag. We were so much more interested in what was going on at home than we were in the endless seams we had to sew at work. They had rush orders on as well and were starting to get quite annoyed about the amount of time we were taking off. But there was so much to do to keep things going at the Centre that we had no choice.

Every evening there were meetings we had to attend. It was a very busy time. We were just setting up, so we had our own committee meetings, the Centre was just setting up and there was endless work to be done up there, then there were fund raising meetings to attend as well as meetings about the strike and meetings which helped us to learn what to do. As well as all that there were hundreds of informal meetings in someone's house or up at the Centre, just to discuss all the other meetings and what we thought about them. We weren't just going to meetings and saying our piece, we were learning all the way along, we were breaking new ground, not just for ourselves but for the whole labour movement.

Increasingly numbers of people started dropping into the Centre, people came to see how we'd set up, to follow our example or just out of curiosity, others came to offer support. We started to meet so many people and make new friends.

On May Day bank holiday there were two rallies, one in Mansfield and one in Nottingham. Our group decided that the men would go to Mansfield and the women and kids would go to Nottingham. To get us there we hired a mini-bus and paid for it out of the funds. We were quite surprised, it was a big rally and because

of the one in Mansfield as well we'd not expected so many people
to be there. We had a banner by now that Margaret had made and
we set that up and all marched in our own little group. The kids
took the leaflets that we'd produced and they had collecting tins. They
dished hundred of leaflets out and collected seventy-six pound. They
had a smashing time, dashing about handing out leaflets and collecting money. They kept running up to us and shaking their tins saying,
   'Look how much I've got.'
   'Hey, Mum, someone put a fiver in my tin.'
   'So what, I got a ten pound note before.'
They made it into a competition between themselves to see who
could get the most, some of them even knocked on the doors of houses
we were passing. They were ever so good, we marched a long way
and they never complained at all. They caught the mood of excitement and loved the singing and chanting. We were all learning the
songs that were sung on rallies and we enjoyed singing them, it was
a way of saying what we were there for; a really alive way. After the
march we walked all around Nottingham looking for the Market
Square where we'd arranged to meet the bus, eventually we found
it but we were a couple of hours early. We all sat on the steps of
County Hall eating sandwiches that we'd brought. The kids were
running about trying to catch pigeons and one of the older lads caught
one, necked it, put it in a plastic bag and presented it to us.
   'Here, you can make pigeon pie up at the Centre.'
There were pigeon feathers everywhere and we were all panicking
because the place was crawling with police from the rally.
   'Andrew, don't do that again, the cops'll 'ave us.'
   'You can just imagine the newspapers–**Striking miner's son
necks pigeon in Market Square**.' He was a bit disappointed, he'd
thought it was a good idea and would actually be a help to us. After
that he continued to catch pigeons but he'd stick a 'Coal Not Dole'
sticker on their breasts and let them go. We thought that was a much
better idea and thought it quite novel that all these pigeons were flying around Nottingham with 'Coal Not Dole' stickers on their breasts.

   It seemed hours that we waited. Some men who were selling
newspapers came up and started to talk to us, saying that we were
doing a good job and to keep it up. Then some young lads came up

and started to say the opposite but the men said to them.

'They're fighting for your jobs too, you know. You're on the dole, how do you like it?'

One of the youths was very cocky and he said, 'Get off, it's great on dole, getting paid for doing nought.' But the rest of them shut up and went away.

That night, Snenton Labour Party had organized a social to raise money for us. We all went into Nottingham. There was a bit of a buffet and we were all given a free drink when we got there. They raised money on the door and at the end of the night they gave us and another village seventeen pound each. I got up and thanked them very much for their support and then we all sang, 'Arthur Scargill' and chanted 'the miners, united, will never be defeated' over and over again.

When Pip and me got home, there were vegetable peelings and bread crusts all over our front yard. As we walked in the door we saw a letter that was pushed through. It said, 'To all the vegetables.' Inside, it said, we were using Arthur Scargill as our God and were supposed to be followers of Jesus. We were starting to get used to such childish abuse, but even so it was a very unpleasant feeling knowing that your next door neighbours were so hostile towards you. Still we knew we were in the right and they had sold their principles and would never be able to hold their heads up again. More than that, we knew that we were learning so much and experiencing so many new things, but they were still tied in the same rut and not able to see further ahead than pay day.

The next night a meeting had been called in Nottingham by the Strike Committee, it was to discuss fund raising in the county. There were mostly men there and they were saying that everything raised must go to a central fund and then be distributed equally among every village. Somebody stood up and said, 'I've heard that some groups are beginning to twin, I'd like to know what the pro's and con's of it are.'

So I stood up and talked about our twinning and about how well it worked. I said, 'As far as we're concerned it's the best way to raise support in Notts., we haven't got a central organisation to make sure that everything is distributed because we haven't got the NUM here. I think that it's different in Notts. than it is in other places. We also support twinning because when you get to know the people in a personal way that are raising the money for you they feel more involved and work harder to raise more. In the Labour Party Branch that we're twinned with there are two old ladies. They go around Nottingham, knocking on doors and get lots of abuse. When they come out to our Centre to see us they tell us about it, but they also see our kids and they're getting to know them. And I know that the only thing that keeps those two women going, is knowing our kids and not wanting to see them go without.' But no-one else seemed to support me, they were all dead against it. I came away feeling that it was a disastrous meeting.

Later I talked to Paul Thompson about it. He said, 'What do you say about us setting a meeting up, to discuss twinning?' I thought that was a good idea and took it to our Committee, everybody agreed and we arranged a meeting in the Village Hall for the 20th May and printed some leaflets to advertise it. The leaflets put the argument in favour of twinning, they were headed 'Blidworth Community Council. Twinning of Communities.' They said:

We are in the process of twinning each mining community in Notts with a city community. There are many community organisations and political groups in the city communities who want to help support the struggle of the mining communities. They realize that we are fighting for them as well as for ourselves. They want to support us to make sure that we are not starved back to work. If we are beaten, they are beaten. Let us all get together as miners' wives and communities to work together in Nottinghamshire to win this strike. We are having a meeting next Sunday, may 20th at 2.00pm at the Blidworth Village Hall, Belle Vue Lane, Blidworth to organize the twinning of communities. At Blidworth we are feeding all striking miners and families three nourishing meals a day and have regular funds and food parcels coming in because we are basing our struggle on communities and not just on a central strike fund. Anybody who needs financial advice or help of any other kind can get it from out Welfare Rights Department. The Community Council gives leadership to the Community and keeps people together. No-one stands alone!!!

*Although trades unions should make regular donations to the Notts.
Miners' Forum, we also know from our own experience that much more
support will come if we go out ourselves to fight for it in the communities. That is why we are organizing this meeting - to show other communities what we have done and the success that we have had. Please
come to this meeting if you need help or if you want to help.*

Paul distributed the leaflets throughout Nottingham and we contacted everybody we knew who was starting to get organized. The
trouble was that not all the groups were prepared to go out and speak
at meetings and make twinnings work. A meeting had been arranged
at the Radford Labour Party for Rainworth to attend, but the women
there were too nervous to speak, so I ended up going and speaking
on their behalf. Hucknall/Linby, another Notts pit wanted to start
organising and they asked us to go to their first meeting and talk about
what we'd done. We did that and invited them to come to a meeting
that had been organised in Nottingham at which I was speaking. They
came and when the collection was done at the end of the meeting
I asked if the group would like to twin with Hucknall. They agreed,
so Hucknall got the collection money and went on from there.

For some time there'd been talk about pickets coming down from
Yorkshire. We all thought it was a great idea and the few contacts
we had in Yorkshire let us know that it would be possible. In
Yorkshire the strike was solid and we all looked up to the Yorkshire
miners and their strength was evident. They perhaps faced greater
economic hardship because there were so many of them, but their
spirits were higher than ours because they weren't always surrounded
by police and scabs like we were.
Relations between working miners and strikers had broken down
completely and hostility was breaking out all over the place. One
night, just after we'd talked about arranging for some Yorkshire
pickets to come down, Pip and I went down the road to the Jolly
Friar for a drink. A couple who we sometimes used to sit with were
there. We'd stopped sitting with them because he was scabbing. Just
for a bit of fun I said in a loud voice,

'Yorkshire pickets are coming so we can have mass pickets in Blidworth. We've had all Derbyshire, now we're going to get all Yorkshire and I'm going to go to the Notts. border in relays and bring them back here in the car.'

The Notts. border was cut off to try and stop anyone from outside getting in. I was only joking but these two took me seriously. Before long it was all around the village that I was going to bring relays of Yorkshire pickets into Blidworth. The next day this bloke saw Pip and said he was going to smash our car up.

'You do,' said Pip 'and I know who'll come off worse, ours is an old banger and yours is a W reg.'

A few days later, Dennis Browne came up and asked Pip if we would put up some Yorkshire pickets. It had been organised, about forty of them were coming down for a few days. When I got back Pip told me that they were coming.

'Where are they going to sleep?'

'I thought we could put the tent up and they could sleep in that.' They were due to arrive the following Monday evening after they'd been to a big rally that had been organised in Mansfield.

The next day we all went to the Barnsley Women's Rally. Some women in Barnsley had organised the rally, Arthur Scargill was speaking and his secretary had asked if Annette and I would speak as well. They were expecting about 300 women and got about 10,000. Lots of men came as well but they all marched at the back. The women were divided up into areas. There was a sort of feeling that all Notts. were scabs and so when we arrived we made sure we were noticed, we all marched along in our own group singing, 'Notts. are here, Notts. are here,' and everybody in the street cheered us and shouted support. There were women everywhere, carrying banners and chanting and singing, it was a great feeling of strength just to be there, especially because it was largely all the women who were involved in the strike. We saw the strength of women that day and that was very inspiring and encouraging.

After the march there was to be a meeting in a hall, but there were too many people and they overflowed onto the street outside. Loudspeakers were set up so that everybody outside could hear the speakers. Me and Annette couldn't get to the front of the hall, it was so packed. Somebody shouted our names over the loud speaker and we pushed ourselves through the crowd. I was the first speaker.

I said, 'I don't know what sort of reception we're going to get, coming from Nottinghamshire.'

Everybody cheered and yelled to let us know that we were appreciated. I talked about the strike and about Blidworth Pit being threatened with closure and I talked about the scabs. Then I said, 'The working class is like a sleeping lion. It's been sleeping for some time, but now it's been prodded and woken up and it's waking up with its claws out, its coming out fighting and it will fight and it will never be defeated.'

It was Annette's birthday that day and I asked Arthur to present her with a card, he did and he thanked us both for coming and speaking. After that a woman came up to me and said she was a journalist from the London Guardian. She said, 'I just heard your speech and I'd like to do an interview with you.'

I said that would be all right and she interviewed me for three quarters of an hour, she asked all about how we'd got set up, who was supporting us and things like that. Later we found out that she was a cop. At the time, I wasn't suspicious at all, but that made me a bit careful about who I talked to.

The Barnsley Rally was on Saturday the 12th of May and on the Monday after that was the Mansfield Rally. The Mansfield Rally became for the men what the Barnsley Rally had been for the women. It was really enormous, miners came from all over the country. We thought the Barnsley Rally was big, but at Mansfield there were 35,000. The march was so long that when the head of it had walked four or five miles around the city of Mansfield and returned to the place they had started the end of the march hadn't even started to move off.

In a car park after the rally, the police started a fight and arrested many of the men. We'd noticed a change in the attitude of the police in our village. When they first arrived they had tried to be very friendly, especially with the children. Of course the kids thought that was great. The police used to let them sit in their vans and play with the handcuffs, helmets and even the riot gear, they used to give them any spare snap they had and swap badges with them. Sometimes one of them would give a uniform button for an NUM badge. At first it was just puzzling to us why the police would want to collect badges, but it was such a strong craze among the miners that we thought the police must just have caught it. Then one day a couple of the men saw a man who'd been on a picket line with them and was dressed like a miner, with a denim jacket sporting a decent number of badges. After the picket, as our men were getting in their cars to come home, they saw this bloke talking to two uniformed cops in the corner of the car park, they realised then that he was an undercover cop. After that more stories started to spread and the NUM Newspaper, 'The Miner,' published some photos of undercover police on the picket line. We realised why the police were so keen to trade badges and buttons with the kids. We told the kids to stop swapping badges with them, at first that didn't do much good, the kids just seemed to think that we adults were trying to spoil their fun.

Then the attitude of the police suddenly changed. They victimised the kids whose Dads were on strike. One day they stopped some kids going to school and asked them if their Dads were on strike. When the kids answered, yes, the cops said:
'Well you tell your Dad to get back to work or we'll arrest him.'
This sort of victimisation became common place and so the kids themselves became frightened of the police and began to hate them as much as we did. They were everywhere, it was like having an invading army in our own village.

Up at the Strike Centre after the Mansfield Rally about eighty Yorkshire lads were waiting to have their billets sorted out. One of the conditions of having the Village Hall was that we didn't feed visiting pickets so I said, 'Well lads, we can't feed you here, follow me and we'll get you some snap.'
Pauline and I came back to my house with a load of them and started cooking them chips. Pip came up and after they'd had something to eat he drove them around to the different houses they were staying in. One group were staying with one of the single lads and when they got to his house he wasn't there. They went looking for him

and then found out that he had been arrested in Mansfield.

About twenty of them stayed in the three houses in Thorny Abbey Road, ours, Pauline's and Annette's. Here and next door they were on the back garden in tents and Pauline and Alan's caravan. I didn't really spend that much time with them I was so busy, but Pip did and he became friendly with them. They used to play cards in the caravan and Pip used to love joining them even though he's not normally a great card player.

By then Pip was taking on most of the cleaning up in the house and as he's very houseproud, he was almost fanatical about it. No-one could leave a cup, plate, a stray piece of clothing or a letter out of place but Pip would have it snapped up and out of the way, moaning all the while at the culprit. After he'd hoovered, any crumb or bit of fluff that appeared on the floor seemed to cause him great distress. It became a sort of family joke, but underneath the joking, Pip was quite serious about it. While the Yorkshire lads were here, Pip even ignored his housework, he seemed to enjoy talking and joking with them so much. I remember one of them was very short and they used to call him Garden Gnome, another one was called Mother because he seemed to be the one that cleaned up the caravan and made cups of coffee and things.

They couldn't get over us having a scab living next door, they were fascinated by our attitude to it. They found it hard to believe that we seemed to ignore him. They were always asking about him.

On one occasion, some of them who were staying in another house came to borrow some washing powder. I had a plastic bag with some instant potato powder in it. I wasn't here, and the pickets looked in the pantry and thought this potato was soap powder. They went back and put it in the washing machine. We ribbed them about that the whole time they were here. The first morning they were here a lot of them were arrested on the picket line. I didn't go up but Pip came back and told me that some of the Yorkshire lads had been lifted. It was just a normal picket and the police suddenly moved in and took a few, then of course there was a bit of scuffle with people trying to pull them back from the police and one of our lads was arrested as well. Then another two of ours were arrested that morning going home from the picket. One of them was walking up the street on his way home and he passed two scabs and shouted at them, 'It's a bit of a bugger when you've got to get Yorkshire lads down to get you lot out.' Then another one was arrested for shouting to scabs after the police had told him to go home. The next few days were fairly trouble free, we enjoyed having the Yorkshire lads here and we enjoyed the sense of solidarity that came from getting to know each other.

·6·
DOREEN DISTURBING THE PEACE ?

On the Wednesday night the Yorkshire lads asked us if we'd go out for a drink with them. Because Pauline and I had been working we hadn't had much chance to talk to them so it seemed like a good idea.

The six of us from the three houses in Thorny Abbey Road and the lads who were staying with us arranged to meet Margaret, Yorkie and the pickets that were staying with them at the Jolly Friar. The police were in and out of the pub much more than usual and each time they came in they seemed to have their eye on us. Our next door neighbour was in as well and one of the Yorkshire lads wanted to say something to him.

'It'll only come back on us, if you do,' we said. 'He'll cause trouble for us later.' Paul Thompson had come up to interview Yorkie and Dennis Browne for an article he was writing about the strike. He asked Yorkie what he thought of the policing. Yorkie had been in the army before he became a miner and he'd spent some of that time in Northern Ireland.

He said to Paul, 'As far as I can see the police occupation here is exactly the same as what we were doing in Northern Ireland. The only thing that's missing is house to house searches and I don't think it'll be long before they start them.'

When the pub closed we all went back to Annette's for coffee. I dropped in home to see how things were. David was looking after Mark and said he wanted to go to bed.

'Go on then, but leave the back door open for Paul and Laggy, they're not in yet. We're just having a coffee at Annette's, we won't be long.'

At Annette's one of the lads was on the phone to his wife in Yorkshire. The others were all larking about, shouting into the phone, that he was at an orgy. I knew how I'd feel in her situation so I took the phone to have a chat and reassure her.

'Don't take any notice, duck. He's quite alright, we've just been

out for a drink and now a few of us are having coffee.' I went on
to tell her how much we'd enjoyed having the lads down to stay and
how much we were looking forward to coming up and meeting her
and the other wives as soon as we could arrange it.

While this had been going on one of the lads went out to the
tent on the back of our garden to fetch some bread. Just as we hung
the phone up he came back and said,
'Hey, we're snided out with coppers.'
We all just looked at him for a minute. Then he looked at me and
said,
'They're all over the place, I only got as far as the fence and I saw
two standing on your back doorstep and another two coming out of
the house. Then I looked down at the tent and there was two more
coming out from behind it and one from inside. You better get off
home, 'cause they're in your house.'
I went straight out of Annette's and across the back way to our
house. As I got to the middle of Pauline's yard one of the coppers
passed me. I didn't speak neither did he, I just walked straight past
him. Then I saw another two coming down our drive and turning
towards our back door. I just went straight into the house to see if
everything was alright.
David came downstairs when he heard me and said there'd been
police in the house, he'd heard noises, looked out of the front window and seen a police van out the front and coppers walking down
our drive. he'd been terrified and stayed upstairs.
When I got back to Annette's everybody had come out of the house
to see what was happening. They were all being edged up the drive
towards the road by a load of coppers and Terry Dunne who was
a Union Official in Yorkshire and one of the lads staying with us
was near the top of the drive surrounded by about six or eight coppers. One of them was leaning on him and saying,
'If you don't get the Yorkshire pickets away from here and out of
these houses by tomorrow, we'll arrest you, your wife and your
neighbours.'
Terry said, 'I think you've got the wrong bloke.'
We were all objecting and asking what it was about.
One of them said, 'You lot have been creating a disturbance, we've

had a complaint.'

They pushed Terry out onto the road and tried to grab him. He ran around the police van and tried to jump over the wall back into the front garden but about seven or eight coppers flew at him, pulling his arms up behind his back and then pushing his head down. Then they all started bashing him, all of them punching and kicking as they dragged him into the middle of the road. We could see blood all over him and then they bundled him into the back of the van. The rest of the cops all raced over to the van, the Yorkshire pickets following.

'If you take him you take all of us.'

But the van drove away at top speed with the men running down the street after it. Chasing it was useless so they came back and we all stood around for a minute, flabbergasted. It had happened so quickly, none of us had been able to act, only to stand shocked and watch.

We were just about to go back inside when the bloke across the road came out of his house brandishing a great long knife and started ranting and raving about someone chucking stones at his lorry. He was quite crazy, he went on about all the noise upsetting his wife and children. His wife came out then and tried to calm him down, she was obviously embarrassed by the way he was carrying on. Pip went over and told him to calm down, that nobody had any interest in his lorry. He told him what had happened and said,

'You'd better get back inside in case the coppers come back. You'll be in a right mess if they find you out here with that knife.'

Margaret and Yorkie's teenage daughter was babysitting Pauline's kids so they went in to see if she was alright. She was sitting on Pauline's couch sobbing her heart out. Police had been to the door asking her where the Yorkshire pickets were and they'd terrified her. We tried to phone a solicitor from Annette's but her phone was dead, you couldn't get out at all. I went home and got through to Berry Hill and they said they'd send a solicitor out straight away. I also made a few more phone calls to people who might be able to help. The solicitor never got here. We don't know what happened to him, someone said that he'd been picked up by police near Mansfield, but we never really found out.

It took a while for us to feel angry, we'd been so shocked at first, but by now we were furious. They'd come, they'd said, because of a disturbance, but the disturbance was so loud, they'd had to look in two houses before they could find us. They'd viciously bashed Terry in front of us all and then carted him off for absolutely nothing. Where to we didn't know, for all we knew we might never see Terry again.

Paul and Laggy had come home soon after the police had left and Paul went out and looked around the tents. He came back with a police torch he found in the tent. We were quite pleased, at least it was evidence that they'd been on our property searching the tents without a warrant. Pip took the torch and went and hid it in our house.

All this couldn't have taken more than ten minutes, then, thirteen transit vans came back up the street and parked one after another across the road. Twelve cops got out of each one and lined up along our front walls. They were all calling out to us to come out onto the street. We told them to get off the drive, that we weren't coming outside our yards. Pip said to them,

'I know what you've come back for, you've come back for your torch and I'm not going to give it to you.'

'If you don't give it to us, you're stealing police property.'

'I'm not stealing anything, you shouldn't have been stupid enough to have dropped it. You were in my tent on my property and I'm keeping that torch for evidence.'

I raced around to our drive to shut the gates and they were all on the street saying to me, 'Come out here and talk to us.'

'What! Do you think I'm balmy? I'm not coming out there, we saw what you did to last 'un that came out.'

Yorkie started to talk to their gaffer. He asked what was going on and they told him that they'd had a report of a police van being attacked and there was an expected riot.

We were really terrified, there were so many of them and we'd just seen what they'd done to Terry. I went down home to phone Mal Howarth. When I told him what was going off he said he'd come up. Then he looked out of his window, he said, 'Doreen, there's hundreds of 'em marching up the street now, headed towards your place.'

I went outside again, then him from next door came out with a few policemen that had been in his house with him. I started to scream and shout.

'Look who you're protecting, them who leave their poor little kid alone in the house at night while they go out drinking. And you're supporting the likes of him.'

Then he started coming for me and the coppers stopped him. They all stood there looking straight at us, hundreds of them. You couldn't see across the road for helmets, Mal and Pip Browne arrived and asked them what they were doing. They told them about the disturbance. Mal and Pip came inside, they were quite shaken as well, they'd had to walk through hundreds of police to get here. Later we heard that there was another dozen vanloads just around the other corner. The street was blocked off, there were police everywhere, you couldn't tell how many or where they were coming from. But one thing we knew, they were Notts. coppers and it wasn't Notts. coppers they had up at the pit on picket duty, so they must have come into the village especially for whatever they wanted to do that night.

Then as quickly as they'd come, they disappeared. But still we were petrified. Pauline and Margaret decided to walk down to Margaret's. There were a couple of Yorkshire pickets staying there who hadn't come out with us and also Margaret's kids, she wanted to check that they were alright. They took Goldie, Pauline's labrador for protection.

They seemed to have been gone ages, so Pip and Yorkie decided to go looking for them. I broke then and started creating.

'Please don't go Pip, what if they come back, what'll I do?'

He said, 'I've got to, I've got to go and look for Pauline.'

'But I daren't stay here on my own, I'm petrified.'

'Look, we've got to go, stay here and lock the doors and don't open them to anybody. I shan't be long, I'll come straight back.'

I sat in the kitchen terrified, I couldn't even keep a limb still. I daren't even go next door, I just sat here, smoking one after the other and kept getting up and looking out of the window to see if they'd come back. I was convinced Pip would never come back. But he did, he wasn't really away very long at all. We went to bed, but we didn't sleep, we lay in bed all night listening to police vans going up and down the street.

All the Yorkshire lads slept in Annette's lounge-room, none of them were prepared to sleep in the tents or caravan.

The next morning all of our men and just two of the Yorkshire lads went up to the picket line, we wanted to see if they'd be arrested, but they weren't. Everybody was prepared for anything to happen, but it was very quiet.

I was just getting dressed when some newspaper reporters arrived and wanted to do an interview and take some photos. The night before I'd made a few phone calls to people I thought might be able to help, someone must have phoned the press because as soon as the newspaper reporters left a television crew arrived. They asked us to tell them what we felt about what had happened, we were still very amazed and upset.

I said, 'What the police did here last night was really out of order. We'd done nothing wrong at all, all we'd done was to put Yorkshire pickets up and the police had no business going through my house and all through the tents. It really brings home to me the extent that they will go to just to frighten and intimidate us. If they think that we'll back down so easily they've got another thing coming. We believe in what we're fighting for and we've a right to our beliefs and to have anyone we want stay in our houses. I'm really beginning to see just how far they're prepared to go to stop us from standing up and saying what we believe in, in a peaceful manner.' I went on for a while like that and the interviewer said to me.

'I agree with you completely, I'm a trade unionist and behind this strike all the way, but there's no way we can put that sort of speech on. We just want you to tell us exactly what happened last night.'

So that's what we did, and I said that we were going to put an official complaint in to the police.

At about one o'clock we went to Pauline's to watch ourselves on the television news, it had just started when Terry walked in. He looked a sight, his face was black and blue and he showed us how cracked and swollen his ribs were from the bashing he'd had. They'd driven him down one of the country lanes on the way to Mansfield and then transferred him to another van which took him to Mansfield where they kept him overnight. As they handed him over he heard someone say,

'We've got to go back and get some more, we haven't done yet.'

He'd been charged that morning and told to make sure he was out of the county within the hour. So he'd come back here to collect his things and then drove back to Yorkshire with one of the other lads.

Just after they'd left the police came back again. About three van loads pulled up outside the houses. We were all in Annette's and when we came out, they started pushing and shoving us in Annette's drive, they were really nasty and aggressive, and were even pushing the kids around.

We said, 'Get out of here, this is private property, you're not allowed to come on this drive.'

'We're staying until we see every document that those Yorkshire pickets have got, we want their car documents, their licences, everything.'

Annette said, 'Get off this drive, it's my drive it's not yours and I haven't given you permission to come onto it. You're trespassing.'

'Have you got proof lady, that you are the occupier of this house, we don't know who you are. We want to see your rate book and your mortgage book to prove that you're the legal occupant of this property.'

While Annette went inside other police ordered the lads from Yorkshire up to the top of the drive to account for their cars. They were told to produce all their driving documents and stand by their cars to prove legal ownership. They stopped Alan and asked him for his name, address, date and place of birth. Pauline passed word around that all the Yorkshire lads should go into her front room and lock the doors. At the back of her house, there are double glass patio doors, the police started banging on the doors asking if they could come in. No-one moved to unlock the doors so they said,

'We'll go and fetch a warrant.'

'You do that ' Pauline said.

I went into my house to try and ring Mal again, I'd just got onto him at the club when I heard loud banging on my front door. It was the police and they were banging so hard I thought they were going to smash the door down.

As I opened the door, I said, 'What the bloody hell do you want now?'

'Who owns that car out there?' They were really horrible, their attitude was very aggressive and bombastic.

'I do.'

'We want to see all your papers.'

'I'm busy right now, I'm on the phone, you'll get the papers when I can find them.'

'How long you had it?'

'Three years.'

Then he grinned a really sickly grin and said, 'I want every document for it and I want them now.'

'You can have 'em when I find 'em.'

And he said, 'I'll be back.'

As they got to the top of the drive Pip was coming back from the Strike Centre. The copper said to him. 'Hello Phillip, what are you doing around this end of town?'

By calling him Phillip they made it obvious they had checked up on who the owners of our house were because no-one ever calls him Phillip.

Pip said, 'I'm coming home.'

'Why, where do you live?'

'I live there, anyway how do you know my name?'

'Oh, come on, Phillip, you don't live there.'

'I do.'

'All those weeks you've been on that picket line, you've caused no trouble yet. We've had a lot of trouble with these people in these houses. It couldn't be you, you wouldn't cause any trouble.'

'No, I've never caused any trouble, but I'll tell you sommat. I never believed in violence, I believe in this strike and I've always believed in peaceful picketing and standing up for my beliefs, but after meeting you bastards I'm beginning to turn, because all you are is bastards, the lot of you. There's no way I'll be right with you again, the lot of you, you've really turned me.'

'Oh come on, Phillip, don't be like that, what are you Dr. Jekyll and Mr. Hyde?'

At that point Mal Howarth came up the street and the TV crew who'd been here that morning were with him. The cops started to walk away.

I yelled after them, 'What's up, afraid somebody might find out what you're really like?'

We all stood on the street talking with the television crew. We'd been hearing lots on the news about the intimidation of working miners by striking miners and so we asked the TV crew why they didn't show the other side. They agreed to take some film of a car which belonged to one of our lads which had been ruined. It had been smashed up and covered with brake fluid which had wrecked the paintwork. We got the car up here and parked it in the street. The TV crew took film of it and interviewed the owner and a few other striking men. They said it'd be shown on BBC News at 6 o'clock.

All the while the TV cameras were filming the car, the police were walking up and down at either end of the street, but they weren't coming too close. The Yorkshire pickets came out of Pauline's house and said they'd decided to leave because they were causing us so much trouble. Then a solicitor arrived from Yorkshire and went inside Annette's house to talk to them all. It was too much for the police, they walked down the road and said,

'There's too many cars in this street, some of them will have to be moved.'

The solicitor came out and told the police that he was taking the Yorkshire lads back to Yorkshire in convoy.

'They are not to be stopped, they're coming with me. And you're to leave these people alone, they've broken no laws.'

So the Yorkshire lads packed up their things and drove off all together, we all stood in the street and waved them off with the TV cameras whirling. The departure of the Yorkshire pickets was shown on the News that night but the ruined car wasn't. The TV crew came back again that afternoon and told us that their editor had cut it out. We were all sad to see the Yorkshire lads leave and especially under the circumstances, in their short stay they'd become great friends. But we had made arrangements to visit them very soon and we all looked forward to it.

The next day I was up at the Centre sitting and talking to two journalists from the left-wing press. There weren't many people there, we'd just had dinner and most of the men had gone. The old age pensioners were in, so there were just a few of us sitting in the back room. As I was talking I saw a van load of police go by. The van stopped and two police got out and stood on the corner just opposite where we were. One of the newsmen said he was going.

I said, 'No, don't go now, them two are here to cause trouble and I want step by step photographs.'

One of the men, John Fletcher, walked out of the Centre to go and visit his Grandma down the street. He lived in Mansfield and used to ride into the Centre each day on his bike, so he took his bike and started to pedal down the road. As he got to the bottom of the street he saw a scab who said something to him. This same scab had waved his pay packet in Fletch's face that morning as he walked past the official picket. Some words were exchanged between them and the next thing the scab had kicked Fletch off his bike. The two coppers standing opposite the Centre saw it too and they started straight away down the street. Pip Browne and someone else from the Centre followed them down and said,

'We'll be witnesses to this one.'

The police say, 'You can piss off, we don't need you as witness to anything.'

Fletch was getting up off the ground by this time and was pulling his bike up and one of the policemen grabbed him. They started to walk him up the street towards the Centre when Eddie Rhodes, another of the strikers came walking up behind them.

He said, 'What have you got him for, what's he done?'

One of the police said to him, 'You can shut up or you're nicked too.'

Eddie said, 'Oh stop getting so aeriated.'

The other cop grabbed him and said, 'Right, you're nicked.'

As the little party neared the top of the road my step-son, David, was standing on the corner, he said,

'You lot got nought better to do, what you arrested them for?'

The copper let go of Fletch and grabbed hold of David and said, 'This is Doreen Humber's son, we've got him.'

Fletch ran off, we all ran outside the Centre then and I went for one of the coppers. I was going to punch him I was so mad and sick of it all.

I said, 'Here I'll give you something to arrest me for, let him alone.'

The cop brushed me aside and said, 'Oh clear off.'

David said, 'I'll be alright, leave it, leave it, let 'em take me.'

They took Eddie and David and put them in the van parked up the street, then they drove them up to the pit and put Eddie and

David in the cell van. After that the van came back to the Centre. Two coppers got out of it and started towards the Village Hall. One of the journalists was outside the hall and he overheard one say to the other, 'We'd better drop this one there are too many witnesses.'

They came into the hall and tried to push their way in. But we all stood in the doorway trying to stop them. They were too strong for us and eventually pushed their way in. We were all yelling at them to get out.

I said, 'Are you happy, you've got my son, you only took him because he was mine.'

I was really angry and screaming at them.

'Oh go and make yourself a cup of tea,' they said, 'you're hysterical.'

Later that day, they picked Fletch up at his house. The three of them appeared in court and were charged. David was charged with obstructing a Police Officer and Breach of the Peace. When the charges were being laid, the police said,

'This lad has been harbouring Yorkshire pickets on his back garden.'

The meeting we'd organised about twinning took place that Sunday. It was very successful. We'd sent out a lot of leaflets, it had been very well publicised. Annette was on the door and everyone had to identify themselves as they came in. We didn't want to take any risks that the police would try to sneak in, we'd learned our lesson. The response to our leaflets was much better than we'd expected, there were at least 200 there. People came from different support groups and from other groups like ours and from the Nottingham Strike Centre which had been set up. A lot of other people came too, because they'd seen the leaflets and were interested. I chaired the meeting and started out by welcoming everybody. I talked about the siege and the arrests of the previous Friday. I also talked about how we'd set up and how successful we'd been with twinning. A few other people spoke some more about the strike and about twinning. Then a woman stood up and said,

'My husband is on the Nottingham Strike Committee and they're opposed to twinning. They want all funds to be given centrally and distributed equally between groups. If you insist on carrying on with this twinning lark, then the Strike Committee won't give you anything at all and will discard you completely.'

Then I got up and said, 'We have been going for six weeks now and we've invited everybody here today to see how successful we are, and the reason for our success is because we are twinning. If we'd relied on the Nottingham Centre to keep us going, these men'd be back at work before they even came out 'cause we haven't had a penny or a tin of beans from this Centre you keep talking about. People need feeding now, not in six months time. Twinning works in Nottinghamshire because we aren't united and the number of strikers in each village differs enormously. You can have thirty men in one village like in Cotgrave, and then somewhere like Blidworth has seven hundred. There's no way we could feed that many on what's we'd get from a Central Group. Apart from that lots of supporters want to give their money direct to miners' wives, they want that guarantee that the money will definitely be used for food. If you expect us to cut back on what we've worked hard for, well then, we won't and we know that we can manage quite well if we keep on going the way we are. We've already helped other groups set up, and helped them to find twinnings and we'll continue to do so, because we started early, we've got a lot of contacts now. We think that there's plenty of support for every pit in Notts. to twin with a community somewhere in the country and be looked after.'

There was a lot of discussion after that and we met a lot of new people and made a lot of new contacts. We were very pleased with ourselves, the meeting had been a great success and we felt that we'd put our case in favour of twinning and most of the people there had agreed with us.

We started to settle into a new routine, every morning we'd go up to the Centre and have breakfast. Then the kids would go off to school and we'd start about the work that needed to be done each day. Just running the Centre took a lot of work, there was the cooking, shopping, planning, organizing and cleaning to take care of as well as a never ending number of visitors to entertain. I had taken on the job of Chairperson and I'd said that I was confident about raising money, but that I'd leave the running of the Centre to others. I saw that as my role, but I was also seen as the Spokesperson for the women so any problems any of the men had they tended to bring to me. As well as that I became the main liaison between us and other groups. I was run off my feet. As soon as I walked into the Centre someone would come to me to ask something.

There were about twenty women coming up to the Centre regularly by this time and a lot more who dropped in every so often. Most of the men came to eat at this stage and we were feeding up to five hundred people a day and serving three meals a day. Pauline and I were still working, but it was becoming more and more difficult to get there.

We had organised our trip to Yorkshire for the following weekend. About a dozen of us were going. We set off on Saturday afternoon, all very excited about having a week-end away from everything. The last ten days had been very hectic and we hadn't really had time to take in all that had happened. We were also looking forward to seeing the pickets from Yorkshire again, and meeting their wives and families. Something about the link with Yorkshire was very important for us, after all that was where the strike started and that was where it was solid. Yorkshire, to us, had the ring of the centre of things, we admired and respected the Yorkshire miners and their area Union which had always been very strong. Somehow being isolated in Notts. and surrounded by scabs, we needed to feel the strength that we knew was in Yorkshire and to feel part of it. That had happened a bit by them coming to us, but now that we were going there we knew that would increase our feeling of belonging to something big and very powerful.

We arrived at the Welfare in Edlington, where we had arranged to meet everyone and where we were to find out where we were staying. Mark and Pip and I were staying with Ralph, and his wife Maureen. Ralph had stayed in a van in Pauline's drive during all the trouble. We all went back to their house where we were made very welcome and began to feel at home at once.

That night we all went out, it was absolutely marvellous. We started off at the Welfare, or the Welly as they called it. When we were all there they announced from the platform that they were privileged to have among them a bunch of Notts. Striking Miners and their wives. Everybody cheered and people fell over themselves to make us feel welcome and to let us know how much they appreciated what we were doing. Of course they all knew about the police trouble we'd had and everybody made us feel as if they were really proud to know us. We never bought a drink or anything the whole time we were there. We were given free tickets to get drinks at the Welfare and at the pubs we went into because the pubs there support the strike, it was so different from Blidworth. They had so much organised for us that we were skipping from one social event to another, staying at each one for about an hour.

We were made to feel like kings and queens. People even gave up their own beds for us. Ralph and Maureen gave up their bed so Pip and I could have it and they made a big fuss of Mark. They fed us and treated us as though we were very special. It made us feel a little hypocritical, all we'd done when they'd been to Blidworth was to let them use our tent on the back garden, but they kept talking about all we'd done for them and how much bother we'd had because of them and how we'd stuck by them against real hell from the police.

Maureen doesn't normally go out but just because we were there she came with us. It seems a funny thing to say but it was like going home, it was just as if that house was ours. We've been back up there since and every time I walk into the house I feel so at home I can just put the kettle on and I know where everything is, where the biscuit barrel is and can have a biscuit or get bread and butter if I want it. I could set the table and sit down. If I didn't have any fags I could just take one of Maureen's from her packet on the shelf, we feel so at ease with each other, and yet they're strangers in a way, we don't really know them that well. I think it was because we'd all been through the siege at Blidworth and also because Yorkshire people are very friendly.

Another really good thing for me, was that I was able to talk to Maureen about my daughter Karen, who had just become pregnant. Maureen's daughter had been pregnant at fifteen, and had gone back to school after the baby was born and Maureen had looked after it as if it was her own. It was lovely to see them all together and it helped to increase my confidence that Karen and I could work it out too.

We'd always been quite close and I knew it would be all right but even so, these things take some getting used to and it was good to see how well they'd worked it out. It was also good to talk about it. Karen had only had her pregnancy confirmed a couple of weeks before and I had little chance to talk to anyone about anything except the strike. Although I was quite prepared to stand by Karen and quite happy for her to have the baby if she wanted I did find the situation a little difficult. The father was the son of my very best friend who had died just a few weeks earlier. He didn't want to know about the baby and that put me in a difficult situation.

After we'd been out on the Sunday night we came home to a fantastic spread that Maureen and her daughter-in-law had organised earlier. They had salad, pork pies, cakes and gateaus, they'd got some beer in and we had our own party, which we just walked into when it was all done and ready. It was a lovely surprise, I've no idea how they managed to prepare it all without my knowing anything about it but it was really wonderful.

We left Edlington the following morning, they all tried to talk us into staying longer but we had to get back to Blidworth where there were things waiting for us to do. While we were there we'd talked to the women about what we were doing and they were all very surprised. They had a soup kitchen, but none of the women that we spoke to ever went up to it. Apparently about four women did all the cooking there but it was really only to feed the men, the women and kids never went up. It was much more like the soup kitchen that we had in '72. They all received food parcels and the men were paid a small amount of picketing money which we weren't getting at all at that stage. They were getting just enough to manage, but we weren't getting anything at all and so we just had to throw ourselves into it.

When we got back we went straight up to the Strike Centre and the first thing we found was that one of our men, Chris, was locked up in Lincoln. He'd been in a pub on Saturday night and a scab had come at him and started a fight, then the scab's wife had come for him wanting to slit his throat with a Stanley knife. Chris was picked up. They couldn't make the charge until the Tuesday because it was bank holiday, but when it did come up he got seven days in Lincoln. When his trial came up much later, he was cleared.

That night we all decided to go out for a drink, we had a lot to tell all those that hadn't been to Edlington. Whenever we went out at night we usually arranged it during the day at the Strike Centre and went out in a group. We did that partly because we felt safer in a group. There was always scabs drinking in the pubs and there'd been a few nasty incidents and lots of minor ones. But I think we also arranged to go out together because we were really just getting to know each other and enjoying that enormously, it was good to let a bit of the tension of the strike off together. I was becoming particularly close to one woman, Sue Petney. Her husband Ken had been on strike from the beginning but Sue had only started coming up to the Centre in the last couple of weeks. She worked full-time as an agricultural labourer so she didn't have much time but she was eager to be involved as much as she could. I remember the first day she came up to the Centre. She walked in one Saturday morning looking a little lost and a little shy. There were always people coming and going at the Centre and everybody was always very busy so there wasn't always someone to welcome strange faces. I was talking to someone about something and I saw Sue take her coat off and start to get a fag out of her bag. Betty Savage said to her,

'Here have one of these.' She handed Sue a packet of cigarettes that one of our supporters had left for us. 'No, its alright,' Sue said, 'I'm working, I can afford my own, leave them for whoever's got none.'

Someone distracted Betty's attention and Sue stood for a minute and then looked into the kitchen where her daughter Ann was washing pots. Sue walked into the kitchen and picked up a cloth and started drying the pots and talking to Ann. After that Sue was one of us, she couldn't get up to the Centre on week days but wanted to do whatever she could. She started coming out to meetings with us at night. She didn't have a car and lived quite close to me so I'd often pick her up and we'd drive off to a meeting somewhere together. The two of us started to become quite close friends.

Sue seemed to understand things quite clearly even though she hadn't been involved in a lot of the action. When she heard about the Siege she told me that she wasn't surprised at all, that she'd had some dealings with the police and would never trust them again. Ken's brother had been in some trouble once and he'd visited their house. Just after he'd left the police came asking for him. Sue and Ken said that he wasn't home but the police didn't believe them and just pushed their way into the house and looked through it.

Another time Ken had been picked up for receiving and held for three days. While he was locked up the cops had threatened to arrest Sue as well and put the kids in a home and then they told Ken that if he'd sign certain statements they'd leave his wife and kids alone. Ken ended up signing for a burglary he hadn't committed as well as receiving.

Sue said to me, 'I'll never trust them again and neither will Ken, you should have seen the state he was in when he finally got out after those three days, he was in a right state. I think when they forced their way into my house was really when I began to realize that this isn't a free country at all.'

I used to enjoy the conversations with Sue, I respected her opinions on things.

The night after we got back from Yorkshire we all met as arranged at the Jolly Friar. At first we sat around a table in the middle of the room and then a back corner became available so we moved over to it. The Jolly Friar is a fairly new pub, and the back half of it is divided into two with built-in lounges going all the way around each section which makes it like quite a private part of the pub. We liked to keep to ourselves and there were quite a lot of us so we usually tried to sit around one of these corners. We were all talking and laughing and passing around a poem that Sue had written, which she'd called 'A Question of Loyalty.'

Why do you cross the picket line?
Answer me, every one,
I've searched for the reason,
But answers I had none,
Will you keep on crossing the picket lines
Till all the pits are gone?

There are people on this picket line,
Who have thought their reasons through,
They are fighting for a future,
For me, for themselves and you.
There are men who've stood on picket lines,
They gave their all and died.
We've lost only money,
But you have lost your pride.
So why keep crossing picket lines?
Valid answers have you none.
Will you keep on crossing picket lines
Till all the pits are gone?

We were enjoying ourselves and were quite oblivious to everyone else; before we knew it, it was drinking up time. Because we'd all been talking so much we were a bit tardy with our drinks and continued to sit and finish them when most people around were getting ready to leave. I was sitting next to Ken so I didn't actually see what happened, but Sue saw it all and she told us later.

'I saw this bloke taking his coat off, which seemed strange because everyone else was putting theirs on. But I didn't take any notice, just sort of saw it out of the corner of my eye, you know how you do. Then I saw this same bloke come over and say something to Ken and I thought he must have been a friend of Ken's and wondered who he was. Then I knew something was going to happen, I just knew. He gripped Ken a bit tighter and said something about "outside" or "on your own" or something and next thing he was dragging Ken and his chair back. Then the chair tipped and both men fell, Ken and the chair on top of this bloke.'

As soon as the chair fell another bloke started to leap over tables and chairs towards Ken, on the way he picked up a chair and started laying into Ken with it, Ken was lying spread eagled on the floor, he's a very big bloke Ken is and he was trying to get up but this second man just kept bashing him with the chair. It all happened so quickly, it wasn't like real life it was like a movie, but it was worse because the chair was solid like real chairs are and didn't splinter up into pieces like they do in the movies. Everybody just froze for a minute.

Sue said, 'He's hitting Ken with a chair,' and although we could see it, we were all shocked into just watching and Sue's voice broke through the shock and we all jumped up. There was blood on Ken's head and Sue started to try and help him get up. As she did a woman with a crazy look on her face came up with another chair. Later we found out it was the first man's wife, for a minute her and Sue just stared into each other's eyes, but she didn't see Sue, her eyes were blank. Then she started hitting down with the chair and Sue managed to move Ken out of the way and this woman was hitting down on her own husband and she kept on hitting and hitting.

I said, 'Come on, let's get out of here.' I grabbed Ken and Sue to help them up and get them out. The whole thing had happened so quickly, none of us had seen it early enough to stop it or even to help Ken. Now he was safe, all any of us could think about was to get out as quickly as possible, because we knew we'd get blamed for what had happened if the police came. All the trouble we'd had with them, this would give them the opportunity they were looking for to lay something on us.

As we got to the door, the scab with the chair started to come after Ken again and tried to push him. Ken turned and said, 'Stop now. Can't you see what you've done, look at that man on the floor, you ought to be ashamed of yussen.' A neighbour of ours came up and started mouthing off at us but we continued to walk out and left him talking to himself. We got into the car with Sue and Ken and drove back to our place. Ken was in a bad way so we bathed his head and then he and Sue went home. Ken was quite shocked, he couldn't walk properly and he couldn't remember getting home from the Friar, so he must have had a bit of concussion as well.

A couple of hours later, Pip and I were lying in bed talking about it all when David and Paul came into our room and said,
'Police are here.'
It must have been about two in the morning when they banged on the door. Pip went down and when he opened the door they said,
'We're arresting you on suspicion of assault.'
'Who me? Why me? I've done nought?'
'We've heard different, come on, you're coming with us.'

'Well, I'm going to get on the phone to the union then.'

'No you're not, you're not getting on the phone to nobody.' I came downstairs then and said,

'What's up with you lot now?'

This copper said to me, 'We're arresting him on suspicion of assault.'

'Go to them that should be bloody arrested, not us, we didn't do anything, why don't you arrest them that did?'

'That's not what we've heard, come on, we're not standing here all night.'

I snapped then, I said,

'Why don't you just arrest the whole family at once, it'd save you petrol instead of coming for us one by one. You'll get the lot of us one way or another, why not just take us all now and be done with it.'

'Don't come with your sharp talk here, that'll get you nowhere.'

'You make me bloody sick, who else are you taking?'

'Next door neighbour and next door but one and him around the corner.'

Pip said to me, 'They won't let me make a phone call.'

'I'll see about a phone call ' I said as I walked straight to the phone and picked it up.

After they'd left, I went into Pauline's and then her and I went into Annette's. We phoned Pip Browne and told him what had happened then phoned Sue to see if she wanted to come around and sit with us. She said that she'd stay in her own house until morning, because the kids were there, but she'd come around as soon as they woke up in the morning.

The three of us sat up most of the night talking and comforting each other. We were very scared, we'd heard all sorts of stories by now, we were fully acquainted with the lack of justice available to us as striking miners. We had been shocked by events so many times that we almost felt as if anything were possible and we were worried about what was happening to the men. On the other hand we were very angry about the injustices we were having forced on us. We were learning more about our rights as we were having them infringed. Unless someone attacks your civil liberties, you don't really need to know what they are, so their attack on ours was a double-edged sword.

At about four we all decided to try and go to bed, but Pauline and I came into my house and sat and had another fag and cup of coffee. Neither of us could go to bed, we were too churned up. We heard a knocking on the back door. We were absolutely terrified, we thought either that it was scabs who knew our husbands had been taken, or the police. We looked through the back window and couldn't see anybody so we started getting even more worried. Pauline picked up the poker and went upstairs to see if she could see anybody from the landing window. She couldn't so she crept back downstairs and then went through to the back door. I was still looking to see if I could see anybody. Pauline put her hand on the door handle and was just about to open the door when we heard a little voice say, 'Mummy, Mummy.' It was Amanda, she'd woken up and come to find Pauline.

At about six Sue and her kids came around. As they'd left their house, there was a copper stood outside and he followed them around here and then stood outside our house looking in through the windows. We rang the police station in Mansfield and they said the men weren't in court yet and that we should ring every two hours for information. I rang Martin Walker, we'd met him just after the siege, he was in Yorkshire at that time helping Yorkshire NUM, and he'd been once with Susan Miller to do interviews in Blidworth. Martin had a lot of experience in dealing with the police and so I thought he might be able to help. He wasn't there so I left a message for him to ring back.

We went up to the Centre, there seemed nothing else to do and that was where our friends were. Everybody was shocked, nobody really believed that the four men had all been taken. We tried to get on with chores at the Centre as usual but everybody was preoccupied by the events of the night before and we did a lot of sitting around talking. Close to lunch time somebody suggested getting some booze that they had left over from Christmas, then a few more remembered they had some too. We ended up with half a bottle of sherry and some Babychams and a few other bits and pieces that people had in their houses. We all had a couple of drinks, I remember Sue saying,

'There's nought we can do, so we might as well wash it all out of our minds.' She was speaking for all of us. It was too awful to think about, it was just like a nightmare but it had the added horror of being real and we were beginning to wonder if this nightmare would ever end.

We kept phoning up the police but they kept saying the same thing, that they weren't in court. They'd say terrifying things like, 'Oh yes, they're with the anti-intimidation squad now, but they haven't been charged yet. We have no further information.'

Dennis and Mal went into Mansfield to the police station, but they wouldn't let them see them. Annette had arranged to go to speak in Cambridge with Margaret and Yorkie, they'd been invited to go down there for a couple of days to raise support. She decided to go ahead with her plans because there was really nothing any of us could do just hanging around Blidworth. Later that afternoon Pauline, Sue and I went back to my house and we hadn't been there long when the phone rang. It was Pip.
'They're not charging me, but they're going to keep me because they've still some more enquiries they want to make.'
'They can't keep you if they're not charging you.'
'Well, they say they can, anyway I'm gasping for a fag.'
'If I send some down, will they let you have them?'
He asked someone standing next to him and they agreed. So I arranged to send some down to him. Then the phone rang again and it was Ken. He said they were charging him. Sue spoke to him and when she came off the phone she was very upset.
Straight after Sue hung up, we had yet another phone call from Alan. The police had asked why they were all ringing the same number, so the men told them that we were all together comforting each other, as if they didn't know, they had police here watching our every movement. Alan told Pauline that they were keeping him and Pip but not charging them.
Pauline, who was very angry said, 'What the bloody hell are they keeping you for, what you supposed to have done?'
Alan said, 'Pauline, this is a serious matter, there's a man lying critically ill in hospital and if he dies we could be charged with

murder.'

'Alan, that's a load of shit they're filling you up with, the man supposed to be in hospital is home sitting with his foot on a stool in his back garden, someone saw him this afternoon. They're trying to intimidate you, take no notice.'

Alan said, 'Well who hit him? They keep on at us about who hit him and I don't know.'

'I'll tell you who hit him, his own bloody silly wife, that's who hit him.'

Of course, when Alan told the police that, they just laughed and said, 'This gets better this does.'

It did sound ridiculous we knew, but it was perfectly true. That night we went to bed and the next morning phoned up the police station again.

This time they said, 'Is it to do with the strike?'

'No, it's an assault, one of them was assaulted in a pub on Monday night.'

As far as we were concerned it wasn't anything to do with the strike, it hadn't happened on picket lines and the strike had never been mentioned.

They went away for ages, then they came back and said,

'Sorry, we can't give you any information, you'll have to ring Nottingham Police Station and ask to be put through to Strike Headquarters.

'How come today I have to ring Nottingham, yesterday you gave me information there, why suddenly do I have to ring Nottingham?'

The woman on the other end of the phone just repeated that she couldn't give me any information. So we rang Nottingham. Then we had to wait ages while they got through to Mansfield to find out what was happening and all the while my phone bill was mounting up, Nottingham is in a different area code. Eventually they said, 'No, sorry, no information, they're not in court yet. You'd better ring later tonight or early tomorrow morning, we won't know anything until then.'

I just about went crazy then, 'This is ridiculous, they've done nothing, what are you doing with them, you've got no right to have them in the first place.'

She said, 'We don't hold people for nothing.'

'Well, you've got my husband for nothing. Go and shit.' I shouted as I slammed the phone down.

Just as I put the receiver down, the phone rang. It was Martin Walker returning my call. I told him what was happening and he said,

'Hang up your phone, I'm going to get you the best solicitor I know and you should start to organise a picket of the Police Station.'

The phone rang again a few minutes later and a woman's voice said, 'You don't know me, I'm a solicitor. I've just had a call from Martin, can you tell me what's happening?'

I told her the story and she said, 'Don't go out for a bit, I'll get back to you.'

While we were waiting for her to phone back we decided to get as many women and kids together as we could and go and demonstrate outside Mansfield Police station. Pauline had found some cardboard and felt pens and we'd made placards to hang around the kids' necks saying, 'We want our Daddy.'

It couldn't have been more than ten minutes when the phone rang again. It was Pip, he said,

'They're letting me and Alan go, can you come and fetch us?'

We started to get our coats on to go when the solicitor rang back and asked what was happening now. I told her we were on our way to fetch Pip and Alan and she said that the other two were going to be in court at two o'clock that afternoon and I should go with a pen and paper and write down everything that happened.

'How's this come about then?' I asked.

'I don't really know, I just phoned and told them who I was, they checked up on me and phoned me straight back and said they were letting two of them go and the other two would be in court at two this afternoon. So you get down there and make sure you write down everything that happens.'

We went to fetch Pip and Alan and Sue kept ringing the court, but they kept telling her that they knew nothing about a case at two.

After dinner we got three carloads together and went to Mansfield Police Station for about quarter to two. We went in and I said,

'Which court are Ken Petney and John Holroyd in at two?'

'No, they're not in court this afternoon.'

'You're bloody liars, I know they are.'

We went over to the court and at two o'clock they came in. Both Ken and John were charged with malicious wounding and causing grievous bodily harm. They wanted to deny them bail and send them straight to Lincoln Prison. As the police put the case to the magistrate for denying the two men bail they described them as vicious thugs who had terrorised the whole village. It took us all a while to realize that they were talking about Ken and John and when we did a few of us just couldn't hold our tongues.

'Rubbish,' we said and the magistrate threatened to throw us out if we weren't quiet and they obviously weren't very happy to have me sitting writing notes all the time, but there was nothing they could do about it. The solicitor from the NUM who was representing Ken and John said that owing to family circumstances it would be wrong for them to be taken to Lincoln, but that they would abide by any bail conditions set. So they were released with bail conditions that they couldn't drink in any of the pubs in either Blidworth or Rainworth and that they were to keep away from the two scabs who'd assaulted Ken in the Friar.

·7·
PAULINE
MOVING OUT

Two days after Alan and the others were released, we were all invited to spend a day in Cambridge with expenses paid. It had been arranged when Margaret, Yorkie and Annette had gone to Cambridge. The whole thing surprised me quite a lot, I had no idea where Cambridge was but I thought it was just a college and wondered why they wanted to support us. The trip was to take place on a Saturday when two coaches had been hired to take us there.

The journey was very noisy because of our excitement. It's always exciting to go off in a big group somewhere and this time it had the added flavour of mystery. We weren't quite sure what we'd find at the other end but we knew it would be fun because whatever else, we were all determined to make it a great day.

When we got there it was nothing like we expected at all. We were met by some people who struck us at first as being a bit weird and very different from anyone in Blidworth, but they were very friendly and made us feel very welcome. The woman who seemed to be organising everything was called Alison, she was probably in her early forties but she was dressed in a big baggy top and baggy skirt with scarves and jewellery hanging from her ears and neck. She didn't look anything like a woman of her age would look in Blidworth, where they'd wear a proper dress and stockings and probably high heeled shoes. But she seemed very nice and although she sounded very posh when she spoke, she didn't look posh and she didn't act posh towards us.

As we got off the bus we saw a great big sign that said, 'Welcome Notts Miners and their Families.' A procession was getting ready to leave, at the head of it was a great big dragon head with colourful material flowing from it. The kids all lined up under the material and formed the body of the dragon which wove in and out of the rest of us and from one side of the road to the other. The dragon led the way and we all started walking off around Cambridge. By now we'd been on quite a few marches where there'd always been thousands of people so this one seemed very small because there was only us and a few students who were all dressed up as fairies and jesters. One man was dressed up and walking on stilts and another rode a one-wheeled bicycle. Everybody was following the dragon and singing,

'Follow the dragon to Strawberry Fair,
'Strawberry Fair is over there.'

The kids thought it was absolutely fantastic dancing and weaving the dragon about.

We started chanting, 'Maggie, Maggie, Maggie, Out, Out, Out' and singing 'Arthur Scargill', but the students at the front gave us quite a dressing down, telling us that this wasn't a political rally and we weren't to chant political slogans. We stopped singing out because we'd been invited there and didn't want to make a bad impression but we were quite put out about it and groaned a little under our breath to each other.

Walking around the streets of Cambridge I began to realise how beautiful, how big and how clean it was. The streets were small and narrow and the houses were all very old, it struck me as very quaint and I loved it. There was so much green, I'd never seen so many beautiful parks, there seemed to be grass in every direction. I was really surprised, we must have passed lots of the colleges, but I had no idea what they were, I kept looking for a group of big pre-fabricated buildings which is how I imagined the college. I came away thinking that we hadn't seen the college at all.

The march finished at the Fair; that was a surprise too. We'd all imagined that the Fair would be just like the ones that came to the green in Blidworth at Whitsun with their mechanical rides and sideshows. This was more what we'd call a Fete. There was a magical atmosphere about it. As we walked around none of us could get over what we were seeing around us. There were stalls and tents everywhere selling all sorts of things. There was loads of odd food on different stalls. Strange rices, beans and all sorts of vegetables chopped up were being sold like salads, but they were not the sort of salads we had. Then there were all sorts of breads and cakes made out of things like carrots and bananas. I'd never come across food like it before, because I like food so much it was great to have so many new things to taste. The tastes were quite strange, quite nice for a change, but I wouldn't like to eat that sort of food regularly. We bought some fudge I can remember which had a very peculiar taste. I thought it was carrot fudge and wondered how they made carrots into fudge, later I found out it was carob fudge, but then I'd never heard of carob at all.

All the people looked really weird, almost everyone had bare feet, and all the clothes were big and baggy and looked several sizes too big except the trousers worn by some of the women which were very colourful and tight and looked several sizes too small, more like what we'd call tights than trousers and no-one would dare wear them out in Blidworth. There was lots of long hair and all the women had scarves, beads, ear-rings and bangles hanging all over them. Most of the ones that had glasses on had small round wire frames like the old fashioned ones you got off the National Health. Everybody looked like hippies or flower people that I'd seen on television years ago and thought were all gone now. If you wore any of their clothes in Blidworth, people would think you'd gone crackers. One of the tents did head massages and in another you could pay to have your face painted. The kids thought that was just great. As they came out one by one with love-hearts and stripes all over their faces, I was dead keen to get mine done too, but Alan thought it would be too much and stopped me. There were lots of buskers and jugglers and people dancing about, making weird movements and playing instruments. I can remember Dennis Browne standing with his mouth wide open, staring at a bloke who was dressed up as a jester, dancing around as he played a flute. He had a long colourful hat and really long pointed shoes with bells on them.

There were a few rides for the kids, things like bouncing castles. We had our own stall too, the miners stall, where we sold badges and collected money. We had a game on our stall, people threw bean bags at cardboard cutouts of Maggie Thatcher and Ian McGregor to try and knock them over. Later on the bean bags broke and we replaced them with wellingtons which I thought was even better. Then we sang out, 'Come and throw a boot at Thatcher.'

At lunchtime we went across the road to another park for our picnic. It was wonderful, we all got a package of food, there were egg and cheese sandwiches, cakes, sausages, biscuits, pop, tea and coffee. We all had more than we wanted to eat and drink. It was a beautiful warm sunny day and there were lots of people but as I looked around the green I realized that it was mostly just us from Blidworth and I felt quite emotional seeing everyone there, having the time of their lives. The kids played on the swings and climbing frames and we all sat around on the grass relaxing. It was so peaceful and so different to Blidworth where we were still basically under siege and not able to walk about without being questioned by police. Blidworth seemed like a far away nightmare and to actually be away from it, in such a beautiful place with so many new and exciting things to see made the strike seem a world away.

In the afternoon some of the kids were taken swimming, those that hadn't brought kits had them provided, other kids went for a tour of the colleges. We stayed at the Fair, our kids were too young to go off on their own but we were perfectly happy to continue walking around taking everything in.

At about four o'clock we were all rounded up to go off and have tea with the Lord Mayor. An upstairs room had been reserved for us in the Y.M.C.A. We expected that tea would be a proper meal, a salad or something. Some of the kids expected a hot meal because they're used to having one every day and lunch had been sandwiches. Not that any of us were hungry, we weren't, but we were surprised when we realised that 'tea' was a cup of tea or coffee and a scone with jam and cream. The Lord Mayor came and walked around the tables talking to everybody, the kids played with his Chain of Office and he seemed very sympathetic to our cause. That increased our feelings of being a world away, where some authority figure actually supported us.

When we got back to the Fair lots more people were arriving. A band had started playing peculiar music and they'd started selling beer which lots of people were drinking. The police arrived, apparently something had been stolen from a car. They started to question a young black lad who looked very upset and scared. We had no idea whether he was guilty or not, but from our own experiences we felt fairly sure he wasn't and anyway our hearts went out to him. Eventually they let him go and we all cheered. But it had brought us all sharply back to reality.

By now it was getting close to the time we were leaving and lots of us were so tired that we went to sit on the bus. Just outside the bus window a group of people starting passing a cigarette to one another. Somebody said,
'That's a joint, that is.'
We all stared out the window. I'd never seen anybody smoking a joint before and I don't think hardly anybody else on the bus had either from the way they all looked. We thought, 'Ooh, they even smoke pot.' But the important thing was that we'd got lots of support at the stall we'd had, raised lots of money and been given an absolutely fantastic time. It was clear that even if these people seemed different to us in many ways, in others they were very close and that made us all think quite a lot about judging people by what they look like.

The buses and food had cost £749 and we were taking home £226 with us, on top of that we'd had the time of our lives. Going home on the bus we were very tired but contented people still in high spirits. To round everything off in our own way and to re-establish our sense of the struggle we were all involved in, and going back to, we sang all the songs we'd learnt since the strike started and more that we made up.

During the week of the siege and then while the men were being held by the police Doreen and I hadn't been into work at all. We kept sending sick notes and in the end we decided to send in our notice. Our involvement with the strike was then so strong we could only work the minimum number of hours anyway and so we were earning little more than we would have if we'd applied for Social Security. Alan went over and collected our cards and some pay we were owed.

Margaret had taken on the responsibility for Welfare Rights and she had become an adviser to us all. She found the whole thing so interesting that she started taking a course about it at the Nottingham Polytechnic. Doreen and I asked her what we should do to make our claims.

The Government had said that miners' wives were entitled to Social Security for themselves and their children but not for the striking men. On top of that fifteen pound was deducted from what we would normally have got because it was claimed by the Government that all strikers were receiving fifteen quid a week strike pay. Not only were they receiving nothing at all at that time, but even if they had received it, that should have only covered the men's living costs which we weren't claiming anyway. Margaret gave us a form to fill in for claiming, so we sent them off. A fortnight later I got a cheque for twenty-three pound. As it turned out we were entitled to claim a heating and diet allowance for Michael. We didn't know that at first, so for the first seven months we didn't claim it. When we finally did we got it back paid, so that was a bit of welcome relief, which came just at the beginning of winter so we could afford to buy some coal. Doreen had a struggle for her money. Because some of the lads and Karen were paying her board, she had that deducted from her entitlement, which was really unfair, she wasn't claiming for them, but still had to keep them.

With more time I started to go up to the Centre a lot. In fact the Centre became the main focus of our lives and like a home away from home. I used to help in the kitchen with the preparing and serving of the meals and then washing the pots and cleaning up. We were serving three meals a day, seven days a week to anything from one hundred to five hundred people and one of the biggest problems was estimating how many to cook dinner for at midday. It was by far the largest meal, it was always a hot meal, usually some sort of meat and vegetables and there were always more people for dinner than for any other meal. A lot of men would come up to the dinner picket and then come into the Centre for the dinner. There were quite a large number of single men and a lot of others whose wives and kids didn't come up very often. Some lived outside the village, some of the wives worked or had other responsibilities such as sick relatives, and others just preferred to cope on their own for one reason or another. The amount of time that each person spent at the Centre was entirely up to them. There were about twenty of us women who had made a complete commitment to the Centre and we went up there every day. Lots of others came regularly but less often.

We always had a cooked breakfast, usually beans, sausages, sometimes eggs and bacon, depending on what we had in stock. The numbers that came in for breakfast varied a lot too, but that wasn't a problem because we just sort of cooked on the spot for whoever wanted it. Teas were fairly static, roughly the same number of kids came in every day after school and we usually made sandwiches and soup and gave everyone a packet of crisps. So our only real problem with the cooking came with dinner.

About a week after we went to Cambridge, Martin Walker rang Doreen, the booklet he and Susan had written had been printed and he asked Doreen if she'd go to the NALGO Conference in Brighton to promote the sale of it. She wasn't able to go and so I agreed to go with one of the other women, Maureen North. Martin came up to the Centre to talk to us about it and gave us twenty quid to spend between us. All the expenses were being paid and I said to him, 'No, Martin, we can't take your money, we'll be looked after.'

He laughed, 'Oh, go on, ' he said, 'Get the fuckin' thing in your pocket and be done with it, you'll find something to do with it.'

He'd arranged for us to stay in London and then go to Brighton on a coach with people from NALGO who were also going to the conference. Maureen and I set off on the train. Neither of us had ever stayed away from home on our own before so it was quite an adventure. We giggled and chatted all the way on the train, wondering where we would be staying. We had no idea, we just knew that someone was meeting us at King's Cross Station. We kept speculating about who it would be, how we would know them, whether they'd be there and what we'd do if they weren't. We wondered if it might be a black person, neither of us had ever stayed in the home of anyone of a different race and although a lot of our prejudice had gone we were still quite nervous at the prospect of staying with someone whose food and domestic life might be different to ours. But most of all we just felt smug that here we were, just the two of us on a train going to London. Neither of us had been to London since we'd been children, when we'd been taken by our parents.

When we pulled into King's Cross we were met by Gay, we were wearing all our badges and she came up to us and said,
    'Hello, I'm Gay, are you from Blidworth?'

She led us through a maze of tunnels down to the Underground. I wondered how ever she found her way around. I'd never been on the Underground before and the first thing I noticed was how beautiful the music of the buskers was in the tunnels. I thought it was great, it was exactly like I'd seen it on telly and the only part that surprised me was the way the wind blew through the tunnel just before the train came in as if it was a cork pushing the air along in front of it.

Gay's house was very close to the tube station, and it struck me as very different from any house I'd been in before. It was a big old house, and inside everything wasn't neat and tidy like in our houses. There was no matching three piece lounge suite or fitted carpets, there were lots of odd comfortable looking chairs and a great big long table. In the kitchen there was lots of wood, there was no cupboards to hide things away in, everything was out on the shelves which were everywhere and covered with plates, cups, saucepans, jars and packets of food and I especially noticed lots and lots of spices. Gay's daughter came in from school and we sat having a cup of coffee and chatting to her. She collected badges so we gave her some of ours. These people were friends of Martin's and they had one of our leaflets there, so we talked about the Centre and how it ran. Then Martin rang to make sure we were alright, and we talked to him on the phone. Chris, Gay's husband came in, we had tea and then they said they'd take us out to see some of the sights of London.

Big Ben, Trafalgar Square, Buckingham Palace were all passing us by, it was magic. We stopped by the Thames and walked across

a bridge then went to a sort of art gallery on the other side of the
river for a drink. I don't know what it was, it wasn't a pub, it was
more like a library and art gallery, but there was a bar there and we
had a drink. As we walked back across the bridge to the car, we felt
enchanted. We kept taking deep breaths to try to breath it all in. The
stars were shining, there were wonderful lights on the bridge and
a gentle warm breeze blowing up from the river.

I said, 'This night could last for ever' and that's exactly how I felt.
I felt wonderful, it was so nice to be away, just me, just Pauline, not
Pauline Radford or Pauline Saint, but just me, a person in a place
she was enjoying and not worrying about anything else. It was all
so enormous and so different. Blidworth, boring old Blidworth seemed
miles away, here we were, seeing new places, meeting people from
different walks of life and I was soaking up everything around me.

Two mattresses were put in the front room for us to sleep on,
it was a sort of music room, there was a baby grand piano in it and
some violins. When we lay down to go to sleep we started being really
silly, we felt just like a pair of children again. I started telling Maureen
all these ghost stories and then I said,

'You see that grand piano, it's haunted you know.'

We'd pretend to be really scared and I suppose in a way we were,
then I'd say,

'Hey, that plant there might wake up when we go to sleep and eat
us.'

It was ludicrous, but we both giggled away like a pair of schoolgirls
sleeping at each other's houses for the first time. We couldn't get
to sleep. At one time Maureen said,

'You'd better turn the light out.'

'Shall I?' I said.

'No, leave it on a bit.'

We had to get up very early the next morning. Chris woke us
with a cup of coffee. We got dressed and he cooked us breakfast then
took us to meet the rest of the people who were going on the coach.
They were all really friendly, when we first started out, we didn't
know them at all and felt a bit strange, but by the time we got to
Brighton we had taught the whole coach all the miners' songs we

knew.

We set up our stall with Martin and Susan's books in the lobby of the conference hall. We met some Kent miners and talked to them and they made us feel very welcome and gave us some of their badges. After a bit we went upstairs and listened to some of the conference, then we went into the bar and had a drink. People kept coming up and talking to us because we were miners' wives, asking how we were getting on and how we thought things were going.

We got a collection bucket and collected as people were coming out for lunch. Then we decided to have some lunch and then look around the shops to spend the ten quid Martin had given each of us. It was such a luxury to have money in our pockets to spend on what we wanted. We decided to take something back for our kids and for our husbands who were looking after our kids for us. I bought some Brighton Rock, a skipping rope for Amanda, a gun for Michael and, I'm ashamed to say, a coffee mug for Alan which was shaped like a woman's breast. We bought a police hat each, when we saw them I said, 'Ooh, I want one of those to wear on picket line.'
Maureen thought that a good idea, so we both bought one. My feet were absolutely killing, the only shoes I had were worn out and the soles of my feet were aching so we decided to buy some shoes with our one remaining pound. We got a pair of plastic flip-flops each. So there we were walking around Brighton, with police hats on, flip-flops and all our badges and stickers. We even had collecting tins and leaflets.

When we got back to the Conference Hall someone asked where we got the hats from.
'We had to kill two policemen to get 'em.' I said and everybody thought it was ever so funny.
When we left the conference we felt quite pleased with ourselves. We'd sold twenty-five copies of 'State of Siege' and taken orders for another hundred as well as that we'd collected quite a bit of money for our Centre as well.

We stayed that night in London again and then caught the train home the next morning. Back to Blidworth, back to reality, back to the picket line, back to the police and back to the Centre. Funnily enough, it was lovely to be home, it's always nice to be home.

The cooking at the Centre was getting more and more under control, we were learning how to cater for so many with the limited equipment we had. At first I didn't get very involved in the cooking itself, there were women who were already doing it and they seemed to be coping alright. I was interested though, I've always been interested in cooking. For me it's an art form.

At first we did everything in pressure cookers, but we never had enough room, not only were the pressure cookers not big enough but we only had a normal cooker, with four hotplates, an oven and a grill. It was always the potatoes that suffered, because we could always substitute powdered potato instead. There were three large electric water boilers and we only used one for making tea and coffee. One day someone had the bright idea, that if the boilers boiled water, they should cook potatoes as well. We tried it and it worked, so that helped to overcome the problem of not enough cooking space.

A chef who lived nearby and was on the dole came up one day to see if he could help. He brought up some of his knives and cooking implements which was a big help and he also gave us some very useful hints, but in some ways he was as confused as we were because trained chefs are used to having proper equipment and tools at their fingertips and our equipment was so basic. He used to do a lot of pastry baking and I watched him carefully, he made cakes, sponges, flapjack, treacle pudding and egg and bacon flans. He was only with us for a couple of weeks because then he got a job. But his presence helped a lot.

After he stopped coming up I took over the pastry baking and I really enjoyed it. While he'd been with us, he'd made dumplings and they were a disaster, they all just disintegrated into the stew. One day after he left, they were making stew again so I said I'd have a go at making dumplings. Dumplings can be very temperamental, but in fact I've always prided myself on being able to make a good dumpling. I was quite nervous that they wouldn't work but still I tried.

I was delighted when they turned out OK and everyone complimented me on them. It was a real boost to my confidence, that my dumplings had worked, I started to do them more and more. Two of the women who had been doing most of the cooking went away for a fortnight, so I became much more involved with the actual cooking of the main meal. I was working with Mary, but she had different ideas to me about how things should be done. They always say that two women can't work in the same kitchen and it's true that everybody has a different way of doing things. But we proved that saying wrong, we had to, we had no choice, it was much too much work for just one person and I felt that she'd been there since the beginning and so I should accept the way she did things.

A sort of pattern started to develop in our lives. Most mornings Alan would go on the morning picket. If we had a baby-sitter staying over from the night before we'd both go, but normally one of us had to be there for the kids. Sometimes all of us women from Blidworth would arrange to go up and give the men a lie in. I used to enjoy picketing. It was a chance to let my hair down a bit, shout at the scabs and make nasty remarks to the coppers.

My attitude to the coppers had changed since the siege. I'd resented them being on the picket line from the beginning, then I'd been angry at what I'd seen them do, since the Siege I hated them and thought them capable of anything at all. I didn't trust any of them, not one little bit. I'd been brought up to respect the police, I always believed that they had a hard job to do and that they did it quite well, I even felt sorry for them, when I saw them on telly trying to control football crowds or disturbances. When I was a teenager I even wanted to be a policewoman, the only reason I didn't apply was because I knew I would have to move away to train and didn't want to. Now that we'd experienced hundreds of them and the tricks they got up to, I lost all respect for them and all that was left was hatred. They had lied to us, pushed us and our kids around for no reason, the most brutal bashing I'd ever witnessed in my life was the one I'd seen them give Terry Dunne. They'd threatened my husband and neighbours and then they'd held Alan for two days without any grounds at all and tried to make him believe that somebody with a minor injury was in a critical condition. All this had happened in front of my own eyes, and it came as quite a shock. I'd really always believed that the police were neutral, that the law was the law and if somebody was breaking it the police would step in. I'd always believed that if you didn't break the law, you wouldn't ever have any trouble with the police. But I found out all that had nothing to do with it. I was shocked and appalled to discover that the police are not neutral at all, they do take sides. You stand there on the picket line and they're there to support the working miners and it doesn't matter what the scab does, whether he breaches the peace or attacks one of the pickets, uses abusive language or whatever, he never breaks the law. But a picket only has to shout 'scab' and he's breaking the law. The realisation that there was no such thing as the hallowed British Justice we always heard so much about was horrifying. During the siege, after the police had left and we'd all gone to bed, I can remember lying there and thinking, they could come back and do anything. Who could we turn to when it's the police who are terrorizing us?

After the morning picket, we'd get the kids up and dressed and then we'd all go up to the Centre for our breakfasts. The Centre was becoming a more and more important part of our lives. We were all becoming a very close community, and our own community, sort of like one big family. We shared everything with each other, we were all in the same boat and we all had financial problems, we all knew that each other had sacrificed a lot for their principles. All of us had suffered enormous economic hardship. Now we were managing to feed everybody really well, and lots of clothes were coming in, but you could never depend on it and although those basic needs were met, you had no money to pay your bills, or get repairs done on things that needed them. Nearly everybody had lost something. I had had my phone cut off because I hadn't been able to pay the bill, and we couldn't afford to pay our television licence, so officially we weren't supposed to be watching telly. Eventually it broke down anyway and so we were without one.

Different business people took different attitudes to our plight and it was just a matter of luck whether you were dealing with sympathetic people or not. Most housing loans and rents were given a moratorium although the terms of it and how easy it was to acquire varied enormously. With other things, it was just the luck of the draw and we all suffered in some ways. For example Doreen had a rented television and video, the company she had dealt with were prepared to place a moratorium on her payments until the strike ended. At one stage the video actually broke down and she contacted them not expecting anything to be done, but they came and collected it as if her rent was up-to-date and replaced it with a good machine. Yet much later in the strike when her dog was sick she rang the Vet who she's dealt with for fifteen years and in that time developed quite a close relationship with and for whom she had quite a lot of respect. When she asked him if he'd come to have a look at her dog, he said,

'Can you pay?'

'Not right now, but I'll pay as soon as the strike's over.'

'No you won't, I'm sick to death of you bloody strikers, expecting everybody else to help you through, the whole lot of you bloody idle buggers should get back to work.'

Because we were all in the same boat we understood what each other was going through. I know that some people would say, what does it matter to be without a video, but that's not the point, if you chose to spend your money on a video, when you want to defend a principle, you shouldn't have to lose that thing. It's as if, as a miner, you're allowed to have little luxuries like videos as long as you're prepared to accept whatever the Government wants. We, it seemed, suddenly had no rights at all just because we disagreed with a plan which promised to destroy our communities, and deprive us and our children of our way to earn a livelihood. In any case videos were extremely important to us during the strike, we were out so much and there were so many current affairs and discussion programmes about the strike, that the only way we had access to that information often, was to video that programme.

Many of us at the Centre had lost family through the strike, and we found a new one in each other. I began to love the people at the Centre just as I love blood. We had our disagreements and falling outs, but just as a family does. Basically we all trusted one another and enjoyed being together and getting to know each other.

Everything came out up there, if a husband and wife had a fight, the whole Centre usually knew about it and would quite often interfere, telling one person that they were being a bit pig-headed or stupid. Usually when that happened it was all right, because we all knew that we must all pull together. If anyone's financial problems got too great, they would always bring them to the Centre and we would try to help out. People were always mending each other's cars, or washing machines, or doing whatever we each could to help the others.

By this time our committee was quite well established, we met every Sunday morning at the Centre. At those meetings we discussed everything that was happening, there was always a report on what money had come in and how it was spent. Meetings people had gone to were reported on, and it was decided who would go to which meetings that were coming up. There were always loads and loads of things coming up, not just meetings, but rallies and socials as well. We felt that as a group we should try to support as much as we could because we had received such fantastic support ourselves.

The committee meetings also discussed any problems that were arising in any of the work, things that came up at the Centre often needed discussion, if any conflicts between people couldn't be settled between them, they would be brought up at the meetings as well. The work load for the committee was getting very hard, especially for Doreen and Annette, who were really doing all the paper work between them. One Sunday morning, Doreen said,
'I think that Annette and I are taking on too much of the responsibility and it's time that we shared it around a bit more. I think some of the jobs could be taken off us, it's better anyway if we all learn how to do different things.'
Everybody agreed with that, but I think everybody was nervous about taking any of the jobs on. Doreen said that the Treasurer's job had become a very big one because there was so much money going through the books every day, she suggested that we appoint two new Treasurers, who could work together and relieve Annette. She also suggested that we appoint a Minute Secretary, up until then, Annette was doing that too. Doreen then proposed Mary and I as Treasurers. I was a bit hesitant at first, but I didn't like to refuse. I wasn't confident that I could do it properly. I had been quite happy just being a member of the committee and helping with the cooking and I was

quite afraid of this added responsibility, unlike any I'd ever had. That suggestion was seconded and then voted on and that was it. I was one of the Treasurers.

Mary and I took our job very seriously, it really was an enormous job, not a day would go by without some amount of money being received, usually quite a lot, at the same time money had to be given out to cover the costs of living day by day. There was food, which was always the main cost but on top of that there were other expenses always cropping up. For example if someone was going to a meeting or a rally, the money for petrol and expenses would come from the cash tin. We set up a special hardship fund and if anybody had a very pressing need for some money it would be given to them, either as a loan or because the Committee decided that we should help out. Apart from the few quid we got from Social Security, it was the only money that we had. A big expense turned out to be cars. As time went by, more and more of them needed repair work and the Committee would often pay for them. Cars were vital if we were to travel around and so it was necessary to keep at least a few of them on the road.

Mary and I decided to ask the NUM Branch Auditors, who were both strikers, if they'd agree to help us to set the books out properly and to audit them every fortnight, so we could be sure everything was being recorded properly. We spent hours with them, learning how to keep books. It was quite involved but eventually we worked out a system which worked really well for our purposes. That was fantastic for me then, I had taken on a responsibility I wasn't sure I could meet, and when I realised that I could manage it my self confidence really grew. I had also started to speak at meetings which was another breakthrough, at first I was very nervous but I soon got quite relaxed about it. I knew what I wanted to say, all I ever did really was to talk about what we were doing, so it wasn't hard.

The men held an open meeting every Friday morning, everybody usually attended it. There were always reports about the strike, what the Union was doing, and a report on the situation in the Notts. Area. Doreen always gave a report from the Women's Committee, she'd tell the men about what we were doing, sometimes she'd ask them for some help for something, sometimes she'd give them a rollicking because she thought they weren't pulling their weight in some way. As time went by Doreen got better and better at organising things. She was recognised by everybody as the leader of the women, she always seemed to know where the problems were and mostly she worked out solutions to them. Some of the men came to our meetings too and brought up things they thought we should know about and sometimes asked us to do things for the men. Pip Browne had become for the men what Doreen had become for the women and the two of them consulted daily to make sure that the work we were both doing fitted in with each other.

We decided at one of our meetings that the men should help more with the kitchen work. Some of them were already helping with peeling potatoes and washing pots, but it was only a few and it was always the same ones. We decided to make a roster for them. So it became official that the men peeled all the potatoes and washed the dinner pots. When we told the men about it, most of them took it well, although they made lots of jokes about it, they were all good natured and they all seemed to accept that it was quite a fair request. After that it became part of the Strike Centre routine that every afternoon two men would sit in the back room surrounded by plastic garbage bins full of spuds preparing them for the next day's meal. And then after dinner every day, two men would come out to the kitchen and wash the pots.

I thought the attitude of the men to these chores was a good indication of the extent they appreciated what we were doing and respected us. We were coming into our own, really, the men were beginning to realize that without us, they wouldn't be able to go on. We were no longer simply supporting our husbands, we had become a vital part of the strike and without us I couldn't imagine the men being able to stay out as long as they had.

Things were beginning to change between the men and women, we were the ones who were raising the money and somehow that changed things. I think it was very important to all of us to see to what extent the men respected that and it made us all feel more equal to them. The men had to accept it and most of them did, although some also complained about it from time to time. I remember the first time we actually went out, just the women, to a social we had been invited to. We had received an invitation from Barnsley in Yorkshire to go to a women's social. We were all quite excited, it seemed nice that just the women had been invited and that we would all go out together. A coach had been provided to take women from several Notts pits and we had been allocated twelve seats. We told the men we were going to a meeting, but they were a little put out.

'Why can't we come?' they'd say 'What's this just women business?'

'We can't see why men can't go on this bus trip.'

But we kept telling them that they couldn't, that they hadn't been invited. Then they started asking us what time we'd be back, we told them we didn't know.

'Oh, whenever the bus drops us off,' we said.

We all got dressed up in our best and went up to the Forest Folk where we were to meet the bus. It was a great night, we all larked about on the bus, at a stop in Ollerton we charged off the bus and into the nearest pub where we each bought ourselves a can of beer and a packet of crisps. When we eventually got there we were the guests of honour. The social had been organised for Notts. women, they said that we were marvellous because we'd been so strong and supported our men in spite of all the scabs and so they had thrown this social in our honour. We had a fantastic time, there was a disco and we all danced, ate and drank and when it was over we piled back into the bus. We noticed a chip shop open, so we got the driver to stop the bus and all piled into the chip shop. The chippy wondered what had struck him, a bus load of very high spirited, mostly tipsy women suddenly filling his shop. By the time we got back to Blidworth it was about two o'clock.

The men were having to change in other ways too, because we were always out, either up at the Centre working or out fund raising or attending meetings, we never had any time for housework. Alan had always helped me with the housework, but gradually he was doing more and more and eventually taking full responsibility for it. We had a few rows about it, occasionally he'd say that I was never at home, that I wasn't paying any attention to the kids. I'd point out how important what I was doing was for the kids and everybody else too. And really, that was the truth so Alan gradually accepted it. Alan started to take Michael home in the afternoons and clean the house. It was funny to watch the way he did the housework, he worked completely different to the way I do, and he used to moan about it all the time. All the men did. They did the housework quite willingly but they'd moan as soon as it got dirty or messy again. It used to make us women laugh. For years we'd done the housework and expected it to get messy and have to be done again so we never moaned, but the men moaned all the time. Alan and Pip both hoovered every day. They were quite obsessive about it, if they hadn't hoovered they wouldn't think they'd done the housework. I wouldn't hoover every day, in fact I'd only hoover the bedrooms about once a week, but I did other things that Alan never seemed to notice, like clean the stairs and wash the kitchen floor.

Pip's hoover broke down and so he started borrowing ours. That was all right because he'd always wait for Alan to finish our house and then he'd do theirs. But after a while that hoover broke down too. Pip made one working hoover by putting parts of the two broken ones together, so then they had a joint hoover. Then they started to have petty little fights about it. They always seemed to want it at the same time and they'd argue about whose turn it was to have it first, and Pip would moan because it was always full of dog hairs from our house.

The other part of housework they took seriously was the washing. Both Pip and Alan washed clothes nearly every day, I don't think either of them had ever realized how many clothes a family goes through. They'd moan about that too. Often up at the Centre the men would be looking at the sky saying, 'I hope it doesn't rain, my washing is out.' They'd have long conversations with each other about it and if it did start to rain, they'd all be off to get their washing in.

One day we underestimated the number that would come in for dinner, so we served all the meat and potatoes up to the men and kids and the women made up some powdered potato and just had that with some of the vegetables that were left. That afternoon at tea, there was a little bit of pork pie so the women decided to have pork pie and salad and we made soup for the men and kids. Some of the men saw us eating our salads and got quite mad. They brought it up at a meeting, that the women were eating salads and feeding them wishy-washy soup. They gave us quite a dressing down. But once we explained the situation, they accepted it. I really think that men just don't have any idea how self-sacrificing women naturally are.

The number of visitors who came up to the Centre increased as time went on. Lots of people came from all over the place for one reason or another and most of them would go up to the dinner picket and come back to the Centre for a meal. They were usually very impressed by what we served and that was always very reassuring for us.

One day at about this time, we had a very special guest, Arthur Scargill was coming to a union meeting with the men in the morning. Margaret went up to the Welfare where the meeting was and asked him if he'd stay and have dinner with us and he agreed. We were so excited and nervous, we knew he wouldn't mind what he got, but we felt we wanted to make sure it was nice. We were having a salad that day. When he arrived he sat opposite the kitchen hatch and was immediately surrounded by all the kids asking for autographs. He must have signed his name a thousand times that day, all the kids treasured the signatures and probably will for the rest of their lives.

When the dinner was ready everybody started to queue up as they always did and I served one dinner and gave it to someone to give to Arthur. He stayed for about an hour and a half and spent most of the time chatting with the kids, who were asking him questions, he seemed perfectly at home, and we all felt very privileged that he'd come.

Our relationship with the Cambridge Support Group had grown since our day at Strawberry Fair, they were working very hard raising money and things. They adopted four pits, us and Rainworth in Notts. and two other pits in South Wales. They were very creative and had lots of fantastic ideas about the sort of support they gave us. They started to send a car load of food up very Saturday, quite often those that drove the car would stay and talk to us, so we were getting to know different ones.

One of their ideas was to offer holidays in Cambridge to families. Different ones there made their houses available and quite a lot of us took up the opportunity at different times. At first we were all a bit shy about it and so no one had accepted the first offer. A few holidays had been offered for the second week in July and no one had taken them up. Doreen got a phone call asking what was happening so she came in and asked Alan if we'd go the following weekend to stay for a week. He said we could.

When I got back from the Centre, he said,
'We're going to Cambridge at the weekend for a week's holiday.'
I was a bit taken aback, I thought, fancy him making arrangements without telling me. I realized I really didn't want to go, I was worried how everybody at the Centre would manage without me and I didn't like the idea of going off and not really knowing where we were going. I had no idea how the kids would get on or how the people we were going to stay with would treat them. I was really worried that it would be a posh house and I'd have to be telling the kids off all the time and stopping them from touching things. Alan had made a commitment and so we had to go, but I was a bit off with him about it.
He said, 'I don't know, I thought you'd be pleased to get the break.'
I said, 'Well, I suppose I am, but I don't know them. I'll only go if we can come back on Wednesday if we don't like it, I don't want to have to stay there a whole week unless it's all right.'

On Sunday, we set off, the Centre packed us a great big food parcel, all sorts of stuff because we didn't know whether we needed food or not. Much to our surprise we had no trouble finding the house once we reached Cambridge. When we first arrived we were taken out the back to a beautiful glass sunlounge which was shaped like a fifty-pence piece. Sue, whose house it was was sitting out there with a friend and with her six-week-old baby daughter Kate.
From the minute we arrived Sue made us feel very welcome and

very relaxed, we didn't feel uncomfortable at all. Sue introduced us to her friend and then showed us our room. It was fantastic, it was upstairs in a sort of attic room, it was really big, like our own little part of the house. We had a cup of tea and chatted about the strike.

Sue said, 'You're supposed to be on holiday, if you don't want to talk about the strike, I understand.'

'Oh no, it's quite enjoyable talking about it, it's a break just not being there,' I said.

She asked what is was like being on strike for so long and I said, 'It's hard at times, especially when you've got family that's working.' And I told her about my family and how none of them were speaking to me.

She said, 'That must be very hard, it's one of the worst things that has come out of this strike is the way it has split families in Notts.'

Then she asked about the support we were getting, she asked if the support from Cambridge was helping us, if it was substantial support.

I said, 'Yeah, without Cambridge we wouldn't be managing very well at all, they've become our main source now. The thing about the Cambridge support, is that it's regular and we can count on it each week.'

We continued to talk about the strike for the rest of the week one way and another. Sue and I became really good friends, we ended up talking about everything, she'd just had a baby and we talked about that, we talked about Michael and his illness and I told Sue about the beginning of the strike and how hard it was for us to make a decision when the Notts. Area had declared the strike unofficial.

I was very keen to have another baby at this stage, ever since Michael had been born I'd wanted another one and I'd wanted to have a home birth. So it was fantastic to be with such a young baby and to be able to talk to Sue about the birth and everything. I loved playing with the baby, nursing her, playing with her and changing her. In fact I was happy to do everything I could. She was breast fed so I couldn't feed her, but I would have loved to.

Sue's husband Simon came home for dinner that night and we all sat and ate and talked. He went off to a camp with their son Joey the next day so we didn't see much of them that time. The next day we went to Great Yarmouth with Sue and her friend. The kids were so excited to be by the sea, we went to the beach, then we went down to where all the rides were and Sue's friend paid for the kids to go on rides. It was only 10p a ride and so they went on everything. They thought it was great, the sun was shining, it was red-hot. We thoroughly enjoyed it, we had one of those great big ice creams with fresh cream in it. Sue and her friend wanted to walk around the shops, so Alan and I stayed on the beach with the kids. It was just gorgeous. It was like a bonus, we didn't expect that going to Cambridge would include a trip to the sea. On the way home we stopped at a pub and sat outside in the glorious sunshine with a drink each and the kids with glasses of pop and a packet of crisps having the time of their lives.

The next day, Sue took us walking around the town, she had Kate in a harness on her back and we walked all round, so we would know how to get about ourselves. We stopped for afternoon tea and Sue bought us all a cake, I had a beautiful piece of chocolate gateau.

The rest of the week passed fairly uneventfully, we spent lots of time walking around the beautiful parks and sometimes riding bikes that Sue had borrowed for us. We talked to Sue endlessly, we must have told her everything about the strike, about the Centre, the siege, taking over the Youth Club, everything came out over the week. She talked a bit about her life, she wasn't working then but her last job had been as a researcher for Yorkshire Television. That seemed very interesting to us, it was also interesting to hear her talk about the television stations from the inside and about the bias of the media in general. I liked Sue, I felt that she was a very genuine person, at first I'd wondered how I'd get on with someone who spoke in a way that sounded very posh to me, but it didn't make any difference at all. We were two women who talked easily to each other about all sorts of things. Alan liked Sue too, they talked quite a lot while I played with the baby. Alan asked Sue lots of questions about her life, he was quite fascinated by the difference between their life and ours. In some ways staying there and getting to know Sue and Simon as we did made Alan a bit restless. It made him feel that perhaps there was a more interesting life for him outside the pits. But I think we all taught each other a lot, our lives were very different and we all knew about different things.

Sue talked to Alan about how she saw herself as a woman, and Alan was quite impressed with what she had to say. Later, he said,
'Sue feels that she wants to play a role in life which is not just staying at home with children, she said she thinks having babies is all right, she said she likes having babies, but also she wants to have time to do other things, which she thinks are of value to her and to her kids.'

Sue did a lot of baking, she baked bread and apple pies, it was raspberry time when we were there and they had raspberry bushes so we picked lots of raspberries and ate them with ice cream. Sue made some jam and froze a whole lot. I talked to her about the problems of cooking for so many at the Centre, I can also remember saying,
'It's so different cooking for hundreds, when you're used to cooking for four. I wonder what I'll do when strike's over I can't imagine cooking for four again.'
The food that Sue cooked wasn't really that different to ours, she used a lot more herbs and spices and she served it all in dishes on the table for you to help yourself to. I remember thinking that was nice and that if I had nice dishes like she did I'd do that too.

At the end of the week we left feeling that we were leaving a very close and dear friend. We knew we'd see Sue again soon, she'd said to come up any time we liked and that she and Simon would visit us in Blidworth. Our holiday had been so successful that when we went back and told everybody, they were all keen to go too. So bit by bit lots of families went to Cambridge to stay and it sort of worked out that everybody got close to one family in Cambridge and so that is where they always stayed whenever we went there and also the Cambridge people stayed with us when they came to Blidworth.

On the way back in the car Alan and I had a bit of a discussion about the difference between life in Cambridge for Sue and Simon and life in Blidworth for Alan and I. Alan was very impressed by what he saw as a calmness in their lives. He saw our life, in contrast as being full of effort. Everything revolving around work.

He said, 'The trouble with us is we whittle too much, I do especially, I'm always whittling about something. I whittle in case the car breaks down, I whittle about paying the mortgage and having enough money to buy the things we think we need.'
'Yes Alan, but I think that's because we're not as secure as they are.'
'No, it's more than that, it's a way of life, they both have jobs that are relaxed and bring contentment, so they can be relaxed when they are at home.'
'It's not just that either.'
'They have more money, it's the constant lack of money, the constant worrying that it won't go far enough that worries us. When you haven't got money you just can't think for yourself, you don't know which way to turn, things come in on you, clam up on you, and then you start to panic and whittle, and say, "What shall we do." You start to blame yourself and then everything gets worse.'
'Yes maybe, but money doesn't buy happiness, I'm happy as it is.'
'But I feel I'm missing out on something in life, there's something out there waiting for me, not just pit, going to pit, I mean more intellectual, there's something underneath.'
'I don't feel like that.'
'No, maybe you don't, but I do, I want more, I don't know what but more out of life.'
'You can go on forever wanting, no matter what you've got there's always something else that you want. The time to worry is when you're not happy.'
'Yeah, I suppose you're right ' Alan said.
For the rest of the way home we were both quiet and I was lost in my own thoughts, I was thinking about what Alan had said and I was thinking about my own impressions of the differences in our lives. I wouldn't really want to change my lifestyle to theirs, although I enjoyed it when I was there, but I was also quite happy with my own. Then I started to think about choices and I realized that the difference was that they had choices about what they did, we didn't have those choices. There shouldn't be any classes. I don't think we should individually try and become middle class, that's not the answer.

It's a fight for the whole working class.

We are entitled to a standard of living that is comfortable, instead of a living that is hard. We shouldn't have to work seven days a week to be able to afford a comfortable house. If we had just five days working and a comfortable life, living would be a lot more pleasant. We'd have time to do things we enjoy instead of always doing things we have to. A lot of it has to do with the education system, the working class children aren't given the same opportunities as the middle class children are. Working class children aren't expected to go to college, or expected to do well. Nobody gives a damn whether the working class kids do anything or not, the teachers don't give a damn, nobody gives a damn, the parents don't give a damn because they don't expect their kids to go to college anyway. They expect them to finish school and get a job and be able to help towards the upkeeping of the house. That is one of the main problems, it shouldn't be that way. We should let our children do the best that they can do and the teachers should expect the best from the working class kids as well as from middle class kids. Just because you're born into the middle class doesn't mean that you have more brains that the working class, it just means that you have a better chance. Anyway if you're working class and want to go to college, usually your parents have to pay for your upkeep and working class wages usually don't run to that sort of thing.

I was beginning to think it was a vicious circle, I'd never really thought these thoughts so clearly before but the injustice of the whole system was presenting itself to me. I realised what I'd thought earlier again. It has to be the whole working class, you've got to stand up and say, no more, we want things different and the sooner that the working class find out that they are strong enough to do that, then the sooner things will change. For too long we've been made to believe that we're not strong and as good as other people.I realised that was what the strike was all about, we were standing up and fighting and showing our strength. We were fighting this Government because it was hell-bent on maintaining the rule of the higher classes.

·8·
DOREEN BRUISING

Since Pauline and I had stopped work our involvement in the Strike had become total. As the time went on we both became absorbed in different ways. Pauline was becoming more and more involved with the cooking and organising at the Centre itself whereas I was spending a great deal of time liasing with support groups, raising funds and other types of support as well. As a result of the siege and the Jolly Friar incident I had started to learn a little about the legal process and as a result I became the unofficial legal adviser in the village.

After we'd got the men back from Mansfield Police Station, Martin Walker rang and asked me what had happened. I told him and mentioned that I'd taken a note pad to court and written down everything that had happened. He said,

'That's good. Can you get everybody to make a statement about what happened during the seige.'

'What do you mean, a statement?'

He said, 'Just write each person's account down as if it were a letter, but try to put as much into it as you can. If you can do that then we'll have something to go on.'

When they were all finished I sent them to Berry Hill to have them duplicated, but they weren't right at all. I hadn't included the right sort of information. Martin decided to hold a meeting of people from all the different villages around Notts to teach us how to write statements. He told us what it was necessary to put in and the form that they should take. When I went to our next Sunday morning meeting I talked about how important it was to have the information written down about exactly what had happened at any incident with the police. I suggested that we issue all the men with a small notepad and pencil so they could always write an account of any incident as soon as it happened. Then I would help them to form it into a proper statement.

It had been decided to make a video for the NUM about our experiences during the siege and the Jolly Friar incident. It was going to be made at the Edlington Miners Welfare, so several carloads of us went up. Martin had rung me saying that it was important that these things are publicised so people know what's really going on. He also told me that Gareth, the solicitor who had helped us get the men released after the Jolly Friar incident would be there. I was really looking forward to meeting her.

When we first got there I was sitting chatting to Sue when a tall slender woman caught my eye walking through the double glass doors that were the entrance to the Lounge.

I said to Sue, 'Bet you any money that's that solicitor.' She looked lost and seemed to be looking around for someone. I went over to her and said,

'Are you a solicitor?'

'Yes, I am, do I know you?'

'I'm Doreen, you're Gareth aren't you?'

'Yes, how did you know?'

'I don't know, something just told me you were as you walked through the door. Are you looking for Martin? I don't know where he is, come and sit with us, he'll be around soon.'

We went back to our table, I introduced Gareth to Sue and we all chatted about the strike, straight away I knew that we would form a strong friendship. We talked about the things that had happened to us and about the importance of writing everything down as we went along, especially statements about any contact we had with the police.

After they'd made the video, Pip and I drove home and stopped at the chippie when we got to Blidworth to take some supper home. As we walked into the shop two CID men followed us in. One of them said to Pip, 'We've got reason to believe that you've got a torch that belongs to the police.'

'No, we haven't,' Pip said.

'Yes you have,' the police went on, 'we've followed your sons on their paper rounds and they're using it.'

'What would they want to use the torch for, it's daylight when they take the papers.'

'Well, we've got reason to believe that you've got it and if you don't hand it over we'll arrest you. You're stealing police property.'

I could feel anger starting to well up inside me. How dare they start questioning us in a public place like this.

I said, 'You're joking aren't you? The silly stupid cop dropped it in our tent, how can we steal it if he dropped it. You shouldn't have dropped it in the first place, you shouldn't have even been in our bloody tent.'

'That don't make any difference, we're going to arrest you.'

'Well, we haven't got it,' said Pip, 'we gave it to the Yorkshire NUM.'

'We'll phone them to check, if they haven't got it we'll be straight back to arrest you.'

The anger I'd been trying to contain, burst. I screamed,

'Solicitor's got the torch, in fact Martin Walker's got it and he's working with the Yorkshire NUM. Now piss off.'

Pip was embarrassed by my yelling at them, he said,

'Calm down. ' I probably would have, but as the police started to turn around to leave, one of them said to me over his shoulder.

'If you want to take that attitude, take it. But you'll soon find out, you can't afford to take that attitude with us.'

I snapped, I started really yelling, 'Do you know what's been bloody going off, of course you know, but I'll remind you anyway. Is it any wonder I don't bloody speak to you. First you enter our tent and house without our permission, then hundreds of you surround our houses, then you arrest and charge my son just because he's mine, then you lock my husband up for three days without any cause at all and you even have the gall to admit you've been following my kids around on their paper rounds. And now you're intimidating us again, while we're only trying to get some fish n'chips for our supper. And then you talk about attitude. I'm telling you now, we've just about had enough, I'm sick and tired of the bloody lot of you, I'll never trust another one o'ya again.'

'You never put any complaints in, if you'd put a complaint in we'd check it out.'

'You're joking aren't you? Right then next time I get a complaint I'll bring it straight to you.'

'Well, do it, I'll leave you my card.'

They left and we bought our fish n'chips. Pip said, when we were back in the car. 'Why did you have to go and lose your temper with them, it don't help any.'

'Well, it's bloody time somebody told them, bloody pigs, they think they can walk all over us and I'm not gonna lerrum.'

'I know, but I still don't think it does any good to do your block wi' 'em.'

'Well, that's the way I am, I'm sick and tired of 'em annoying us. I know one thing for sure, there's no way I'd take a complaint to them, if they think I'll ever trust 'em with anything they can sing.'

The next morning when I woke up I was worried about having told the cops that Martin had the torch. I rang him straight up, he wasn't there so I left a message. When he rang back a couple of days later he said,

'It doesn't matter, I've given the torch to someone else anyway.'

He went on to ask me if I could go to a meeting at Ollerton on the following Friday night to help set up a Legal Centre for the Notts. region. Setting up the Centre was very important. Going to the meetings about it, I learned a lot about the law and the right way to go about organising defence. A lot of London solicitors came up to work in the Centre and I got to know them. Martin always seemed to have a lot of faith in me and trusted that I was capable of doing things I didn't think I was capable of doing, mind you I always did them; he gave me confidence.

Once the Centre at Ollerton was set up I often went there with people who had been arrested. I became our own on-the-spot legal adviser. I don't mean that I gave advice, but I always helped people write their statements and went with them to the Legal Centre to see solicitors and went to court to give moral support. This legal work became a large part of my responsibility in our group.

At that first meeting about the Centre, Martin told me that Gareth had taken an injunction order out on the police to keep them away from me and Pip.

'Does that mean they can't intimidate us any more?' I asked.

'Yes.'
'Oh great. Can you do that?'
'In some circumstances you can, yes.'

The following Monday I arrived home from the Centre, tired and looking forward to leaving the strike behind for half an hour while I watched the taped episode of my favourite TV serial, 'Sons and Daughters.' As I walked into the house Karen said to me, 'The police have been looking for you.'
'I thought they were supposed to be keeping away from us, what the bloody hell do they want now?'
Nearly every day for the next fortnight the same thing happened. The police must have known I was at the Strike Centre, but they never went there, they continued to call at the house.

The Monday fortnight, I got home, no-one else was in, I'd just settled down by the fire with a cup of coffee and there was a brisk knock on the front door. When I opened it, there were two plain clothes coppers there,
'We're CID can we come in?'
'No, I'm sorry you can't.'
'You Doreen Humber?'
'Yes, I am.'
'Well, we want to come in.'
'I'm sorry, you're not coming in.'
'We've got reason to believe that you want to make an official complaint against the police for entering your house.'
'Oh do I?'
'Well, that's what we've got reason to believe.'
'Where did you pick this piece of information up.'
'We read it, ' they hesitated and said, 'In the Morning Star.'
'Oh did you?'
'Yes, can we come in and talk about it.'
'No, you can't come in.'
'Well this is our job, how can we talk about it if you won't let us come in.'
I said, 'I'm talking to nobody but my solicitor.'
'Who's your solicitor?'

'That's none of your business.'

'You're not being very co-operative are you?'

'No, I'm not.'

'Do you realise we've been chasing you round for a fortnight?'

'Well, ' I said, 'You've been wasting you bloody time then haven't you. Piss off.'

And they did. Soon after this, Gareth came to the house to have a talk to me about things. She'd agreed to act as our solicitor. When I told her what I'd said to them, she was amazed and asked me where I got my strength from. I've no idea where I got it from really but if anything it came from talking to Martin and Gareth about what my rights were.

At about this time, we had a set-back that none of us expected. Margaret Groves had been getting more and more involved in the welfare rights issues. She had started a course at the Nottingham Polytechnic to learn more about it. She was also going to a series of films they were showing at the local library about all sorts of issues. One night she went to see a film about Women's Health and it went into some detail about cervical cancer. Margaret recognised all the symptoms. She was suffering herself. After a few visits to her doctor and lots of tests, it was confirmed that she had cervical cancer and she was rushed into hospital for an operation. The first operation wasn't completely successful so she had to have another one. Of course it put Margaret out of action and sent a shock through all of us. Margaret had been with us from the start, she was one of the most active members of our group and so apart from feeling for her and her family we were also made brutally aware that the normal pressures of life were still with us and had to be dealt with on top of the pressures of the strike.

The support we were getting from outside was increasing all the time, it had started to come from all around the country. In Nottingham a Central Women's Group had started. It was called the Notts. Women's Support Groups, every Monday night delegates from all the Notts. pits met and discussed their problems and planned and co-ordinated activities and support. The Notts. Branch of NUPE gave them use of an office, a phone and all of the facilities in NUPE. We attended these meetings, at first we had a difference of opinion with some of the women there about twinning, they seemed to want all groups to give all the money they raised to the Central Group and then have it all distributed equally among the groups. I argued against that.

Our experience with Cambridge had been very successful, we were increasingly learning all sorts of things from them and they felt very involved with our struggle and were learning from us. The exchange between the two communities was a very rich one and I think it benefitted everyone in many more ways than just the material support we got from it. Of course that was important, but the friend-ships that were developing between people were important too. I thought that arranging all the money through a central fund would destroy that.

We managed to reach an understanding with the group and con-tinued to be part of it. At times there were tensions of course, but they were always overcome. We were better off than some groups, but we were always prepared to help out if any group was desperate. I thought that we worked hard for the support we got and that it had been a good experience for us.

In the last few weeks I'd made some important contacts with two groups in London and they'd both become regular supporters. The Thursday after Strawberry Fair, Pip and I were sitting at home wat-ching television and relaxing when there was a knock on the front door. One of the miners from Ollerton had brought three men from the National Graphics Association in London. They said that they supported the strike and would like to help, could they come in and talk to me about it. We talked for about two hours, they told me that their union branch would be able to raise quite a bit of money and asked if I'd distribute it to groups who needed it. They'd been refer-red to me by a Kent miner they'd met in London. They weren't prepared to give the money to a Central Group, they wanted to know exactly where it was going. I said that I wasn't sure I had the time because I was always busy fund raising for Blidworth and that they should give the money to the Notts. Women's Support Group because I knew they were doing a good job. They asked if I knew of any pits that were especially badly off. A few days before that Pip had been on the picket line with a bloke from Harworth and he'd come home saying that they were really struggling. I gave them the Harworth telephone number and they left saying that they'd think about things and let me know what they'd decided to do.

They rang me back a couple of weeks later, just before a London rally and told me they'd raised six hundred pound and that they wanted to hand it over to someone at the demonstration and have it distributed. They asked me if I'd do that and ensure that the money was distributed to groups that needed it and make sure that Harworth got a hundred quid. I agreed and kept a hundred pound for Blidworth, gave a hundred pound to Harworth and the other four hundred to four other groups that I knew needed the money.

I asked each group if they'd make sure they wrote to Doug Shaw of the NGA thanking him and his union branch for the support. That was a check for me too, because he would know that I was passing the money on and where it was going. We formed a trusting relationship. He became a regular supporter and used to ring every so often and say, 'We're coming at such and such a time.' And he'd tell me who he was bringing with him.

One week, at the end of June, Doug phoned and said he was bringing two carloads up on Sunday, the 1st of July. He said they had so much money and asked if there was anything we particularly wanted him to bring up. I said,
'Yes, we do need baby food badly.'
'Righto, I'll get some and bring it up to you and there'll be some money as well. We should be there at about three on Sunday afternoon.'

Five of them arrived on Sunday in two cars and unloaded the baby food. We had a cup of tea at the Centre and then some of them went for a walk around the village. When they came back, Doug said to me.
'I can't believe it, every time we've been here before you couldn't move for cops, the place has been covered with them, but we didn't see a single one today, is it because it's a weekend?'
'Oh no, they're there somewhere, don't you worry.' As I said it

two policemen walked past the Centre.

We went back to our house to look at the videos of the news broad-casts of the siege which none of them had seen. After that, at about ten to six, they started to get ready to leave. Doug was going on to Harworth with some more baby food and the rest were going straight back to London. After he'd left our house, Doug turned left at the bottom of the street to get onto the A614 which would take him straight to Harworth. He was only about 200 yards up the road when two police cars pulled out. The first one waved him down and told him to follow them, the second one followed him so he was sand-wiched between the two. They drove up the road to a roundabout and proceeded to drive round and round it. By this time it was dark and Doug's sense of direction was confused by the continual circles they'd been taking. Then the coppers took him up a country lane and eventually stopped the cars. The coppers came up and opened the doors of Doug's car asking him who he was and whether he sup-ported the miners.

He said, 'Yes, I am supporting the miners, I'm from the National Graphical Association and I've brought some baby food up.'

The police said, 'Oh, so you're in a union, are you?'

'Yes.'

'Get out and go and stand over by that wall.'

Doug walked over and stood facing a brick wall which was just beside where the cars were parked. The police searched him and then they searched his car. Then they got hold of his head and dragged it down the wall so his face was grazed, next he felt a truncheon hit-ting him on the elbow and he felt something hitting his legs. They really roughed him up, when they'd finished he was so dazed he didn't know what day it was. Then they told him to get back into his car, that they were going to escort him to the A1 and he must get back to London and if he ever showed his face in Nottinghamshire again they'd lock him up. They took him to the A1 but they pointed him in the wrong direction. It took him ages to work that out because he was so dazed. Eventually he did get back to London. The first I knew about it was a phone call from Doug. He rang a few hours after he'd left here and asked me if I'd ring Harworth and let them know that he wouldn't be able to make it tonight.

'What's up Doug, what's happened? You left here to go to Harworth.'

'Yeah, well I had a bit of trouble with the police, they wouldn't let me through, but tell Harworth that their baby food will be there soon. Don't worry about it, it'll be alright.'

I was quite worried about it, it was very strange, Doug hadn't sounded like himself at all. Anyway I rang Harworth, they were worried too, they'd been waiting for him. Almost as soon as I hung up the phone, it rang again. It was Mike Green, Doug's friend in London. He said,

'Doreen, has Doug phoned you?'

'Yes, what's up, he didn't say much.'

'No, he wouldn't want to upset you, he was badly beat up by coppers just after he left your place. They picked him up just by the Jolly Friar. They wouldn't let him get through to Harworth, he's quite badly shocked and shaken. It happened just after he left your place. But don't worry about it, we're printing it in all the papers, it's already been on the television news. He had photos taken of himself as soon as he got back to London. He's still with solicitors now, he's going to take the police to court about it.'

A few days later Doug phoned me again and we talked about it, he knew that my phone was tapped but he said,

'Listen, you bastards, I'll be back, there'll be loads and loads of us with loads and loads of food, you can't stop us.'

We'd also been contacted by the National Union of Journalists' Book Branch, they had asked if they could raise money and send it to us. Towards the end of July we arranged to speak at an NUJ Book Branch meeting in London. We had been receiving quite a lot of money from them and I wanted a chance to thank them for it in person and to meet all the members who'd been donating from their weekly pay cheques. I asked the Treasurer of the branch several times if he could try and arrange it. In London on Saturday the 28th July there was to be a large women's rally in support of the strike. The NUJ arranged a meeting for the Friday night before and six of us went down on the train. A coach was bringing people down on the Saturday to the March, so we were going to stay overnight and meet the others the next day.

It was the first time some of the women had been to London
during the strike and I suppose because there were six of us, we left
Nottingham on the train in very high spirits, laughing and joking
about everything around us. I had been a few times to speak at various
meetings but each trip had just been for a day at a time.

As soon as we got on the train Ann Penny started to take things
out of her bag. Most of the work Ann had done for the strike up
to now had been in the Centre. She'd become one of the mainstays
of the Centre. She was a very hard worker and was always somewhere
busily taking care of some chore. As we watched the things she was
dragging out of her bag, we all started teasing her and killing ourselves
laughing. She had curling tongs and a complete change of clothes
which she'd brought to change into on the train. Our teasing didn't
stop her spending half of the journey in the toilet getting changed
and curling her hair. She still has to live that down, it's become a
standing joke now, whenever we want to tease her we say that when
she dies she'll have her hair in curling tongs, to make sure she looks
beautiful in the coffin.

The train pulled into King's Cross station and we started to get
off. The great high curved glass roof makes the place feel very grand
and we felt very important arriving there, with a busy timetable in
front of us. Claire, the branch President and Mike, the Treasurer
met us. We weren't hard to recognise, six of us, looking around and
wearing badges. They'd arranged for us to have a meal before the
meeting.

The restaurant they took us to was just near Covent Garden, it
seemed very select with dark plush curtains at the windows and lots
of dark polished wood. It was in a wine bar and there were loads
and loads of bottles of wine around. Some tables in one of the corners had already been booked for us and as we sat down and ordered
pints we looked at the wine bottles around us, some of which had
prices of more than sixty pound. We laughed amongst ourselves about
who would pay that price for a bottle of wine, Pauline said,

'I bet it's horrible wine anyway.'

We all laughed and then Claire and Mike came back with our drinks and we all looked at the menus.

My eyes were drawn straight to the steaks, I could have murdered a steak, the thought of one was driving me mad, but because I knew that Claire and Mike would pay the bill I thought it would be rude to order the most expensive thing and so I ordered seafood. Later we all admitted that we would have liked steak and Claire said,

'Oh, you should have had whatever you wanted, you all deserve a treat.'

The meeting was just around the corner, in another pub, but this time in the upstairs room. The room reminded me a bit of an old Church hall, it had dark wood panelling on all the walls and the seats at the back were old pews. I sat at the table in the front of the room with Claire. The others all sat in one of the corners at the back of the room. We were the first ones there and I wondered if anyone was coming but gradually people started to arrive and by the time we started the meeting there were about sixty there. I talked about the strike, explained how we'd set up the Strike Centre and about the heavy policing we'd been getting and I thanked everybody for their generous support. The discussion afterwards centred around twinning and politics and at the end of the meeting everybody agreed that the branch should adopt us which was wonderful for us, it would mean some more regular money coming in. I'd talked about the refusal of our Labour Councillor to support us over the Youth Club and they asked me what I was going to do about it.

'I'm going to have his job,' I said. 'We've all joined the Labour Party.'

That led to a discussion about the Labour Party and what was wrong with it and what we wanted from it.

After the meeting we were all offered accommodation at various people's houses. I'd arranged with a London solicitor who I'd become friendly with when she was working at the Ollerton Legal Centre to go to a party at her house after the meeting, so I said, 'I'm sorry, but we've been invited to a party.'

It seemed to make things quite complicated but eventually it was arranged that we took the telephone numbers of the people who were offering us beds and that we'd ring if we needed the accommodation.

The party was in a big three storey house. It was a bit of an eye opener to us because the whole house was full of women and lots of them were cuddling and stroking each other. We'd never seen lesbians being so open before and we carried on a bit like a bunch of school kids, running about with our eyes nearly falling out of our heads and then running back and reporting to each other about what we'd seen. We met lots of women and everyone was really nice to us. There was a great buffet laid out which really caught Pauline's eye. She put some smoked fish on her plate and said to someone.

'Look at this, smoked salmon, I've never had real smoked salmon before.'

But it turned out that it wasn't salmon at all, it was smoked mackerel. Still Pauline enjoyed it enormously and enjoyed laughing and laughing and telling everyone that she'd make a fool of herself by mistaking smoked mackerel for smoked salmon.

There were lots of people there who'd been up to Blidworth at different times and it was interesting to see them, at home, among their own friends. Lots of people asked all of us lots of questions. The last time I was in London I'd stood on the picket line of the South London Women's Hospital, the day it was officially closed. I'd said then that I'd come back with some more miners' wives and support them by doing a lie-in. The hospital was the only one in London where women could guarantee that they'd be treated by women and lots of women were really angry that it was being closed down. I suggested to the others that we go over there and do a lie-in that night and they were all enthusiastic so it was agreed. At about one o'clock people started offering us accommodation for the night.

I said, 'We've already been offered accommodation by NUJ people and we don't want to offend anyone, but we'd like to stay the night at the South London Women's Hospital. We want to support them, we believe in what they're doing.'

Louise drove us to the hospital and dropped us off. From the outside, so late at night the hospital had a certain daunting air about it. As we approached the two women who were on the door, we all noticed that they broke an embrace to talk to us. We all looked at each other, already feeling wise about these things, but some of us still smirked. We were directed up to the wards. The first one we went into was nearly full and we asked if there was another one we could sleep in. The second ward was nearly empty and as we walked in Pauline spied a water bed.

'That's mine, ' she said. Then she jumped onto it. 'Oh, look how lovely and soft and warm it is.'

The women who showed us to the ward told us about an intruder who'd come in drunk a couple of times and assaulted some of the women, he'd been nicknamed 'Twine.' They told us that a teapot had been balanced on the door he used to get in, so that if the door was opened it would fall and set off an alarm, everybody was to run to an appointed place when the alarm went off.

I was absolutely shattered and all I really wanted to do was to go to sleep but the others, who'd never been to the hospital before, were keen to explore. I started to get ready to go to bed, and they all started teasing me.

'You going to bed now, don't you want to explore?'

'Oh, leave Grandma she needs her sleep.'

'Are you going to stay here on your own, better take your stilettoes to bed to hit Twine if he comes.'

I thought they were joking but they insisted that I take my shoes into bed with me. Then they went off like five girls on a big adventure. For ages I could hear them wandering around, laughing and giggling.

Eventually I must have dozed off, but I was woken up by an enormous clatter followed by the pounding of running footsteps above me. Bang bang bang, it was like an earthquake, the whole place was shaking. The next thing the five of them came running in, slightly white in the face but giggling at the same time.

They plonked themselves on the beds all breaking up with laughing, and they all started talking at once, telling me what had happened.

'Doreen, you should have seen us. It was so scary out there, so empty, just like one of those horror films, where the bombs dropped and everybody's just left everything. The baby incubators are there.'

'And the babies' food in the fridges, all going sour and out of date.'

'Oooh, it's so weird, everything's here just no people.'

'Shurrup and get into bed and go to sleep. I've seen it before.'

'But listen, do you think they'll be cross with us for knocking the tea pot off.'

'How do I know, we've got to get up early. Get to sleep.'

'We were just walking along these corridors, switching lights on as we went. We walked around looking through doors and working out what things were. Then we came to this door, pulled the handle down and then there was this great clatter.....'

'I know, I heard, now go to sleep. ' I was irritable with tiredness. But the others were still very excited after their adventure.

'But then, when we started to run downstairs, we got to this lift and it was coming up and somebody was in it, whistling. That freaked us right out, we just ran and ran until we got back here.

They kept on talking to each other about it, then Pauline got onto the water bed and gave everybody a running commentary on how terrific it was. It must have been four o'clock before anyone got to sleep.

Next morning I was woken by Sue, moving about opposite me, she was getting dressed.

I said, 'Sue what time is it?'

'Six o'clock.'

'What are you getting dressed for, get back to bloody bed. I'm shattered we can have another hour before we need to get up.'

'I can't sleep, Doreen, there's too many noises and too many funny things happening.'

'Why, what's happening.'

'Well, there's aeroplanes going over, I can't sleep for the noise they make.'

'You're dreaming, there aren't any aeroplanes.'

'There is and there's women running about naked.'

'Don't be silly and go back to sleep.'

'Doreen, I can't sleep here, it's strange and eerie and there are noises coming from all over the place.'

I eventually drifted back to sleep, when I got up an hour later Sue was already dressed and sitting in the day room where we all made ourselves coffee and toast after we'd showered and dressed. Ann Penny was still getting ready when we were ready to go, so we sat talking to some of the other women. They had all heard the teapot fall, but from the giggles and pounding footsteps that followed they'd known it was our women and also that they'd scared themselves half to death. We talked about the strike and they told us about the hospital and the battle to save it. We also talked about the connections between different groups of women like us and Greenham Common Women. It was always quite inspiring to meet other women who were involved in different things. It gave us a sense of being involved in something much bigger than the Miners' Strike. The fight was taking place on a lot of fronts. The women at the hospital were all very supportive to our struggle. They gave us fifty pound donation and the ward we'd all slept in was afterwards known as the Miners' Ward.

After we had breakfast we met the bus from Blidworth, some of the kids had gone to a creche which had been arranged by the march organisers. I was worried about that, I wasn't sure how Mark would fit in because he doesn't normally mix very well. But I soon stopped worrying because the march was so demanding itself. There were thousands and thousands of people there, lots of women, lots of miners' wives and miners. Everybody was singing and chanting and we really felt very powerful, as we walked past the houses of Parliament we talked about taking them over because there was so many of us. As we walked past Downing Street, somebody took a wreath and put it outside of No. 10. and we all observed silence as we walked past, we were mourning the passing of democracy in this country. I was really surprised and very pleased to notice that Louise who was marching with us, really enjoyed the singing, she sang out at the top of her voice. 'You can shove a National Ballot up your arse.' She's got a fantastic house and is very well spoken and good with words, it was wonderful to see that she obviously felt the meaning in the songs just as we did. We heard Arthur speak at the rally, then picked up the kids. They'd had a ball, I need not have worried about Mark, he came back very excited and painted like a spider man, he'd thoroughly enjoyed his day too. I was exhausted and not really sorry that tonight I'd be sleeping at home, and could relax and hopefully get a good nights sleep. It had all been very tiring but also enjoyable, we felt very tired but fulfilled as we sat back in our coach seats on the way home.

Our mail increased dramatically, both our personal mail and mail to the Group. Most of it was letters of support and encouragement usually with a cheque as well. The messages were often very touching and would bring tears to my eyes. Pensioners who had nothing themselves would write and say they believed in what we were doing and wanted to help. People described us as courageous, spirited, brave, and our struggle as vital, momentous, essential, critical.

Sometimes I felt very humble in the face of all this praise but at other times I felt very proud. In some ways I just seemed to be the same old me, and it was hard to realise that all these people from all over the country, many of whom I'd never even met were using these words to describe our struggle. In another way I knew that what we were doing was of the utmost importance, not just for ourselves but for the whole country, somewhere inside I felt the gravity of the situation and a sense that our struggle had vital implications for the future.

Letters of support often confirmed these feelings, it was clear that lots of other people felt the same. When I felt low these letters would pick me up, they'd give me the strength to continue by reminding me of the importance of our fight. The problems that were making me feel low would shrink to apparent insignificance. Some of the mail would arrive opened and we suspected that the police were reading it.

Other letters brought information about things that were happening in other areas and other villages, letters from other groups like our Central Groups or Groups of Supporters. Dealing with the mail became a major part of the work. Our Committee had appointed a new Secretary, Chris Tucker. She had a difficult job just answering the correspondence that came in and sending receipts and thank you letters for all the money that was received.

One morning a letter arrived from some women in Yorkshire. It was very short, it just said, 'We're coming to Calverton to do a picket on Wednesday night, could you please try and support it.' As always in these situations, I felt that if women were coming all the way from Yorkshire to help us here in Notts., then it was important that we give our support too. I brought it up at our next Committee Meeting, stressing the importance of supporting it. About eight of us decided to go.

Calverton is only a few minutes drive from Blidworth and we got there half an hour early. The most sensible thing to do seemed to be to have a drink in a pub and then leave the cars in the pub car-park when we went to the picket. We were all decorated with our badges and it must have been a scab-pub because they didn't like it. We stayed to have our drinks and as we left they all came out shouting abuse at us.

When we got to pit lane we met up with some of the women from Yorkshire and decided to start picketing straight away because some of the men were coming off the afternoon shift. There were only about twenty of us and we stood opposite the canteen on the pavement. A bus load of scabs went past us and they all pulled their trousers down and bared their bums at us through the windows. We felt disgusted and then the police came up. It's funny because despite all that we'd been through as the police approached old habitual expectations flashed into my mind. I actually thought for a second or two that the police would try to stop the scabs from being so disgusting, but of course, it was us they were coming for. They asked us to move. We said, 'No, we're not moving, we're staying here.'
They left.

Twenty minutes later bus loads of Notts. coppers, identifiable by what we called their 'tit-hats' with their silver nipples shining on top of their helmets, started to arrive. They were standing across the road from us and then one of their gaffers came over and said to us,
'Come on Ladies, you'll have to move.'
'Where do you want us to go.'
'Up the other end of the lane there.'

We all chorused, 'No, why?'

'We're not doing any harm here, we'll stay.'

'We can't shout at people going to work from up there.' He tried to keep it all friendly, he said, 'Sorry Ladies, you've got to move, we're not gonna let you stay here.'

'We are staying here, if you want us moved, you'll have to move us. We're not breaking any laws.'

'If you don't move we will move you.' There was no pretence at friendliness any more.

We all started singing, 'We shall not be moved.'

He went over the other side of the road, talked for a moment to the coppers lined up along the edge of the pavement and then they all came marching across towards us.

There were still only thirty of us and we linked arms and watched them marching towards us. They positioned themselves right around us. A line about three deep and then they started to push. We heard one of them say,

'Treat 'em just like men.'

Another woman heard one say, 'Go for their noses, women don't like to get their noses broken.'

They pushed and pushed and we tried to stand our ground but we had little chance, we were just thrust ahead by their pushing and the only way to keep your balance was to lurch forward every so often.

We kept singing and singing, they didn't like that at all, it unnerved them. Annette fell down and they wouldn't stop pushing to let her get up so women were being forced to walk over her. Eventually a couple of us pushed police out of the way for a bit so Annette could get up. The police had determined and vicious looks on their faces and just kept shoving us along as if we were herded animals.

One of our women, Mary, had managed to stay behind the fence, I looked around to see if she was still there and saw two coppers marching her off. Eventually we were pushed right over to the other side of the road and we thought that was it. But they kept pushing us. We started complaining all over again.

They said, 'We want you up the end of the lane.'

It was about two or three hundred yards away from the pit. They said two of us could stay at the end near the pit, as a sort of official picket. We still refused to go voluntarily so they started pushing again. They pushed us, kicked us, thumped us and elbowed us. They did everything they could to hurt us while trying not to be too blatant about it.

Eventually they got us where they wanted us and circled around us. Then another van load of women arrived and we all started singing, 'There'll be more, there'll be more, there'll be more.' More van loads started to arrive and each time we'd sing. In the end there must have been a hundred of us.

They'd put Mary in a van and we were all shouting to her, 'Can you hear us Mary? Are you orright Mary?'
At about nine-thirty some of the women were desperate to go to the loo. The police said,
'Sorry you can't go.'
We were hemmed in and couldn't go anywhere, they explained that they were desperate and so police said,
'All right, we'll take you two at a time.'
The first two set off with two police, but they never came back, then another two went and they never came back either and we realised then that they were being put in the van with Mary. At a later picket at Calverton, because we knew what happened when the police took people to the loo, some women squatted behind a hedge and were arrested for indecent exposure. It was disgusting, the scabs were dropping their trousers and exposing themselves at us from the buses, but no-one arrested them.

That picket went on till about eleven. The whole experience had been horrific. Later when we saw Mary after she'd been released she told us that while she was in the van, the cops that were there with her, tried to embarrass her by telling revolting jokes about parts of women's bodies. At one time she wanted to go to the loo, and asked them if she could. At first they told her that she'd have to wait for a woman police officer to arrive, time passed and she'd asked again because she was getting desperate, they'd tell her the same thing.

Eventually the woman copper did arrive, Mary asked her if she would take her to the loo and she said to Mary,

'Piss on the floor that's all you're good for.'

When they got her to the station, they asked her hundreds of questions, about the Centre, who runs it, how much money we've got, who supplies the money, who were spokespersons and so on.

After the Calverton picket the Notts. Women's Central Support Group decided to start organising mass women's pickets at different pits around Notts. We decided to hold one at Blidworth. The organisation was kept as secret as possible, so in Blidworth even the men didn't know it was going to happen. Most of the scabs went in the main gates of the pit by the canteen and so there were always six official pickets next to those, either standing or sitting on the wall, and then there were two at each other gate. The men were always very choosy about who the official pickets were going to be and quite jealous of the privilege.

This morning we women all turned up, we went up to the men on the gate and said,

'This is a women's picket.'

They said, 'Ya what?'

'This is a women's picket, so will you all demonstrate over on the green please. We're taking over the gates.'

They sort of looked baffled and mumbled, but they did as we asked. I think they must have known we were determined, we'd never asked before to be among the official pickets. They seemed to know we were serious and that we had our reasons so they moved over to the green and six of us took our places along the wall. Lots of women turned up from all over the place. One group arrived in a blue Bedford van just like the police ones. They'd not been stopped once on a road block they just sailed past them. We thought they were police when we saw the van driving up and then when a bunch of women got out we all cheered.

Standing at the gate was interesting too, you'd get some chat from some of the scabs, they'd say,

'Get off back to washing pots, get off back to the kitchen. You're not an NUM member.'

I'd say, 'I'm more of an NUM member than you are. You're a bloody scab.'

Others said, 'What you doing here, you've no right to be stood here picketing?'

'We've every right to be stood here, you're taking food out of our kids' mouths.'

One guy took a hand rolled fag out of his pocket as he walked towards us and started to light it.

I said, 'That's right, light your fag, you need some courage to walk past us.'

He said, trying to be smart, 'Why, do you want a drag.'

'No thanks, I needn't take one of your crumby rollies, I've got real cigarettes here that our supporters give us.'

Whatever they said, we had an answer for them and we actually succeeded in turning a few back. Overall it was a very good picket and the men were pleased too, they kept asking us when we were going to have another one.

·9·
PAULINE
CHANGING STATES

By the middle of August we had settled into life on strike. It was becoming hard to remember what life had been like before. The Centre was running efficiently, money was always a problem but we now had a number of regular supporters who we could depend on to provide a certain amount each week. Our relationships with these supporters had grown, they all visited the Centre regularly, sometimes just for a few hours, and sometimes for a few days. Most of the supporters would help with the chores and we would always talk endlessly about any recent events. We talked about events in the village and they talked about their fund raising and organisation and we all talked endlessly about what was happening in the strike at a national level. There had been an attempt at talks between the Coal Board and the NUM, but they had broken down. We felt very strong, we had been out for nearly six months and in that time we had managed to organise so that everybody was fed and clothed well.

At about this time, Doreen came back from a trip to Cambridge saying that some of the women in Cambridge had asked if they could come up and stay with us for a few days and help with the work. We all thought it was a great idea and after a bit or organising they arrived on a Sunday. Four women came and two of them brought their kids, so altogether there were four women and three kids. On Monday morning they went up on the early picket and then went to the Centre and cooked breakfast, then they helped us with lunch and clearing up. By two o'clock they were back in the houses where they slept until they'd stagger up to the Centre for their teas. This became the pattern of their stay, some days they'd even miss their teas, they were so tired by the pace. It was great for us to have them, they really helped take some of the burden from us and it made us realise how hard we worked to see how tired it made them. We'd been doing it for nearly six months by this time and we'd got used to it but it was a very hectic pace. It wasn't just the work, there was always something unexpected coming up, something which would make extra work and cost extra money. On the Monday night we threw a party for them at my house. It was quite funny really because by ten o'clock they were all fast asleep and we were all merrily enjoying the party. They stayed until the following Friday. During the time that they were here we took them to a women's picket at Bilsthorpe and to one of the court cases which resulted from the siege. They all sat up the back and the Magistrate asked,

'Who are those peace women, sitting in the back row?'

He wanted to move them but Gareth said they were supporters and he couldn't make them leave. We had a lot of discussions with them. They all called themselves feminists, and a lot of our discussions were about what they meant by that. We agreed with a lot of what they said, they just talked about wanting to live their own lives in the way they wanted to. There was a notice board in the kitchen at the Centre and when they left they had written on it,

'Women not Ladies.' We all laughed and laughed, all the men called us the ladies, they would walk into the Centre and say,

'Mornin' Ladies.' And we'd all answer. We called ourselves ladies as well, and while the women from Cambridge were here they were always referred to as the ladies from Cambridge and we always addressed them as 'ladies.'

'Would you ladies like a cup of tea?' It had obviously really annoyed them, but they hadn't said anything, they'd just written the note in the kitchen. But the thing about the note was that we all knew what they meant. It wasn't something we'd talked about, we'd always used the word ladies. Suddenly we realised that the men were men and not gentlemen and therefore we were women and not ladies. Suddenly we saw that we didn't want to be connected to those ladies who sat around and did nothing. Although it's only a word, it made quite a difference to the way we saw ourselves. We recognised a strength in the word women, and we recognised our own strength so from that time on we have always insisted on being called women.

At first the men didn't know what had struck them, they'd walk in and say, 'Mornin' Ladies.'

There'd be a chorus of us saying, 'Women, not ladies.'

Some of the men asked why and when we told them, they agreed, they saw the sense in it. Some of the men never stopped calling us ladies, but every time right throughout the strike we'd always tell them. Even visitors, or people who came into the Centre on business of one sort or another, any man who called us ladies, was told we were women. It meant a lot to us, it was our way of telling the men that we had changed.

And we had changed, we could feel it within ourselves. We talked about it a lot between ourselves. Everybody around the country was talking about the strength of the Miners' Wives. Margaret Thatcher had thought that the women would send the men back to work, but the very opposite had happened. It was the women who had so solidly backed the strike that had made it possible for it to go on for so long. People often asked us why that was. The women had been totally inactive in the Strikes of '72 and '74, but this time we'd become the backbone of it. I thought it might have something to do with the fact that the strike was really a community issue, if the pits closed, we lost our whole way of life, our children's future was at stake and the villages we called home. We all knew what happened to mining villages when the pits closed. They became ghost towns, none of us want to see that happening to our homes.

I think women have been gradually asking more and more questions over the last ten years or so. In the last strikes the women didn't ask any questions, it was all left to the men. If the men were involved in a dispute, then it was their dispute, just like it was their work. But now women wanted to be more involved in the decision making, we wanted to know why the men were going on strike, so we could understand and support them. We wanted to find out more and more, it was like wanting to know what's beyond that fence. When we first went on the picket line, it was because we wanted to know what was there, what was over that fence. Once you step over the first fence you want to know what's over the next one and the next. That's what it had been like in this strike we didn't just get over the fence, we went over the next one and the next one and it was like going downhill. The more we found out the more we wanted to know and the more we wanted to do as well.

Also I think, because Margaret Thatcher's a woman we expected something better from her. I didn't vote in the elections but when I heard that we had a woman Prime Minister I thought that might be better, I expected that as a woman she would be more compassionate, but it was just the opposite. When I watch her on television it makes me really angry and I don't think I'd be so angry if she were a man. I wouldn't expect him to understand, but I do expect a woman to. Of course now I realise that this is not the case, now I realise that she is a Conservative and that is the difference.

We all knew that we had become fully active people, who had to be reckoned with not just ignored as we had been when we were housewives.

Some of the women started to go out every Friday, they called it the Women's Night. I didn't go with them, I thought that was taking it all a bit far but there were lots of discussions about it and about women's roles in life. We also started to talk about what life would be like after the strike and every single one of us knew that we'd never go back to what we'd been before. As for me, I knew that the only interests I had before the strike were my house and my kids and I knew that my views about all sorts of things had changed. Before the strike I thought I was quite content just to be in my own little kingdom, or my own little cell, whichever you want to call it, at home looking after the kids, doing washing, ironing and general chores. I was quite content some of the time, but at other times I used to ask myself if this was all there was to life. Sometimes I'd get quite fed up of it and Alan and I would have words about it. I'd say to him,

'It's alright for you, you can get out of these four walls, you see people, you see friends, orright, they might not be ya best mates, but at least you're seeing someone different to talk to. I'm stuck, in this house, in these four walls with these two kids who you can't have a decent conversation with.'

But once we were well into the strike I started to realise that there could be a lot more to life than that and that it didn't necessarily have any bad effects on anything. I'd always believed, I'd always been brought up to believe, that a woman's place was with her family. Not necessarily doing everything that her husband tells her or at the kitchen sink slaving all the time, but taking care of her children, and being with them when they needed her. I'd always thought that children needed a mother to be there before they went to school and then before and after school once they'd started school.

But all that had changed. My involvement in the strike and my continuing commitment to the responsibilities I'd taken on meant that I wasn't spending as much time with my kids. It didn't seem to be having a detrimental effect on them, in fact I think it was quite good for them. They've learnt to fend for themselves more, to become more independent. I also found out that Dad can look after the kids just as well as Mum could. If someone had suggested to me before the strike that Alan could look after the kids as well as me, I would have been quite hurt. I would have felt that they were attacking me as a mother. Being a mother was the only thing I had to do in life which I thought was important. It would have been hurtful for someone to say that Alan could do that as well as I could. But it's true, my involvement in the strike meant that Alan took on a lot of the looking after the kids and they were just as happy as when I did it. In fact I realised it was good for them, good for Alan and good for me. Lots of men became closer to their children through the strike and lots of them were pleased to have the opportunity. Many men said to me that they hadn't known their children before the strike, that they were always at work and then when they were home they were too tired to bother. Suddenly all these men had a lot to do with their kids.

Just as the adults at the Centre were learning to live together and to see each other as family, so were the kids. Because the village was divided over the strike, that of course was reflected at school so the kids quite often got into scrapes, but they would defend each other. One day all the kids came racing into the Centre excitedly singing out that one of them had been threatened by some other kids. They all supported him. It had become quite a thing for the kids to be part of the Centre. They were identified by the outside kids as 'the Strike Centre kids', and they were really proud of the label. They all understood what the issues were, they all knew that their Dads had taken a stand and their Mums were supporting it. They knew that we women were travelling around the country speaking at public meetings and they knew that we had lots of visitors. All sorts of people from all over the country came to the Centre to see us and talk to us about what was happening. Suddenly I think the kids were forced to see their parents in a different way and that was very good for everybody. The older kids set up their own committee. They claimed that the women had one, the men had one and they needed one too. So it was set up. They had a very large number of office bearers, I think they wanted to make sure that everyone had a title, but they were quite serious about it. They called themselves 'Kids Against Pit Closures' and whenever they were unhappy about something they sent a notice to the women's committee meeting and their complaints were usually taken seriously.

As far as I was concerned, it was quite good for my two kids to find themselves in the middle of something much bigger than just our own family. They learnt to be part of that bigger organisation where they couldn't be the centre of things all the time. At the same time, I missed not having any quiet time at home to ourselves. Sometimes I longed just to be at home and to cook food for just the four of us. I was spending very little time with the kids and sometimes I missed that.

I was surprised at how complete my involvement was. I had no idea before that anything could become so important to me or that I could get so involved in anything. The issues of the strike really ate at me inside, really made me want to stand up and say, 'All right, enough is enough, I won't take this, I will do something to change it.'

Once you've felt that once, you can feel it again over other things and we all knew that we'd never be the same again, that we'd always fight, when we saw something that we thought was wrong. Already there were other issues which we knew we wanted to get involved in. Mainly they were the peace movement, and campaigns against cuts to the health service, but there were lots more. The situation of black people in Britain and the situation in Northern Ireland both worried us now because we knew what was causing those situations and we knew that the only way they could be solved was by everybody standing up and fighting. Just as we knew we could only win our strike if everybody stood up and fought.

I'd always accepted things even if I didn't like them because I didn't think I could do anything to change them. But now we had all joined the Labour Party, suddenly realising that we weren't totally powerless, that we must try and change things wherever we could. I hadn't even voted in the last elections because I'd never thought much of politicians, I'd thought they were all the same. Now I had joined the Labour

Party, we all had, we all believed that if we joined it we could have a say in its policies and in who stood for Parliament. The Blidworth branch was shaking in its boots because they all knew that we'd joined to change things, but they couldn't stop us.

At the same time it was quite terrifying, because we had such a lot to learn, and we were frightened of putting our feet forward and stepping in shit.

I also learned I was capable of doing many things, apart from just being a mother. I could still do that, but I discovered that there were other things which are important for me and which give my life more meaning. I had no idea that anything could become as important to me as the strike did. The strike was twenty-four hours a day. I went to sleep with the strike and I woke up with the strike. Some nights I'd go to bed and wonder what it would be like if I woke up the next morning and the strike was all over. I usually thought that when I was depressed. It was easy to get depressed because there were so many tensions. It had been six months and we had no idea how much longer it would go on for. Just that created a tension in all of us, then there were conflicts that arose at the Centre that were hard to put right and on top of all that we never knew what lay around the next corner. We'd heard rumours that the Government was going to send troops in to break the strike. We had no reason to suppose they wouldn't, anything seemed possible.

At the same time, whenever I thought about the end of the strike, that was sad too, it had become such a way of life and my life had expanded such a lot as a result of it. I knew that when it ended I would stay politically involved but I also knew that life would have a balance that it didn't have now. I could go out and do the things I saw as important, but I could also switch off sometimes when I wanted to.

At the beginning of September the Trades Union Council had their Annual Congress. A coach load of men from Blidworth went down to Brighton on the first day to lobby the conference to give more support to the Miners. The first afternoon of Congress had been given over to a debate on the strike. We heard that a motion had been passed which called on the TUC to co-ordinate industrial action in other unions to support us. We began to hope that the end was near.

Some of the Labour Party women in Nottingham were so fascinated by the way we had changed that they decided to do an interview with us about it. They came out one Sunday afternoon with their tape recorder and asked Sue, Doreen and I a whole lot of questions. We all sat around one of the wooden tables in the main hall with the tape recorder in the middle of us. The kids were beginning to get used to people coming and interviewing us, but still everytime they made more noise than usual. I think that was their way of trying to get in on the action. One of the women, Mary, had been out to Blidworth a lot at the beginning of the strike. She arrived one day and stood on the picket line.

It was a dinnertime picket and three men were arrested, Mary said to us,
'I've never seen the like of that sort of intimidation by police before and I've been in politics for thirty years. I recognised the Miners' Strike as one of the most significant fights against capitalism for some time in Britain, and as important as many of the struggles being fought out in third world countries around the world. But I hadn't understood the full impact of that struggle until I stood that day with you and watched the treatment the cops gave out to you.'

Mary asked us about the changing roles between the men and women. Doreen said,
'Men are having to do washing and cleaning up, I've not washed a garment for six month, men are having to do all that. I'm going to Blackpool next week for three days. Most weeks I go away and the men have to look after the kids.'
Sue added, 'And they accept it, I've been married for nearly nineteen years and we never went anywhere without each other. He was the man of the house, he was the breadwinner, we just sort of fell into that pattern as things are. I went to London with Pauline last week for three days, and Ken just accepts that. Well we've been liberated really haven't we.'
'Yeah', said Doreen. 'And men don't mind.'

'After the strike we'll never go back to what we were before, ' Sue said, 'men will just have to accept that.'

'Thing is, ' Doreen went on, 'the men know that through this fight it's the women who've come to the forefront and it'll be the women that'll win it. And the men know that. They've said times many in here, that if it weren't for us and this place a lot of them would go back to work. When this strike first started Margaret Thatcher thought that it would be the women that would send the men back to work. She was convinced, she'd told us to buy our houses, get our cars and our H.P., Visa Cards, get up to your eyeballs in debt. This is not a thing she's had in mind for the last year, she's had this in mind for years and that's why she has allowed the country to get into the state it's in. She thought when the Miners' Strike does come, she knew it was going to be a big battle and she was prepared for it. The Tory Government have been preparing for years. She thought the women would send the men back to work. But she's wrong.'

'She underestimated us ' Sue said and Doreen continued.

'She's wrong with the women involved in the strike, there's a lot of women involved just like us and we know, we're in contact with them, from Yorkshire, Derbyshire, Wales. This is one big mistake that she's made.'

We continued talking about the changing role of the women and how widespread it was. We talked a bit about other groups in Britain that were suffering at the hands of the Tory Government and the links that we were making with them. Then we started to talk about attitudes to work. Sue said,

'I'll give you an instance. I went strawberry picking last summer, it's hard work, you're on your hands and knees. Last summer we earned about eighty or ninety quid a week, not this year we're working just as hard for about forty quid because there's no bonuses. One day I was there and I was crawling along this row and there were a woman and her friend next to me and one woman said t'other, 'It's not so good money this year is it?' Her friend said, 'No, but still you've got to be grateful for a bit extra, haven't you.' I knew that I might have thought that a year ago, but this year I was so angry. I thought it's not right, we should not have to be grateful for a bit extra, we're working hard for less money this year than we did last year, and it made me stop and think. And it made me angry. That's what this strike has done for us, it's really made us think. If you work hard you deserve your money.'

Then someone asked us about the Women's Movement and whether we thought it was important. Sue said,

'It's like a lot of other things, you read bits in the paper and you think what a load of fanatics, going over the top. But we didn't really look at back of it to see what it all meant, now we're learning about it, we're learning about a lot of things every day.'

Doreen said, 'This country's in one big bloody mess, do we lie back and let it get worse and worse or do we stand up as women and fight. The thing we've got to do is stand up and fight. If we lose, what have we got to lose. Nothing, if we win we've got a lot to win.'

We discussed events in other countries and compared them to England and then they asked us if we thought the Labour Party had the answers.

'No, ' said Doreen, 'Not at the moment.'

'I don't think they realise,' Sue said, 'That we're ready for somebody that's going to stand up and say what's true and not worry about images, not try and sell themselves like a box of chocolates. There's a lot of people that are ready for somebody that's got the guts to stand there and say what's what. And we haven't got that yet.'

Mary said, 'What would you say to the arguments of the right wingers who say we're going to lose votes?'

'Let them say it and have a go.' Sue said.

'The Labour Party, ' Doreen said, 'are supposed to be working for the working class. What are they worried about, they shouldn't worry about votes, if they were doing their jobs for the working class they'd be throwing their full support behind this strike, instead of sitting on the fence and seeing which way it's going to go.'

'It would get them votes, wouldn't it?' Sue said adamantly.

We talked about joining the Labour Party because we wanted to change it, then we started to talk about what we would do after the strike. Betty Savage had joined us by then, she said,

'After it will be good to get women together to form peace groups, and get this over to other action groups as well. We've had contact from other groups that are thinking about the same things. We'll definitely continue after the strike.'

With the beginning of September we approached the six months point of the strike. It was a strong time for us all, we felt that we'd been out now for six months and that was quite an achievement. A social was organised at the Ollerton Miners' Welfare for Blidworth and Rainworth Strikers and their wives. It was one of the most amazing nights of my life. About six hundred of us danced and sang with so much self respect and pride. There were two acts arranged, the first Glenys and Colin, who were on strike and from Blidworth, they played in a band and sang lots of sixties songs which we all knew. We all sang along, it was fantastic to have our own musicians, the audience were all striking miners and it was great to have strikers who we all knew providing us with the entertainment. The other act that had been arranged was a pair of folk singers from Cambridge. They sang lots of songs about strikes which were very moving and it was quite emotional to listen to these songs which we'd never heard before but which described our situation and our feelings.

I had sung a ditty at a party we'd had in Blidworth a few weeks before and everybody had thought it very funny. Without my knowing, Doreen arranged with the performers for me and one of the men from Blidworth to perform the song on the stage. I had never sung to that many people before, but it was a great success, everybody sang along and hooted with laughter. After we finished everybody sang all the miners' songs we'd learnt at rallies. It was great, six hundred of us standing on tables and singing our hearts out. When we started to sing 'We will win, We will win,' we changed the words half way through to 'We have won.' That was how confident and strong we felt, we felt that if we'd been out for six months we could stay out for as long as it took to get a victory.

The next morning a women's picket had been organised at Bentink. We all got up very early after a very late night, and rugged up in all our warmest clothes. I made a flask of coffee to help keep us warm and we set off. Nicki, one of the women from Cambridge, who'd stayed with us before, had come up for the Social. She had stayed the night in our caravan and came on the picket with us in the morning. When we got there it was still dark and freezing cold. There were about sixty women, twelve men and sixty police there. The police set up a cordon around us as the scabs started to arrive for work. Doreen's brother worked at this pit and she said that if she saw him going into work she would get arrested, but he didn't come in on that shift.

After we'd all been standing and singing out things to the scabs for about half an hour we saw a police woman arrive. She stood next to some police vans which were parked across the street from us and next to the pit. As soon as we saw her we knew that the police were going to lift someone. Sure enough, five minutes after she arrived three police moved into the crowd and lifted Nicki. She had screamed, 'Scab.' They took her across the road and put her in one of the vans.

A bit later the van started to drive off with Nicki in it, but it only got five hundred yards down the road when it turned around and came back. Within a few minutes the police had again moved into the crowd, this time they picked up a woman who was sitting on the fence behind us and started to cart her away. Some other women furious with the injustice of the two arrests, threw themselves at the police and they were eventually carted off too. Nicki told us later that as the van moved off it had received a radio message telling it to come back that there would be more arrests. At that stage absolutely nothing at all had happened. We left that picket feeling very angry, you never did get over the feelings of frustration being on pickets when for no reason someone was arrested.

Towards the end of September we went to Greenham Common. We'd heard a lot about Greenham and quite a few of the women from there had been up to the Centre to visit us. They had told us stories about police violence and the difficulties they were having there and we always found it exciting talking to them. They were different to us, but they had put themselves in a situation which had similarities to ours, so we had lots in common. Of course, before the strike I'd always thought that the Greenham Common women were just a lot of weirdos and gypsies, but since talking to them and since learning myself about a lot of issues, I'd realized that what they were fighting for was very important and was really the same fight as ours. The Government was clearly very keen to introduce Nuclear Energy to replace coal and that was part of the reason for the attacks they were making on the coal industry. We therefore wanted to support the women at Greenham Common as much as we could. Some of us had even talked about going there to stay at different times after the strike was over.

There was a Women's Peace Group in Nottingham, they'd been out to the Centre and a few of us had been to some of their meetings. They organized a few coaches to go down to Greenham one Sunday and eight of us decided to go. The coach left Nottingham very early in the morning, it was a long journey and we were very excited. We'd heard that there was likely to be thousands of women from all over the country there. When we arrived we felt a big strange, we didn't really know what to do or where to go. We went into one of the tents by one of the gates and the women told us that there was a blockade on at another gate so we walked around to it. Loads of women were sitting on the road in front of the gate and a lot more were standing along the edge of the road. There were certainly not thousands there, more like a few hundred. We all just watched, we were pleased to be there, but felt a bit out of place, we were so used to being at pickets and demonstrations to do with the strike and this was quite different. Every now and then the police would move in on the women sitting and pick a load of them up and cart them away. Then they brought a couple of horses in and the horses gently walked in among the women but nevertheless succeeded in scattering them so eventually the road was cleared. As we watched all this going on we were amazed by the number of women who were chatting and laughing with the police. Later we talked to some women about it and they said that they thought there was some point in talking to them, because you might be able to convince them of your point of view. We all shook our heads, none of us could talk to police at all after what they'd done to us.

At about lunch time we all went back to the gate at which we'd arrived and sat on the grass to eat our lunch. Soon after we'd finished our lunch it started to rain and we wandered into a small wooded area to look for some shelter. A woman sitting under a plastic canopy outside a tent asked us if we'd like to share her shelter and started to make us a cup of tea, talking all the while about things at Greenham. After some time she asked us where we came from, when she found out she asked us lots of questions. The rain stopped and she took us for a tour around the edge of the base. It was so eerie, miles of fence guarded on the inside every few yards by soldiers who were just young boys, and guarded on the outside by police. Behind the guards on the base itself, the large ominous looking hills which housed the missiles looked more like something from a science fiction movie than something from real life.

The whole day had been quite an experience, it was a world away from our own struggle, but we felt the links between the two very strongly. The other thing we'd learned from this strike was that material things don't matter nearly as much as we'd thought they did. We'd risked all of ours and in doing so we'd learnt that it didn't matter what people had or what they looked like, the important things were what they were as people, how they acted as people and how they fought.

A couple of weeks after our trip to Greenham, Sue and Ken came into the Centre looking white.

'Whatever's the matter,' Doreen said.

Ken had received a letter from the pit Manager stating that he'd been sacked. The letter said that management were convinced of Ken's guilt even though his case hadn't come for trial. They went on to say that they were sure that none of the men employed at Blidworth Pit would want to work with him. We were witnesses to Ken's innocence and to see in black and white that the pit management had assumed his guilt before his trial went against all our ideas of justice. Immediately it made our resolve stronger and at the open meeting that Friday morning a unanimous vote was taken that no-one from Blidworth would go back to work until Ken was reinstated.

Things at the Centre were starting to get quite uncomfortable, a division among the women had developed and although we'd tried to arrange things so that it didn't interfere with our work it kept cropping up. Some of the women had complained at one stage about having to get up to the Centre early to cook the men's breakfasts. That led to a discussion at a meeting about what we were doing. We were after all supporting the men in their strike. That was our first priority. But the division just grew. A small group of women seemed always to be upsetting all the others and there always seemed to be someone upset. Snide remarks would be made about who did the most work and silly things like that but they made it quite uncomfortable. We were all determined to keep the Centre going and to keep our differences away from the men, we felt that we could work them out ourselves and that if the men saw our difficulties it might demoralize them.

By this time I was taking on a lot of the responsibility at the Centre, I was enjoying it but it worried me too. Knowing how many to cook for was still a problem and I was always worried that there wouldn't be enough or that there'd be too much and some would be wasted. I also worried that something would go wrong with the cooking and it wouldn't taste very good, or worse, that there was something in the cooking that would make people ill. I felt that responsibility quite heavily, our facilities weren't very good and although we tried always to be very hygienic, you could never be sure. We had heard stories about some groups accepting cans of food that had been blown, and although nothing had happened the dangers were always there.

I took the Treasurer's job very seriously too, our money was limited and it had taken the people who raised it lots of time and effort. I had the same problem with buying food as I had with cooking, I never knew quite how much to buy. I suppose I must have planned quite well, because we really didn't have any disasters, but I worried about it a lot. Every day after dinner, when I could relax because I knew that everybody had been fed and there were no problems with the food, I would sit down with my cash tin and my books and balance them. There were a lot of transactions from the tin each day. We paid people's expenses if they were going anywhere and needed money for petrol or anything else. Everyday there would be several people taking money for one thing or another. Sometimes if people had special hardship we would lend or give them the money to get them through. When cars broke down, if they were used by the Centre we would pay to have them repaired. There was always money needed for something. As well as that there was nearly always some money come in each day. Most of it would arrive through the mail in cheques, but often people were given money at meetings they'd been to the night before and they'd nearly always give me the money up at the Centre. Every day it was an enormous relief to find that the cash tin balanced. Once that was over I felt I could relax for the day.

Although that wasn't really true because as soon as I'd balanced the tin, I had to start preparing for the next day's dinner.

I started taking a lot of the meat home with me and cooking it there. It was easier than trying to do everything at the Centre the next day. Nearly every night I'd have my kitchen covered with meat, some cooked, some waiting to be cooked and some cooking. I usually didn't finished that cooking until eight or nine at night, by then I was wiped out and ready for bed.

But quite often there'd be a meeting or an outing that I'd somehow raise the energy to go to. Whenever visitors stayed overnight we always went out for a drink with them. It was a chance for everybody to get to talk to them in peace away from the bustle of the Centre. Mostly when I did go out I found a second wind but bed was always very welcome when I got home.

In early October there was talk that the pit Deputies would go out on strike. They had been claiming money from the Coal Board for crossing picket lines, but they hadn't had any success. They made statements to the press that they agreed with the NUM's position on pit closures. New Government legislation required all unions taking strike action to hold a ballot of their members and the pit Deputies did so.

Over eighty percent of the Deputies voted to strike. When they announced the result of their ballot they said that the decision about the strike would be referred to their branches. None of us trusted that they would strike. They had been on strike before and their relations with NUM members in the pits was not good. They were the overseers and most of the time they acted on behalf of management. However the branches overwhelmingly voted to go ahead with the strike, it was announced that they would come out on Thursday 25th October.

Still nobody believed that they would actually come out. Daily the media talked about the end of the strike. If the pit Deputies did come out it would close all the pits, no-one is allowed to work without a Deputy. So although we distrusted this alliance they seemed to be offering us, we couldn't help but hope. It seemed that if they did come out the strike might be over and we might have our victory.

But for seven months all hopes had been disappointed and so we had learnt not to hope. Throughout that fortnight of waiting to see if the Deputies did stand up to their word, tension began to mount. At first we all tried to ignore the situation and continue as we always had done. We all felt quite strongly that we'd been out on our own all this time and that we'd have to finish it on our own as well. But as the days went by and the Deputies were still adamant that they would strike, we started to let ourselves hope, against our own better judgement. No-one dared hope out loud, but inwardly I know I was hoping and could tell everyone else was too because there was a sort of excitement in the air, that hadn't been there since the strike began. On the Tuesday before the proposed Deputies' strike it was as if that excitement suddenly burst out. As a few of us were clearing up the Centre before going home, a water fight broke out. We were all running all around the hall like children waiting for Christmas, screaming with laughter and chucking water all over each other. I got absolutely drenched, I was wet right through, when I got home I had to change everything, right down to my underwear. Although no-one actually talked about the end of the strike there were a lot of conversations about how the end would actually happen, how the men would go back, what would happen to the scabs and so on.

On Tuesday the Deputies met with the NCB, they spent all day talking, but there was no news about what was happening in the talks. We all kept a close eye on the News all day, someone had brought a small portable black and white telly up to the Centre early in the strike and that day it was on all day. Early that evening, there was a news flash that the talks had broken up and the TUC had been asked to get involved. It seemed then that a deal was bound to take place because the NUM had not been invited into the talks. Within another hour it was announced that the NUM was taking part in the talks and again despite ourselves, we hoped.

On Wednesday morning there was still not much news about the talks, but after dinner it was announced that the Deputies had settled with the NCB. We waited for news of the NUM's decision. Arthur Scargill appeared on the television and said, 'We are in exactly the same position we have been in for seven months'. The Deputies had agreed that the decision about whether a pit should be closed or not should be left to an independent tribunal.

No-one said anything particularly, we all felt flat, we got on with what we were doing. The next day a group of the men appeared in the Centre with a pack of cards and sat all day playing cards.

Over the next few days, a despondency started to creep into the Centre, people actually started talking about going back to work. The tensions between the women re-emerged and were worse than ever. Everybody was very depressed, there seemed no end in sight and we started to wonder if we would be on strike for ever. Those that were talking about going back to work were saying that there was no point going on, they still believed in the issues and in the union, but they could see no point in keeping on and putting themselves through so much hardship when they couldn't see an end in sight. There were a lot of arguments between the men about the situation which just made everything worse and more depressing. The NCB announced that it was offering a special bonus to any miner who returned to work before Christmas. Some of those who had been talking about going back argued even more strongly now that it was the only sensible thing to do. It was decided that these discussions were just demoralising everyone and those who were talking about returning to work couldn't come up to the Centre any more. Some of them had said that they were definitely going back.

On the following Monday eight men returned to work. It was really horrible, we all stood on the picket line and watched men who'd been with us all this time crossing our picket line and going into the pit. The official pickets talked to them but they nearly all said that they had had enough and were looking after themselves from now on. Some of those men had been in the Youth Club occupation with us, some had been arrested, they'd all been to rallies and demonstrations with us. They'd all stood on the picket line they were now crossing, most of them every day, they'd all been active members of the Centre. It was only a couple of weeks since they'd all voted to stay out until Ken was re-instated. We couldn't understand them, they hadn't spent the last eight months burying their heads beneath the sand like the scabs who'd been working since the beginning. They had seen with their own eyes what had happened, they had seen the police violence, witnessed the bias of the media, seen the comradeship of the strikers and the strength of unity. They couldn't rationalise their decisions to return to work, they had to admit it was selfishness. They wanted the bonuses so they could have a good Christmas.

As they walked past the picketers, they looked down at the ground, their pride was gone. Someone said a couple of days later, 'You can't believe it, as soon as they start to scab they start to look like scabs.' It was true, scabs all had a certain look about them, they looked sour and miserable, I think deep down they all knew they were doing the wrong thing, but the picketers always looked proud and held their heads high wherever they went.

·10·
DOREEN WINTER

Among those who had returned to work was Pip's best friend, Howard. Pip and Howard had worked side by side for fifteen years, electricians and fitters always work in pairs and Pip and Howard had been a pair all that time. They had worked really well together as a team, and through that, the two families had become very close. For the six years I'd been living in Blidworth, Howard and his wife Marilyn had been our best friends. The two families had been on holidays nearly every year together. When we first moved into this house and I was seven months pregnant Howard and Marilyn came and helped us scrub the house out and move in. Whenever they had problems with their marriage, they would come and talk to Pip and I and we would do the same. Pip and Howard went on strike together and all through the early months we discussed things with each other. Howard taught me quite a lot about socialism and communism.

But Marilyn had never been in favour of the strike. They had moved to a big posh house in Rainworth a couple of years before and so they had a lot of debt. Howard had been working lots of overtime to pay for everything, their house had everything you could want in it and they had a car each. So since the strike started Howard had a lot of financial pressures and things between him and Marilyn got really bad because she wanted him to go back to work.

Six weeks before the Deputies talked about coming out Howard had said he was thinking of going back. We had a number of long talks about things and he decided to give it another month. Then he decided to wait and see what the Deputies would do.

On the first Monday that the men went back there was a National Delegates Conference in Sheffield. Pip and a lot of the other men went up to lobby it Everybody wanted to make it clear that we were still solidly behind the strike. Howard went in on the afternoon shift.

The next day Pip went up and talked to Howard as he was going in. They talked until Howard was nearly crying, but he still went in. Pip was heart broken, he came back to the Centre looking sick, and he couldn't talk about it he was so hurt. That night Pip was as miserable as a dog. He knew this would mean an end to his long and close friendship with Howard and he hated the thought of ever going back to work and having to work with someone else. Pip and Howard had worked together for so long and made a team that everybody in the pit respected and admired. I said I was going up the next day to try to talk to him, Pip didn't want me to go. He thought I'd just lose my temper, but I was determined to go.

When I got up to the Centre that morning I told Dennis Browne that I wanted to stand with the Official Pickets and talk to Howard. He was all in favour of it, he said,

'It might do some good, Howard's a good lad, I can't understand what he's doing.'

'Pip doesn't want me to go. He thinks I'll just lose my temper, but I won't, I don't want to do that, I just want to talk to him and see for myself if I can change his mind.'

The last two days Howard had gone in one of the side gates, a gate they call the chicken run, he'd never gone in the chicken run before, it was as if he was trying to hide. It was pouring with rain and I stood at the chicken run with Dennis and the assistant picket manager, Pete Savage. There were three of us there and two cops and I thought the cops might send me away so I said to Pete,

'If they move one of us will you go?'

I even had it in my mind to say I was a cleaner at the pit if the coppers asked me if I was an NUM member. But because of the pouring rain, the coppers left that gate saying,

'You three will look after this gate won't you.'

So I stood at the gate to the chicken run in the pouring rain waiting for Howard to arrive. Marilyn dropped him off about two hundred yards down the road. He walked towards us, his head down. He was going to walk right past me but I said,

'Howard, you're not going to walk by me are you?'

He said, 'I've got nought to say.'

'Well, I have.' I said, 'What do you think you're doing?'

'I'm doing what I've got to do.'

'What, crossing picket line?'

'I've got no choice.'

'Course you've got a choice, you come back with me now, back into the Centre.'

All the time he looked down at the ground, He wouldn't look me in the face. I said,

'I've never ever stood here before in the pouring rain to talk to anybody, but I'm doing it this morning for you. I've never asked anybody to come back to Centre wi' me that had betrayed us, but I'm asking you, I'm not asking, I'm begging you, turn around and come back now to the Centre for your dinner and come to Sheffield with us to see Arthur Scargill.'

'I can't, I've got to go.'

'Have I got to call you a scabbin' bastard like I do them down there?'

'It looks like it.'

'Because that's what you are, your worse than them that's been going every shift.' He almost looked up at me but not quite, I continued. 'Do you realise what you're doing to me and Pip let alone your own Dad? Do you know what your Dad says to me last week?' 'He says he's got two lads, one's a scab and ones on strike and he's really proud of the one that's on strike. Did you know that your Dad said that?'

'No.' He could hardly open his mouth to say anything.

'Well I can assure you he did, you're breaking his heart and you're breaking my heart and you're breaking Pip's heart, your're betraying everybody.'

He didn't say anything, he just stood there looking ill.

I said, 'All I've done through this Strike and you've sat and talked to me about it in beginning and now you're betraying everything that I've done.'

'I can't help it, I've got to go and sort myself out.'

'You don't have to sort yourself out down there, you can come and sort yourself out with us.'

He looked up at me and said, 'I've got no mates down there, they're bastards the lot on 'em.'

'Howard, you've got no mates up here, not now, but you can have. Do you know what this has done to Pip, he's been your best mate for years and years, do you know what you've done to him?'

He looked as if he was just about to cry. Then he looked down at the ground again and said, 'Yeah, I know what I've done to him. I seen him, other day on here.'

'Yes, but you've not seen him in house Howard, you don't know what you've done to him. Neither of us had any sleep last night we're both so upset. What are you going to do when we've won and Pip comes back to work, he'll not be your mate you know, you've got to work on your own from now on.'

'That's up to him.'

'It's not up to him, it's up to you.'

'I can't help it, it's not him that has to live with this, it's me who's got to live with it.'

'Yeah, if you keep walking, you've got to live with it, but you're betraying everything. Where's your principles? What about Ken Petney, he's got three kids, but he can't go back.'

He just said, 'That's not my fault.'

'Howard, where's your principles? What's the first rule of a trade unionist? You're breaking it, you've been a trade unionist all your working life and now you're breaking the first rule.'

He just shrugged his shoulders, 'Doreen,' he said, 'I can't do anything about it, I've got to go. Do you think it isn't making me badly?'

'I know it's making you badly, but don't do it. What's two months mortgage, we're on the verge of winning, so what's two months mortgage compared to what we're gonna get? What are we gonna get next year, what are you gonna do when they close this pit? It's gonna be one of the first to go you know.'

'I'll have to bury my head, same as them scabbing bastards that's going down.'

'Howard, you're a scabbing bastard and I'm telling you straight, you go across here today and you're a scabbing bastard. I'm telling you that.'

He started to walk away, I said

'That's it then, Howard, I'm done.'

As we walked back to the Centre I started to cry. Dennis said, 'Don't let it upset you duck, you did best thing you could've done, you didn't lose your temper, you said what you wanted and he's got to think about everything you said. He's had more than anybody else's had, he's had an invitation back to the Centre.'

All that day I couldn't get it off my mind, I kept thinking and re-thinking the conversation and wondering what I could have said that might have changed his mind. But in the end I knew I'd done all I could. I hadn't lost my temper and Howard knows as well as anyone what a temper I can have. Once, when we were laying carpet I went for him with a Stanley knife. We had an argument about something and he made me so mad that I just went for him with the knife I had in my hand and he flew out of the house. I knew that he must know how deep my hurt went because I didn't lose my temper, and I knew Howard well enough to know that he'd take what I'd said to heart and think about it. I kept remembering all the things we'd talked about since the strike started and about the night at the Youth Club we'd all spent in the kitchen. Howard was there then and there was this big joke because Howard and I knew each other so well that we'd snuggled up to keep each other warm just like a brother and sister.

When I got back to the Centre, Mick Taylor came in with his wife who'd never been in before. Mick was a close friend of Howard's and Pip's and I knew that Howard had visited him both nights after he'd finished his shift. Mick had said that Howard was sick with worry about what he'd done and could hardly bear to live with himself. But Mick had also been talking about going back to work. Mick was a great joker and at first it was hard to know whether he was joking or not, he kept saying,

'I'll be back by Christmas an' all, I can't manage any more, the kids need a good Christmas.'

'He'd said it so many times that in the end I'd said to him,

'If you don't stop talking like that Mick you can get out of here and not come back, we're not slaving to look after anyone who's going back to work.'

The approach of Christmas was making it hard for us all, none of us wanted to see our kids go without so it was a pressure we were all feeling. We had all talked to our kids, telling them that they would have to wait for their presents until their Dads went back to work. They'd all understood, but it was still hard for us to feel that we were making them go without. It had seemed for a while that we would be looking toward a very bleak Christmas, but suddenly there seemed to be lots of talk from supporters of the strike saying that everybody would make sure that the Miners had a good Christmas. I'd already been given quite a lot of things for the kids from supporters and we'd been gradually buying bits and pieces for Christmas Day. I'd been approached by two of the organisations that supported us asking if they could buy Christmas presents for all the kids, and asking what sort of food we wanted for our Christmas dinner. We'd decided to have Christmas dinner all together in the Centre and then to have a party there on Boxing Day as well. We all felt that whatever it was going to be like we'd share it with each other. And we were just beginning to think that perhaps Christmas wouldn't be so bad after all. We were all fairly sure that we'd still be on strike, there was no longer any hope of a quick settlement.

When Mick and his wife walked into the Centre, I knew something was up, I looked at Mick's wife, Elaine who I'd met a few times and said,
'Hey up duck, what you doing here?'
She looked really miserable and bit shy, I said,
'What's the matter, duck?'
She said, 'Oh, I'm just a bit low.'
'Well, what's making you low? ' I said and she started to cry.
Mick said, 'She's been nagging me to go back to work.'
I took Elaine over to a quiet corner where we could be on our own. She had never been up to the Centre before. They lived at Rainworth and she had three kids the youngest was only about two so I knew it was probably hard for her to get in. I'd seen her at a couple of rallies and demonstrations with the little 'un in a push chair so I knew she was behind the strike. I said,
'What's up, are you worried about Christmas?'
She said, 'Oh it's partly that and also I'm sick of being on my own. Mick's always up here and I see less of him than I do when he's working. I just get very depressed about everything stuck at home on my own and I can't see any end to it all. Debts are mounting up and I'm just not coping any more.'
'There's no need to feel like that you know. Why don't you come

up here and help us, we always need more people to help, there's so much to do all the time?'

'I can't get here.'

'You could come in with Mick in the mornings. Lots of women bring their little 'uns up, they all have a great time, you'd find it much easier than sitting at home on your own. You don't want to see Mick like Howard do you? And that's what he'd be like if he went back, could you live with him seeing him like that?'

'No, I couldn't, I don't really want to make him go back that's why I'm so low.'

'How about you come up to my house with me now? I've got to make a couple of phone calls and I can show you what we've started to get ready for Christmas, it's beginning to look as if Christmas won't be that bad after all.'

Back at my house, I showed her all the things we'd got for Christmas and talked about all the support we were getting. I rang Doug Shaw and he told me that they were raising money to buy chickens, hams and turkeys for our Christmas dinner and he asked me what vegetables we wanted. He said,

'We won't see you go without for Christmas. As a matter of fact, I think I'll come and have my Christmas dinner with you if you'll invite me.'

I told him that of course he would be welcome and then I told Elaine what he had said. She was quite surprised, the thing is no-one knew what support we were getting unless they were involved. I think that a lot of the men who just went picketing and then ate their dinners didn't really understand what was going on. As far as they were concerned meals just miraculously turned up on the table every day. They didn't understand that those dinners were there because thousands of people outside of the mining communities were one hundred percent behind us and wanted to see us win. It made a difference to know that we weren't on our own and that other people were depending on our victory and prepared to back it with their money.

That night a lot of us were going to Sheffield to a rally which had been organised by the NUM Executive as a morale booster after the let-down we'd had by the Deputies. I knew Mick was coming and so I asked Elaine if she'd like to come too and also if she'd come up to the Centre the next day to help with the cooking.

She said, 'Yeah, I feel guilty now, I had no idea there was this much involved, I'd be pleased to help.'

I knew it would be much better for Elaine to be up at the Centre helping us, even if she was just sitting with us making Christmas decorations. It would be better than sitting at home on her own letting all the problems get on top of her. I also asked her if she'd like to come up to London with me the next time I had a meeting there, she said she would.

When we got back to the Centre we said to Mick,

'Elaine's coming to Sheffield with us tonight.'

He said, 'Oh good, we'd better organise a baby-sitter then.'

But Pip said to him, 'Coach leaves here at 4.00, you'll never get a babysitter for that time.'

I said, 'Right then Mick, how about you stay home for change and babysit so Elaine can come. It'll do her more good than it will you at the moment.'

Apparently her and Mick had had a fight that morning and he'd said to her, 'Right get your coat on, you're coming up to the Centre with me and see how hard those women are working for yourself.'

It was the best thing he could have done. It's a shame more of the men didn't encourage their wives to come up. Elaine came up to the centre after that every day and became one of us. It was better for Mick too, it meant that he wasn't divided about whether to spend his time at the Centre or at home with Elaine.

At about four o'clock we all started gathering at the Centre waiting for the coach to arrive to take us to Sheffield. The NUM had organised five rallies each night of that week in different parts of the country, and had arranged coaches to bring everybody in from the coalfields around the centres. At about half past a monstrous double decker coach arrived and as we all piled in, there were lots of jokes about how 'posh' it was and 'riding in style.'

There weren't a lot women going and four of us claimed the upstairs back seat, the others sat with their husbands. As the coach moved off it started to sway and when we looked down we felt very insecure, so far above the ground.

Betty started to talk about the coach overturning,

'They do you know, I've heard they do quite easily when they build up a bit of speed. Ooh Doreen, I don't like this.'

'Shurrup Betty, ' I said, I was feeling as nervous as she was and didn't want to be reminded of it.

'It's bad enough, just try and forget it.'

We laughed, laughter filled the coach, everybody was in high spirits. We'd been so low for so long and we were all looking forward to being part of the night's events. Before any of us expected it we were in Sheffield. It was only six o'clock and the meeting wasn't due to start until seven thirty. The hall wasn't even open yet and so we decided to go and have a drink, one of the men asked one of the hundreds of coppers that were standing around where there was a pub.

'Closed them tonight 'cause they knew you lot was coming to cause trouble.'

But he was lying, we found a pub but as soon as we'd ordered our drinks we all became impatient to get back to the steps of the hall to make sure we all got a good seat. They were expecting thousands and only the first five thousand could fit into the main hall. Everybody else was going to be seated in other halls and have the meeting relayed to them on closed circuit videos. So we rushed our drinks and hurried back to the steps of County Hall.

It's a great big grey stone circular building and just standing on the steps was quite awe inspiring. On top of that it was very exciting to see coach after coach pull up and striking miners pouring out of each one. Some of the groups brought their banners with them. We had brought the Notts. banner and at first unrolled it and stood with it by the wall, but soon it was obvious that we would get crushed so we rolled it back up again and carried it with us. People were crowding in but the atmosphere was very bright, occasionally there were bursts of song and everybody talked to everybody else, we all knew we were there for the same reason so it was easy to be friendly. As we stood there, at the top of the steps, looking behind us at thousands of people all in the same situation we were in it suddenly struck me that we were the masses they always talk about. I swelled with a feeling of pride and in that moment saw more clearly than I'd ever seen before the strength of the masses. I said to the woman beside me,

'We're the masses aren't we?'

'Yes, I suppose we are,' she said.

When they finally opened the doors, they didn't open the central door that we were all expecting to open. They opened side doors instead and so there was a great push from behind us. Everybody was scared that they would miss out on seats in the main hall. The pushing crowd would've been quite frightening but the solidarity we all felt was reassuring and we trusted each other.

We had Willie with us, he was a miner from Blidworth who'd been off on club for some time because he had tumours behind his eyes and was nearly blind. He was solidly behind the strike, he picketed every day and after dinner always cleared up the plates and took them out to the kitchen for the men washing the pots. We were nervous about him in the crowd because of his poor sight so the four of us surrounded him and all grabbed hold of him to make sure he didn't get lost in the crowd. As we were all pushing to get into the hall everybody was singing 'Here we Go' and the noise was so loud that you felt as if you couldn't hear anything. It was a bit disturbing, it was like being blind, we were just going forward because we were being pushed from behind.

Inside the hall the atmosphere was strong. There was lots of noise, people were taking banners up onto the stage and as each banner was displayed there was a great roar from the crowd.

Betty and I took the Notts. banner up which was greeted by cheers and thunderous clapping, we felt very proud. The cheering continued and there were more outbursts of singing and chanting, the sound echoed off the walls and sounded fantastic. As the people on the stage started to come on the cheering got louder and I began to think that we'd never hear anything at all but as soon as the Chairman got up to start speaking he only had to raise his hand a couple of times before everybody quietened down to hear.

He started off by welcoming everybody, he said,

'Could I just open the meeting by welcoming the lads from Nottingham.' There was a great cheer and I sang out, 'And women.'

When the cheering died down he continued,

'And the lads from Lancashire.' There was more chanting. He went on and welcomed everybody from Yorkshire and then from Derbyshire and there were cheers everytime and everytime I sang out,

'And women.'

There were a number of speakers and we all listened carefully to what they had to say. A French trade unionist came and spoke in French which was translated for us. It seemed strange listening to someone talk to us in England in another language and some laughed, but when we heard the translation it brought tears to our eyes. He talked about the situation of the French miners and the struggles of workers all over the world and said,

'To us in France the British Miners are the flagbearers of the struggle against policies of closures and deindustrialisation which have been decided by the Common Market Authorities and which are accepted and carried out by the Governments of both France and Britain.'

He finished up saying that the French unions would do everything to help us to victory and ended up saying, 'And your victory will be ours too.'

His speech was followed by a round of 'Here We Go' and everybody cheered.

The Chairman introduced Betty Heathfield as the next speaker, she said that the women in this strike had taken the Union into new dimensions. Betty was the first woman ever to speak from an NUM platform and the importance and significance of that was recognised by everyone.

She said, 'Like thousands of women in the mining communities all over the country my lifestyle has changed a bit in the last eight and a half months. Like them, I've been in food centres, on demonstrations, speaking at meetings on a scale that none of us ever thought previously we would be able to do. But of all the meetings I've been at, this meeting is the most important meeting in my whole life.' Everybody cheered.

'I'll tell you why, because I consider it a great honour to be on this platform tonight, speaking on behalf of the Women Against Pit Closures movement and the Women's Action Groups. Eat your heart out Maggie Thatcher.' Everybody laughed and cheered and Ken, who was sitting just behind me shouted out, 'She hasn't got one.'

Betty continued and talked about the work of the women in the strike and the example that we had set to women everywhere. She went on to talk about the police activities she said, 'We are also very disturbed at the way our communities have been criminalised in a most brutal way. Our men and women have been arrested on any pretext, there is no joy from the judicial system, which is weighted heavily against miners and their families in this country now. The increasing number of injuries and massive police presence in all villages and their intimidation and harassment of our families should make all lovers of freedom and democracy shudder with horror. But we women are most concerned at how Mrs. Thatcher and her Tory Government has used the hunger and the deprivation of our children to further her political fight against the trade unions and labour movement. And in particular the NUM, whose destruction they need as a first step to this end. The fifteen pound removal from every family's DHSS Benefit's a total of fifty million pounds now, that this Government owes us, that has been stolen from us....This money we paid in taxes to the Government's Treasury it's our money and they've stolen it from us.'

She talked about the importance of solidarity and the scabs who would never know the strength that came from fighting for our union.

She said, 'They might be able to break the picket lines with their buses, but they'll never be able to take away the shame of the word scab.'

Then she asked for trade unionists everywhere to support us, 'We're asking all the trade unionists and all the Labour Party activists and everybody that's on our side, to give us now some more tangible evidence of their solidarity. We are saying to you, we don't care all that much about the half-hearted statements from some trade union leaders and some political leaders. What we're bothered about is the members, the members to come on our picket lines with us. We're saying to you, it doesn't take much to come on our picket lines with us to show the lads that you're there......I want to make a special appeal tonight to the women, to come on the picket lines with us. Just a few women have a very electrifying effect on a picket line I can assure you. Thatcher doesn't like us there, the Government don't like us there and the police don't like us there because they don't know what to do about women who sing and chant slogans and sound very happy and very positive, they just don't know what to do with us.'

I thought about that, in some ways I didn't agree with her, I'd seen women treated just like men on picket lines, but at other times I had seen the police quite put out by women being there. I remembered one night in particular when quite a few of us were on the picket line and it was the first really cold and wet night we'd been there. To keep warm we started singing and dancing along the pavement, not even political songs, we were singing, 'Singing in the Rain' and linking arms and dancing. The police brought their reserves out from the back of the pit to surround us, our frivolity made them nervous.

There were a few more speakers, among them someone from the TUC and a Labour politician. Neither of them had much to say and neither of them got a very good reception. Neil Kinnock, the Labour leader had been invited to attend this series of rallies but he'd declined the invitation. We were all disgusted with him, he wasn't prepared to back us, he wanted to stay sitting on the fence, so we weren't very impressed by the speaker who came in his place and lots of people shouted out, 'Where's Kinnock?'

Then finally it was Arthur's turn to speak, it's what we were all waiting for. We had come to respect the man so much we all looked to him for inspiration to keep going when things were hard. As he got up to speak everybody started singing the song we had dedicated to him.
'Arthur Scargill, Arthur Scargill,
We'll support you ever more.'
Everybody sang it over and over again and he had to wave his hands for quiet before he could start speaking.
'This industrial dispute is now the longest in the history of British trade unionism. And over the past two or three days we have seen in the media time and time again suggestions that miners are drifting back to work. It must be right it's in the Daily Express. "The National Coalboard said today that 53,000 miners are back at work," that's dated the 6th November. On the 25th June, that's before November, National Coalboard said, "Miners drift back to work, 60,000 have now gone back to work." If there's anyone in this union thinks for one second that the media are going to paint a picture in support of miners who are on strike fighting for their jobs, they're living in proverbial cloud cuckoo land. We won't get support from

this bunch of hyenas in Fleet Street. I say to my colleagues in the NUJ, who send us cheques and messages of support, 'Stop easing your consciences with a few quid, stop writing your filth about these brave lads.' The cheers were so loud that I couldn't hear the next few sentences he said, but then he started to talk about the Government and the Coal Board, he said that we were advised by the Government to negotiate, 'Have you ever tried to negotiate with a bloke in a plastic bag?' Everybody laughed. He talked about the pit closure programme, that was supposed to bring supply into balance with demand, that he said, meant the closure of twenty pits, the loss of twenty thousand jobs and the destruction of mining communities, of a culture and a way of life. 'But that,' he continued, 'is not the end of the story, it's the beginning, because this Government's policy and Ian McGregor's tactics are to close seventy pits and destroy seventy thousand jobs and I say to those that are scabbing in Notts., they're your jobs that will go as well as ours.'

'Our demands in this dispute are not very much, in fact our demands are far too modest, the only people demanding in this dispute are the Coal Board, they're demanding that this union become signatories to a closure programme. They're demanding that we decimate the north-east coalfield from seventeen pits to four. They're asking us to become signatories to an agreement that wipes out sixty percent of the Scottish coalfield, they're asking us to become partners to an agreement to destroy seventy percent of the South Wales coalfield and twenty-five percent of the Yorkshire coalfield and fifty percent of the Derbyshire coalfield. I think I'm speaking on behalf of every miner at this magnificent rally when I say, not only will we not become partners to an agreement of that kind but we will not sign away one pit or one single job.'

He went on to say that the NUM wanted an agreement to keep the pits open, to keep Cortonwood open, not for three or six months, but to keep it open until the point of exhaustion, in line with the Plan For Coal.

He talked about McGregor's history, first at British Leyland where he dismissed the senior shop steward for writing a pamphlet on the survival of British Leyland.

'This movement, ' he said, 'to its eternal shame, stood by and saw Derek Robinson dismissed from his position.' Then he talked about

McGregor's attacks on the British Steel Industry. Then he returned to our dispute and said,

'How many times have we heard the saying, "Young people today are not like their forefathers, they've got too much invested in HP or in mortgage repayments." We're sick and tired of listening to the Jeremiahs of this movement who said young people will never fight like the older generations who built the movements. Well I say, without fear of contradiction that if those who built our trade union could look on this scene today, they'd salute our young miners and their families. Not only throughout Britain, but throughout Europe and the world, for the first time in an industrial dispute we've seen women take their place, not in the soup kitchens, not merely giving moral support but in those magnificent Women's Support Groups standing shoulder to shoulder fighting for their jobs, their communities.

'I wonder if Thatcher understands, she can probably sequestrate our funds, she can probably freeze the operations on a day by day basis of our organisations, but she can't sequestrate our minds, she can't imprison our principles and she cannot freeze our will to win.

'I want to see the same commitment to this union from rank and file trade unionists in power and steel and in transport that we've given to them when they've been involved. I'm calling on all trade unionists to examine their consciences, I want to ask our brothers and sisters in the power industry and in steel, how much longer can you stand to one side and see this union battered by a galaxy of the Tories, the Coalboard, CBI and the Institute of Directors. Come and take industrial action now and stop accepting scab coal, scab oil and scab iron ore, practice what you preach and stop....' The rest of the sentence was drowned out by clapping and cheering.

The speech came to a close, Arthur said, 'I've never felt as proud or as privileged to be in a leadership position as I do here today. Members of this union, their wives and families, have displayed a solidarity, have displayed a commitment that has inspired not only workers in Britain but inspired workers throughout the entire world. During the course of this struggle, when once again we've discovered ourselves, we are beginning to understand the meaning of real trade unionism. Never again will this union be the same because of what we've learned and what we've discovered during the course of this eight month strike. When people ask why we should go on, we say to them that Davy Jones and Joe Bean were killed fighting for this union. You are fighting to preserve your right to work.

'You're determined as a result of this action to convey to this Government and to employers that we too have rights. When we talk about investment, we're not talking about financial investment in an industry, we are talking as men and women who have the greatest investment of all, the investment of our very lives in this industry, and that is something on which none of us can ever compromise. Time and time again the leaders of this union have asked the members to respond, never in our wildest dreams have we expected such a magnificent response and time and time again members of the union movement have demanded leadership. Well I say to you without fear of contradiction that you have not got in the leadership on this plat-form three leaders or members of the NEC who will finish up in the House of Lords, but what you have got are leaders determined to take this union, side by side with you to the most fantastic historic victory. Miners I salute you, you're magnificent.'

There were more rounds of the song we all sang in his honour and then the meeting broke up quite quickly. We all piled into our coach which took us home. I was very very tired, it had been a very big day.

But things were becoming harder and more difficult at home. The weather was getting colder and our lack of fuel became a major problem. Our houses were all heated by coal and our allowance had been stopped because of the strike. It was very hard to buy coal and very expensive. We tried to organise any sort of fuel we could. Some supporters helped with money for coal but it was never enough to last very long, it was so expensive. A lot of people borrowed gas heaters from friends and relatives because the cost of gas was less than coal. Everything seemed that much harder when we had to go home each night to a cold house.

The divisions between the women had become quite strong. There was a lot of ill-feeling and four of the women resigned from the committee. I felt that they had been the cause of the trouble and so I wasn't really upset when they put their resignations in. They had upset a lot of the women and some of the men and their presence at the Centre was creating a tension we could well do without. Then I found out in a discussion with one of the men that two of the husbands of these four women were talking about going back to work. Some of the men thought that we shouldn't accept the resignations because that would probably ensure that these men returned to work. I now felt sure that it was because of their failing support for the strike that the women had become so destructive in the Centre. The issue was widely discussed, but all the women felt that the Centre ran much more smoothly without these women and so we decided to accept the resignations. At the meeting that Sunday morning, it was announced that the resignations had been received and no-one made any comment.

After that there was still a lot of nastiness. The women who had resigned would come up to the Centre and sit to one side sniggering to each other. They came up one day and took all of their equipment which suddenly meant that we were short of pressure cookers and other vital cooking implements. But we managed quite well really, everybody was happy to get on with their work.

The two men returned to work the following week and although I hated to see anyone go back to work, I had to admit that their return was a relief, it made the issue much clearer. I hated the feeling that we were turning our back on any of our own, even if they had made life very difficult for us. Now it was quite straightforward and everything that happened before seemed to make sense.

The return to work stopped and we became a solid group again. More and more of our time was spent getting ready for Christmas. We were receiving massive support. Presents for the kids were pouring in. There were ninety kids altogether, sorting through the presents and working out what would be best for which kids became a mighty task in itself. One of the women offered her father's house for storing them and they took up nearly two rooms. We sorted through them all, making sure that each kid got what they would want and each kid got a fair share. We had ninety red plastic garbage bags, each with a child's name on it.

The other side of the preparations, the preparing of the food, was also a massive task. I didn't have that much to do with it, I was busy with the presents, but Pauline and some of the others had all the food preparation under control. Every woman will know how much work it takes to prepare for Christmas. We prepared for a monster Christmas and the work involved was monstrous. But we did it willingly and happily, we were so surprised that the support had been so generous to us. We'd expected the worst Christmas of our lives and now it seemed we were going to have one of the best.

A lot of the men were spending Christmas Day with their families and so it was a chance for everybody to get together. The women decided to have a party of their own and that was prepared for. Then the kids, hearing all these arrangements, made a complaint through their committee that the men were having a party and the women were having a party so they felt left out. We decided to hold a kids party too. The pit always held a children's Christmas party and this year none of us had been invited so we held our own. It was fantastic, the kids had a ball. Father Christmas came and brought them all a little present.

Pauline was in charge of the Christmas menu, the ordering and preparing of the food. It was an enormous job to take on but Pauline was enjoying it. A week before Christmas, she bent down to pick something up and her back went. She couldn't move. The doctor came and told her that she may be laid up for some time. She would just have to wait and see. Pauline was very upset, she felt that she had done so much for Christmas and now when it was getting close she would miss out on the celebrations themselves and on the final organising.

The next day Alan came up to the Centre saying that Pauline was no better. At dinnertime he went back home to see how she was and then returned a half hour later with Pauline. She could hardly walk, but she said she couldn't stay away from the Centre. When Alan had got home, he'd found her crying and she'd pleaded with him to bring her back up to the Centre. We were all very worried about her, we were nervous that she'd do more damage to herself. All that afternoon people were telling her to be careful and that she should really be at home lying down. As it was she was sitting in one of the straight backed chairs with a sleeping bag around herself to keep warm. At one stage she had to go to the toilet which was right up the other end of the hall from where she was sitting, it took two men to help her get there and as she walked back her face was white from the pain. We were all very worried about her. Pauline had become a vital part of the Centre, she had shown outstanding organising capabilities, the work she was doing was equivalent to running a full scale restaurant and she did the bulk of the cooking as well. On top of that her serene personality often had a calming effect on others' very frazzled nerves. Everyone that came into that Centre admired and respected Pauline and the enormous workload she had taken on.

The next day to our great surprise Pauline was back at the Centre as right as rain. The night before she'd got Alan to shift her back into place, she'd just laid on the floor and told him where to push and where to pull. Her courage left us all open mouthed. But we were all glad that she was back with us, it would have been tragic if she had missed out on the Christmas festivities.

Christmas Day itself was fantastic, we hadn't been able to find out exactly how many were coming, in the end there were just over a hundred of us. Christmas dinner was as elaborate as any we've ever had, we went without nothing. Supporters had bought us food, drinks, Christmas crackers and cigarettes as well as all the presents. Even the women had been remembered, one of our support groups had sent presents for all the women, we carefully wrapped them all the day before. As we were doing that I realised that the only people not receiving presents were the men, so I checked with Pauline to see if we had enough money and suggested to the other women that we buy presents for the men out of the kitty. They all agreed so I sent two of the kids' down the street to buy sixty pairs of men's socks and then the kids all wrapped them.

On Christmas Day the Christmas tree was surrounded with all the presents, ninety red bags all full to the brim for the kids and presents for all the men and women as well. It was quite a sight. At four o'clock I asked the kids if they wanted to see Father Christmas.

'Yes,' they all chanted.

'Well then, you sing jingle bells and we'll see what happens.'

Without any hesitation at all the kids all sang at the top of their voices.

> 'Jingle bells, jingle bells,
> Jingle all the way, I'd rather be a picket
> Than a scab on Christmas day.'

We'd all learnt those words some time before and sang the song regularly at the picket line. The kids seemed to have forgotten that the original song had different words. Father Christmas arrived, he spent two hours giving out the presents to everyone. Each name was called out one by one and each kid came up and sat on Father Christmas's knee and he had something to say to all of them. To see the look on the kids faces as they received their bags made all the hard work worthwhile. They had all been told by their parents that Christmas would be a dull affair and that they shouldn't expect any presents and now there were more presents than any of them could ever have dreamed of. Most of the parents had managed to save a little to buy something for their own kids, so this was on top of that. They were ecstatic. Then it was the women's turn. There were enough presents to make sure that every woman in the room got one. When Father Christmas started to call out the names of the men, they were ever so surprised. None of them had any idea that they would be getting anything, we'd kept it a well guarded secret. They were all delighted and there were lots of jokes about sitting on Santa's knee as each of them came up to get their presents.

The celebrations continued until the New Year. Every day someone would arrive to visit us and usually bring something to drink. We had been given lots of wine and beer and a few bottles of spirits, it was like one long party. But once the New Year was over we had to come back to reality and that came with a bang.

More men said they were going back to work, they couldn't see any end to it and they felt they couldn't go on any more. Every day now for two months the media had rammed down our throats how many had gone back. They'd done it all along but after the Deputies' sell-out they had intensified the campaign. Early in the strike it was clear that the NCB figures about the number who'd gone back to work were inaccurate. There was no evidence in the coalfields that there was any drift back at all. But now stories started coming through, first from Derbyshire and then from Yorkshire that the drift back was real.

Our spirits were low. Every week a few more seemed to go back to work. There was still a hard core of us and we were still as solid as ever, but our numbers were dwindling. Ken's court case was due to be heard at the end of February, Ken and Sue started to get very anxious about that, so did we all. If he was found guilty he would face a gaol sentence and would never stand any chance of getting his job back. In the meantime Sue had been sacked from her job. They'd told her that she was a militant and they didn't want her working there. She'd worked in that place for ten years, hard work for rotten pay and they sacked her just when her and Ken were dependent on her money. They were both very low and very anxious.

·11·
DOREEN
WHAT NEXT?

January was a very hard month for me. I had worked so hard to prepare Christmas and now that it was over I was exhausted. Karen's baby was due on the 29th December and as the days went by and nothing happened I started to worry about her. She was very fed up just sitting around and I was scared for her. I kept looking at her and thinking, poor little thing, she doesn't know what's in front of her. We were all wishing it was over and we could relax with our new little baby.

My son, Laggy, was due to appear in court on the 6th January, I was very worried about him. He'd had a fight with the father of Karen's baby which had resulted in him being charged with causing grievous bodily harm. Since the strike had begun our three lads had all been picked up by the police and charged several times. We felt the police were holding a vendetta against us. Only the first incident was directly related to the strike, that was when David was arrested outside the strike Centre. Since then, David had been arrested once again, and Laggy and Paul had both been picked up and charged twice. It was becoming a regular part of life to have the police come around with a summons for one of the lads. We began to feel persecuted and wondered if it would ever end. It was one more strain on top of everything else, constantly worrying if the lads were out late at night about what might be happening to them.

At one time Paul had been picked up in Mansfield with a group of his friends and they'd all been charged with being drunk and disorderly. A month or so later we had a letter from the police that Paul was also being charged with obstructing a police officer. Everybody agreed it was ridiculous, all the lads who'd been with Paul that night were adamant that Paul had been one of the quietest.

During the court case I sat and watched a young police woman stand up and tell some story about Paul dragging her across the road when she was trying to arrest his friends. All the lads had stunned looks on their faces, none of them could believe what they were hearing. I was used to it, I'd heard many of the cases resulting from the strike and I was used to there being no correlation at all between the evidence given by police and that given by the accused and their witnesses. To my surprise, Paul actually won his case, he was let off because they said that there wasn't enough evidence to convict him.

But I was very worried about Laggy, a charge of g.b.h. carried a gaol sentence. Although I knew that because he was so young and because it was his first conviction, the court might show leniency, I was terrified of him being sent down all the same. I couldn't bear the thought of him going to gaol. I knew that he'd been provoked and I also knew that he'd acted out of loyalty to Karen, I couldn't help admire him for what he'd done even though I don't believe in fighting. I wanted to be able to go to court with Laggy and I knew that if Karen started her pains I wouldn't be able to.

As a mother I felt torn in two. Both of my children were in situations where I felt I needed to support them. As it turned out, the two did coincide, Karen was in hospital when Laggy was in court. For two days I lived in a daze of worry and then it was all over. Karen had a healthy and very beautiful baby boy and Laggy was given a fifty quid fine. The magistrate, after hearing all the evidence, had been lenient because of the circumstances. I think it actually went quite well for Laggy that Karen was in hospital having the baby when his case came up, it sounded more dramatic than just saying that she was pregnant.

My relief was enormous, but all I wanted to do now was to stay home with Karen and help her with the baby. I decided to take a week off from the Centre and just spend it at home with Karen and the baby who she'd called Ricki. He was absolutely beautiful and I soon realised how wonderful being a Grandmother was. I could love Ricki in a different way to the way I had loved my own kids, it was like loving my own, but it was different, it didn't have quite the same responsibility.

I got very low with everything except Karen and Ricki and it got so that the only time I was happy was when I was with them. After a couple of weeks I started to get back into work at the Centre. It was fairly depressing though, we didn't seem to be getting anywhere. We'd been out now for nearly a year and the New Year didn't seem to bring any hope of resolution. Towards the end of January my attitude to the support we were getting started to change. We all started to feel as if we'd been left on our own to battle it out. Food and money was still coming in but we needed more, we needed industrial support and it wasn't coming from anywhere. I started to feel resentful towards everybody who was working. The miners had always helped other unions when they were in trouble and now when we needed help no-one was there. I started to hate getting letters of support, they had become meaningless, we had done all we could and now it was clear that we needed more than just letters of encouragement and money. It was clear this dispute was very political and that the Government was not going to back down. If all the people who wrote letters of support to us really wanted to see us win, they would have to take the same stand we had taken, the same risks we had taken.

The court case resulting from the Jolly Friar incident started on the twenty-fifth of February. It became our main concern. The charges were very serious and Ken and John faced prison sentences if they were found guilty. A lot of us were defence witnesses so we couldn't go to court, or talk very much to anybody about what was happening. It was very frustrating for those of us who couldn't go, but a lot of the men and some of the women from Cambridge were going into court each day to give Ken and John moral support. Each day they came back and seemed happy with the proceedings, but it looked as if it would go on for at least a couple of weeks. Ken had been waiting eight months for this court case and had no reason to hope that he would get justice. We hadn't been involved in a case yet that had been conducted in a fair way. But somehow Ken's case was so ridiculous and the prosecution case so fabricated that we did dare hope he'd get off.

At the end of the first week everybody seemed happy with the way things were going. For some reason which none of us understood, the prosecution had Alan down as one of their witnesses and so of course he was able to tell the story as it actually happened, and able to do so as a prosecution witness, which made their case look a bit silly.

Things up at the Centre had become very tense. Our numbers had dwindled and we were all at our wits' end. Suddenly there was another whole year in front of us with no hope for an early victory, we were beginning to wonder if it would ever end. We started to have arguments amongst ourselves about the possibility of winning. Little things were getting people down and so we decided to close the Centre after dinner each day and give everybody a food parcel to make their own teas at home.

There was quite a bit of talk about a return to work. On the Saturday after the first week of Ken's court case I had a discussion with Sue about it. I said that I thought there might be a return to work soon. Sue didn't agree with me, but I think she couldn't face it because she knew that Ken couldn't go back to work. There had been a lot of rumours about a return to work in Wales and we knew that the strike was now breaking in Yorkshire.

The next afternoon I was sitting at home watching television with Karen and Paul at about four-thirty when there was a news flash.
'The pit strike is over. Miners will return to work on Tuesday the 5th of March. Arthur Scargill will be holding a Press Conference a little later.'
I thought, 'Bloody hell.'
Karen was alarmed, she said 'Mum, what you going to do now, strike's over.'
'Oh shurrup it makes me feel sick.'
Pip was outside doing something to the car. I ran to the front door and shouted.
'Pip. It's just been on television, strike's over. Scargill's going to do a press conference later.' Pip said,
'Oh shit, I don't believe it, you're having me on.'
I closed the front door and ran around to Pauline's house. Alison from Cambridge was staying with us because of Ken's court case.

I said, 'Have you seen television?'

'No we've not got it on, why?'

'Strike's over, Scargill's coming on in a bit.'

She said, 'Ooh, bloody hell.'

'Yeah' I said, 'That's exactly what I feel.' Then I started going on about how the bloody trade union movement should have backed us, how this shouldn't have happened, and how the hell can we go back on these terms. I started yelling and going crazy. Pauline had been in another room, when she came in she looked at me, stunned.

Then Pip came in and started talking about the car.

I said, 'Did ya hear what I said to ya.'

'Yeah, but it's not true is it?'

'It is, it is Pip, Scargill's coming on television in a bit.'

'Ooh, I don't want to know then.'

And he went back outside again.

But it was true and we all had to believe it. We cried and cried, all of us, we felt sick and ill. It didn't seem possible that we had been through so much and for it to end like this. We were also very angry, angry with the rest of the labour movement and trade union movement for leaving us on our own and not coming out with industrial support. Ever since the TUC Conference we'd been asking other unions to support us with industrial action and they hadn't, we felt very let down. We even felt resentment about the money we'd received and the letters of support. I felt as if we had carried the whole British labour movement on our backs, they'd given us the money for food and they'd given us words of encouragement but they hadn't got off our back and fought for themselves. We needed other unions and union members to go out on strike with us, but they had let us down.

That night we all wanted to be together so we went up to the club, but it was terribly depressing. The men were all angry and at a loss to know what to do. At one stage Pip and Yorkie were going up to the toilet, they were both so mad that I was worried that they might start a fight, so I escorted them to the toilet and back.

The next day we all went up to the Centre as usual but it was terrible. Ken, John and everybody who could, had gone off to court. The rest of us hung around the Centre not able to think about anything except that the men were all going back to work and leaving Sue and Ken in the Centre on their own. Everywhere there were people in tears. We hardly managed to talk. We tried to comfort each other, but it was poor comfort. None of us had anything to give. We couldn't even share our misery because we were no longer all in the same boat. Ken was on trial and he had no job to go back to and although it wasn't our choice we felt we were deserting him.

All of the men had to go up to the pit individually to have an interview with the Manager to see what shift and what job they were going on. They all got a lecture, they were told to keep their feelings to themselves, not to cause any trouble and not to mention the strike. They were all rostered to work with groups of scabs, so they couldn't even go back and work together.

Sue sat at one of the tables in the back room watching as the men walked, one by one, up to the pit for their interviews. She hardly said anything at all. It was hard for me to talk to her. I didn't know what to say, I didn't feel like telling her what shift Pip was on and what had happened when he'd been up for his interview, but there seemed nothing else to talk about. We all knew how she was feeling and we were all suffering with her, but there was nothing we could do to help.

We'd heard that some of the pits in Kent, Wales and Yorkshire were going to march back in with their banners and we women wanted to make a banner and to march back with our men. Margaret Groves went home to start making one. It said 'BLIDWORTH ACTION GROUP, WE'RE PROUD OF OUR MEN.' But the men were so fed up that they didn't want us to do it. They felt so miserable at the thought of having to go into work with the scabs that they couldn't face any celebration of our twelve months' struggle.

Dennis Browne and Pete Savage had been to a union meeting in Ollerton and when they came back into the Centre they looked as sick as dogs. Dennis looked as if he'd been crying, he was really full-up. As he walked in a lot of the men said, 'We're not going back to work without Ken.'

Dennis said, 'You have to, we've been told to, we've stood by the union for twelve months, and we've got to stand by it now. We've got no choice anyway, if we don't go back we'll all be sacked.

Then he went straight up to Sue and sat down and had a long talk to her. He said,

'You understand, don't you Sue, they've got to go back. Ken wouldn't want them all sacked because of him, would he?'

I couldn't stand any more. I went into the toilet and sobbed and sobbed because I just couldn't think about them all going back and Ken still being out. I was angry and pissed off with everything. I stood in the toilet and I kept thinking, 'Where's God now? Let God come now and show us what's what.If he's really there, he's got to prove that he's really there and he's got to throw Ken's case out of court and let's have one thing to have a celebration for.'

When I got back a lot of the women were crying. Sue's voice said, 'I know they've got to go back, I understand.'

But it didn't sound like Sue talking, I think she was in a daze, I don't think she really believed that it was happening. I looked over at her and Dennis was sitting beside her, quietly sobbing.

Two supporters from London had come up and they took me out to their car where they had two bottles of champagne, they said,

'We've brought these up to celebrate Ken's victory and Karen's baby.' I looked at the champagne and tears started to swell up inside me again.

I went back inside and made myself a cup of coffee. As I did, a car pulled up outside and John Holroyd walked into the Centre.

'The case has been thrown out of court,' he said.

Immediately the atmosphere inside the Centre changed. We rushed back out to the car and got the champagne. The other cars started to arrive from the court and people filed into the Centre as the champagne corks popped and the glasses were filled. Pauline and Sue hugged each other with pure joy. In a few seconds an atmosphere that had been suicidal became filled with excitement and relief. Ken had been cleared, the police case hadn't stood up in court, and most of all, Ken was not going to prison. Two bottles of champagne couldn't have gone very far between so many of us but suddenly we all seemed drunk. Someone had gone to fetch Karen because one of the bottles had been brought for her and Ricki, but by the time she got to the Centre the champagne was all gone.

That night we went out for a drink to celebrate Ken's victory. It was a strange celebration because we all knew that it was our last night on strike. Our excitement that Ken was not going to prison was short lived because he still didn't have a job to go back to.

The next day we went up to the Centre and cooked dinners, most of the men were on 'afters', so they came up and had some dinner at the Centre before they went in. Everybody was very miserable, after dinner the men begrudgingly walked out and off to the pit. Margaret had packed Yorkie some snap to take but before she could give it to him, he had disappeared. No one knew where he'd gone. Someone said they'd seen him walking out the door and Margaret went out to the street and he was half-way up to the pit. She called after him and he came back.

'Where's me kiss?' she said.

'Kiss?' He said, 'I've got nothing to kiss anybody for.'

Pip was one of the last of the men to go in because he had been rostered on late afternoons. He stayed home until dinner-time and did the hoovering as usual, then when he came up to the Centre he was in a foul mood. He kept saying that he hoped there'd be a picket line on, so he couldn't go in. We'd heard that some of the Kent lads had refused to go back and were picketing around the place. At one stage, Pip actually walked up to the pit to see if there was a picket line there. He'd brought his snap box up to the Centre with him and when I opened it to pack his food there were still two chocolate biscuits there from the last day he'd worked. He took them with him that day.

AFTERWORD

Through the struggle which has been written about in this book, we have found a confidence which we never knew we had. We have proved to ourselves and our men that we are as strong as they are. We learnt so much in this, our struggle, and we know now that it is the same struggle as many others, against racism, for minority groups, against nuclear weapons and against the racist regime in South Africa; but the list is endless. They are all just examples of working class people struggling for an equal chance out of life.

Before the strike, we used to think that we couldn't voice our opinion, now we know that we have a voice and we will make it heard. We intend to continue with our struggle and making our voice heard, we are both activists in the Labour Party Women's Section, we have joined our local community centre and we are active in this. We still have Blidworth Action Group meetings and we are now concentrating on issues like Greenham Common and the cutbacks in the National Health Service.

We have both gone back to work in a factory together and the first thing we wanted to know was, 'Is there a union?' When we last worked we didn't even know if there was one. Although the miners' strike was a hard and bitter struggle we know that there are thousands of women whose lives, like ours, have changed for the better. Finally, we are very grateful to Lynn for writing this book, for us it is a chance to let the working class movement of this country know how we feel and how much we realise that the struggle still goes on.

Doreen Humber
Pauline Radford.

Blidworth 1985